Formal Matters

To Papa

Formal Matters
Embodied Experience in Modern Literature

Zoë Roth

EDINBURGH
University Press

Edinburgh University Press is one of the leading university presses in the UK. We publish academic books and journals in our selected subject areas across the humanities and social sciences, combining cutting-edge scholarship with high editorial and production values to produce academic works of lasting importance. For more information visit our website: edinburghuniversitypress.com

© Zoë Roth, 2022, 2024

Edinburgh University Press Ltd
The Tun – Holyrood Road
12(2f) Jackson's Entry
Edinburgh EH8 8PJ

First published in hardback by Edinburgh University Press 2022

Typeset in 10.5/13 Sabon LT Pro
by Cheshire Typesetting Ltd, Cuddington, Cheshire,
Croydon, CR0 4YY

A CIP record for this book is available from the British Library

ISBN 978 1 4744 9750 3 (hardback)
ISBN 978 1 4744 9751 0 (paperback)
ISBN 978 1 4744 9752 7 (webready PDF)
ISBN 978 1 4744 9753 4 (epub)

The right of Zoë Roth to be identified as the author of this work has been asserted in accordance with the Copyright, Designs and Patents Act 1988, and the Copyright and Related Rights Regulations 2003 (SI No. 2498).

Contents

Acknowledgments	vi
Introduction: The Matter of Form	1
1. The Corporeal Urn	51
2. *La Pensée incarnée*: Embodying the Unrepresentable in Anne F. Garréta's *Sphinx*	69
3. "All life is figure and ground": Samuel Beckett and the Politics of Embodied Form	98
4. The Unbearable Lightness of Being: Chiasmus, Embodiment, and Interpretation in Maurice Blanchot	138
5. The Hunger Artist: Testimony, Representation, and Embodiment in Primo Levi	151
Afterword: Against the Unrepresentable: The Common Sense of Embodied Form	193
Bibliography	205
Index	220

Acknowledgments

Formal Matters has gone through a number of permutations and bears almost no resemblance to its chrysalis form. This metamorphosis has been generously supported by various institutions, including the Arts and Humanities Research Council and Durham University, which provided me with research funds and a generous period of leave to help finish the book. A fellowship at the Vienna Wiesenthal Institute for Holocaust Studies (VWI) got me over the finish line of my PhD thesis and laid the groundwork for what would eventually become this book. More importantly, at the VWI I gained the friendship of Elisabeth Gallas and Sandro Fasching, who helped me with this project in both academic and amicable ways.

I want to give thanks to the two anonymous reviewers at Edinburgh University Press, who provided insightful advice that undoubtedly made this book better. I would also like to thank my editors at EUP. Jackie Jones showed immediate enthusiasm and support. Susannah Butler has expertly steered this book through to completion.

I am fortunate to work with intellectually inspiring and personally supportive colleagues across Durham University. My deepfelt gratitude, in particular, goes to Sam Bootle, Marc Schachter, and Amaleena Damlé for both their friendship and feedback. William Schaefer and Marc Botha, too, deserve thanks for helping me with the book proposal and providing lots of LOLs. Laura Campbell, Venetia Bridges, Laura Leon Llerena, and Emily Rohrbach – otherwise known as the Elvet Riverside party bubble – provided crucial moments of reprieve during the dark days of a British winter and social isolation. Special thanks to Emily for responding with grace to my frantic requests to read parts of this manuscript at short notice. More thanks to those I have undoubtedly left out. A hug to Susan Frenk for her warmth and encouragement.

A number of individuals were pivotal in providing early inspiration that helped shape this book's final form. These include Lisa Blackman, who first introduced me to the concept of embodiment; Patrick ffrench, who always read my work with a beautiful attention to detail; and Robert Weninger, for his unfailing encouragement. Special thanks goes to Alice Mexter for helping me overcome my hang-ups about what this book would not be and enabling me to look towards what it could become.

I would not have been able to write this book without my dearest friend, Charlie Gustafson-Barrett, whose brilliant insights and ability to draw out the undisclosed form of my writing and thinking made this book into an entirely different political animal. My friends Denise Grollmus, Cécile Bishop, and Cat Moir have also provided insightful comments and encouragement.

My grandparents, Ken and Bev Paigen, did not live to see this book published, but their presence is felt in its very existence. Without their emotional, academic, financial, and (they would say) genetic support, it would not have come to be. My other grandmother, Lillian (Bubbe) Leiber, was a woman before her time who gained her PhD in her forties and is an early model for female academics. I owe my intellectual curiosity, stubbornness, and French passport (all things that greatly aided the completion of this book!) to my father, Gilbert Roth. He is not alive to see it, but I know he would be very proud. My mother, Susan Paigen, provided all kinds of material and emotional aid throughout this book's various phases, including proofreading an entire early version. The indomitable Roth sisters – Natalie, Nicole, Cassia, and Erica – have been an invaluable presence in my life, providing joy and laughter (and sometimes annoyance). In particular, my fellow academic, Cassia, has demonstrated what can be accomplished in spite of – and in testament to – devastating loss. The memory of her beloved Clayton lives on through her. Patrice Dini has accompanied me in different forms at almost every stage of this book. I will carry his indefatigable curiosity and tenacity with me for the rest of my life.

Introduction:
The Matter of Form

Imagine a scene that takes place over 30,000 years ago in the Chauvet caves in southern France. Prehistoric man presses his hand against a cave wall and blows paint around the edges. He pulls his hand away and leaves an outline of his body – an imprint of absence. The act of blowing paint through an instrument over his hand anticipates writing; it translates oral language into a visual sign. Nearly 25,000 years before the first known writing system, human beings already understand that writing is an embodied act. But bodily expression is not simply a question of signs and representation. It also concerns form. Like the paintings of horses and bison found in the same caves, the hands play with the cave's undulating surface. By transforming the cave's brute matter into a meaningful form, prehistoric man leaves an index of presence; he announces himself as a subject and, most importantly, as a political animal whose existence graces the community's social and symbolic spaces. His primal impulse is not merely for self-expression but for communication to – and recognition by – an other.[1] What unites form, representation, and the political is the body. And the relation between them is the subject of this book. *Formal Matters: Embodied Experience in Modern Literature* contends that literary theory has privileged the body's relationship to representation at the expense of its connection to form. Embodiment, this book argues, is not what resists but what *constitutes* form.

Form and representation are both types of organization, but they organize in divergent ways. Form shapes things into cohesive wholes; it implies organic unity.[2] Representation produces patterns of difference: the sign creates a likeness, and its meaning derives from its difference

---

1 Aristotle writes that "the city [*polis*] belongs among the things that exist by nature, and that man is by nature a political animal," in *Aristotle's "Politics,"* trans. Carnes Lord (Chicago: University of Chicago Press, 1984), 4.
2 For an excellent, thorough analysis of the way concepts of form have changed in philosophical, aesthetic, and poetic enquiries, as well as a historical mapping of the term, see

from other signs in a chain of signification.³ Both form and representation are foundational elements of Western literary theory, dating back to Plato and Aristotle, and they are the essential components of narrative. Form and representation have also always been tied to the body. Form molds elements into an outward shape whose organic wholeness retains a close connection to the figure of the body, as in Aristotle's understanding of form as the holistic container that unifies physical matter.⁴ Representation, on the other hand, refers to something other than itself and thus entails a separation.⁵ From Odysseus' scar to emojis, representations externalize the body's perceptual phenomena into a recognizable but not naturalized sign.⁶ The close relationship between the body and these concepts' modes of organization has also provided the basis for some of the most important political theories. This is evident in the concept of the body politic as the unification of form, signified by the *polis*, and matter, made up of citizens, or in the way representative governments act as bodies that stand in for other persons in the same manner that representation stands for something else.⁷

Angela Leighton, *On Form: Poetry, Aestheticism, and the Legacy of a Word* (Oxford; New York: Oxford University Press, 2007).

3 This understanding of representation derives from Saussure's notion that language is a system of arbitrary signs that do not possess a natural link to the signifier; meaning only emerges in the difference between other signs. For a classic presentation of Saussure's work see Jonathan Culler, *Saussure* (London: Fontana, 1976).

4 This concept in Aristotle has been termed "hylomorphism." For more on the relation between form and matter in Aristotle see S. M. Cohen, "Hylomorphism and Functionalism," in *Essays on Aristotle's De Anima*, ed. Martha Craven Nussbaum and Amélie Rorty (Oxford: Clarendon Press, 1992).

5 Paul Crowther writes that representation is "a formalized semantic and syntactic code through which it refers to some aspect of the world other than itself," in Crowther, *Art and Embodiment: From Aesthetics to Self-Consciousness* (Oxford: Oxford University Press, 1993), 4.

6 Erich Auerbach begins his comparison of the two Western traditions of realism with an analysis of the recognition of Odysseus' scar in *The Odyssey*, which reveals his true identity to his household, as exemplifying "the basic impulse of the Homeric style: to represent phenomena in a fully externalized form, visible and palpable in all their parts," in Auerbach, *Mimesis: The Representation of Reality in Western Literature* (New Haven, CT: Princeton University Press, 2003), 6.

7 The *polis* is literally made up of *polites*, or citizens: "*Polis* designates the 'political community' peculiar to a stage in Greek civilization. [...] *Politeia* [πολιτεία] seems to pose different problems: the *politês* [πολίτης] being a member of the *polis* (hence the citizen), *politeia* designates either, distributively, the citizens' participation in the city-state as a whole, and thus 'citizenship,' or collectively, the organization of citizens into a whole, and thus 'constitution' or 'regime.' [...] If the *politês* is a person who participates in the *polis*, the *politeia* may be either the subjective bond of the *politês* to the *polis*, that is, the way in which the *polis* as a community distributes among those whom it recognizes as its participants (the 'citizenry'), or the objective organization of the functions of government and administration, that is, the way in which the power of the polis is collectively guaranteed (the 'form of government' or the 'constitution')," in Francis Wolff, "Polis," in *Dictionary of*

The body thus intertwines form and representation. But the current critical landscape largely separates them, particularly with regards to the body. The reasons for this relate to their current political associations. When harnessed for political ends, form's drive towards totality, unity, assimilation, and conformity can exclude, sometimes violently.[8] This is particularly the case with groups defined by their bodies. When women, people of color, sexual minorities, and those from disadvantaged economic backgrounds constantly run into ideological configurations materialized into impenetrable forms – border walls, glass ceilings, color lines, and class barriers – then form's unity signals oppression. Organic form threatens to erase different bodies. Representation, on the other hand, depends upon difference: the difference between signifier and signified, or between the different signs that make up language systems, or between the material body and its visual index. In contrast to organic forms, representations do not possess natural meaning. To approach the body through what Michel Foucault calls "the order of discourse"[9] thus helps deconstruct the dangerous essentialisms that associate the body's organic form with innate biological characteristics. The body's materiality can only be grasped through the medium of language.

If associating the body with organic form can lead to essentialism and exclusion, separating the body's physical, material dimension from its discursive expression has created an inverse political problem with distressing ramifications. The body has come to signify the "brutal difficulty of materiality"[10] and a "brute facticity,"[11] which give rise to discursive "intransigence"[12] and a "semantic impertinence."[13] A body that inherently escapes signification ultimately reinforces the mechanics of a political system that discounts materiality and embodiment, because

Untranslatables: A Philosophical Lexicon, ed. Barbara Cassin, Steven Rendall, and Emily S. Apter (Princeton, NJ: Princeton University Press, 2014).

8 Anna Kornbluh, *The Order of Forms: Realism, Formalism, and Social Space* (Chicago: University of Chicago Press, 2019), 3. Kornbluh notes that the association of aesthetics with bounded forms has led a range of critical theorists to connect form with fascism and totalitarianism, as in Walter Benjamin's assertion that fascism constitutes the "aestheticization of politics."
9 Michel Foucault, "The Order of Discourse," in *Untying the Text: A Post-Structuralist Reader*, ed. Robert Young (Boston; London: Routledge & Kegan Paul, 1981).
10 Richard Terdiman, *Body and Story: The Ethics and Practice of Theoretical Conflict* (Baltimore, MD: Johns Hopkins University Press, 2007), 14.
11 David Hillman and Ulrika Maude, "Introduction," in *The Cambridge Companion to the Body in Literature*, ed. David Hillman and Ulrika Maude (Cambridge: Cambridge University Press, 2015), 3.
12 Diana Coole and Samantha Frost, "Introducing the New Materialisms," in *New Materialisms: Ontology, Agency, and Politics*, ed. Diana Coole and Samantha Frost (Durham, NC: Duke University Press, 2010), 1.
13 Gail Weiss, *Refiguring the Ordinary* (Bloomington, IN: Indiana University Press, 2008), 69.

it reproduces the exclusion from the political sphere of people who are most often reduced to their bodies. In other words, the (un)representability of the body has fundamental consequences for the constitution of political forms. Separated from form through representation, the body cannot participate in the body politic – a literal, and not figurative, discursive space. As Judith Butler argues: "those who gain representation, especially self-representation, have a better chance of being humanized, and those who have no chance to represent themselves run a greater risk of being treated as less than human, regarded as less than human, or indeed, not regarded at all."[14] If the body fundamentally escapes expression, those most often associated with the body find themselves shut out of political representation. This logic is evident in the way enslaved people and women were denied suffrage based on the belief that they were governed by bodily impulses and not reason.

The unrepresentable, fragmented body is a poor site for political action. It devalues materiality, reifies discursive violence, and denies individuals agency. In turn, dematerialized concepts of form will lead to weaker political institutions. They will not be able to harness the affective, experiential, and volitional forces of embodied subjects, what Rosi Braidotti has termed the fundamental "desire to be, the tendency of the subject to be, the predisposition of the subject toward being."[15]

Is there a way out of the impasse between form and representation? Navigating a passage cannot entail simply returning to older concepts of organic, unified form. Nor can it uncritically fall back upon representation's political critique. It will be necessary to revise our understanding of both form and representation and redraw the relationship between them.[16] The body – as the material ground of form and the primary index of representation – provides the site for this enquiry. And literature, which brings together form and representation, matter and discourse, is the medium. To move beyond this impasse, *Formal Matters* develops the concept of 'embodied form,' which demonstrates that embodiment is the *matter* of form. Embodiment is the experience of the lived body. It bridges the divide between the body as subject and object, conceiving

---

14 Judith Butler, *Precarious Life: The Powers of Mourning and Violence* (London: Verso, 2004), 141.

15 Rosi Braidotti, *Nomadic Subjects: Embodiment and Sexual Difference in Contemporary Feminist Theory* (New York: Columbia University Press, 1994), 196.

16 W. J. T. Mitchell argues that in order to formulate politically "committed" approaches to form, it "will require not simply returning to the concepts and formalism of yesteryear or restating old commitments. It will necessitate a rethinking of both terms and of the relation between them," in Mitchell, "The Commitment to Form; Or, Still Crazy after All These Years," *PMLA* 118, no. 2 (2003): 321–25, 323. My concept of embodied form contributes to rethinking form, politics, and the relationship between them.

of these two dimensions of the body as inseparable. The concept of embodiment emerged from phenomenology, in particular the work of Maurice Merleau-Ponty, who located the body as the primary locus of subjectivity and argued bodily experience organizes our perception of the world. Cultural anthropology, sociology, and feminist philosophy popularized the term during the 1980s and 1990s, seeking to reengage with the body's materiality in the wake of the theoretical turn to representation, discourse, and text.[17] Whereas the 'body' signifies an object, whether symbolic or political, embodiment entails a sense of agency and locates this agency in materiality itself – in its suppleness, resistance, flexibility, adaptiveness, and pure desire to exist.

The concept of embodied form conveys how our embodied experience is the central site that shapes the flux of sensual perception, kinesis and proprioception (movement and the awareness of the body in space), and the discernment of difference into a coherent horizon of experience. This book argues that embodiment is an *organizing principle* that determines what we are able to know, think, do, make, and say about the world. In this sense, embodiment also underpins the notion of aesthetics, which is first and foremost knowledge through the body. Derived from the Greek term *aesthesis*, aesthetics denotes what is given to sense perception – what is perceived, in other words, by our embodied consciousness. While aesthetics and form are not interchangeable concepts, they are nevertheless

---

17 In cultural anthropology, the work of Thomas J. Csordas has been enormously influential. See, for instance, Csordas, *Body/Meaning/Healing* (New York: Palgrave Macmillan, 2007) and Csordas, "Introduction: The Body as Representation and Being-in-the-World," in *Embodiment and Experience: The Existential Ground of Culture and Self*, ed. Thomas J. Csordas (Cambridge: Cambridge University Press, 1994). The engagement with embodiment in sociology largely came under the aegis of feminist approaches, which sought to understand bodily materiality and matter in order to nuance social constructivist approaches to the body that had long held sway in the discipline. For examples of constructivist approaches to the body in sociology see Mike Featherstone, Mike Hepworth, and Bryan Turner, eds., *The Body: Social Process and Cultural Theory* (London: Sage, 1991); Bryan Turner, *The Body and Society* (Los Angeles: Sage, 2008). For an account of the 'corporeal turn' in sociology, see Anne Witz, "Whose Body Matters? Feminist Sociology and the Corporeal Turn in Sociology and Feminism," *Body & Society* 6, no. 2 (June 2000): 1–24. Sara Ahmed puts concepts of embodiment into dialogue with feminist theory, postcolonial studies, and affect theory. Some representative examples include Ahmed, *Strange Encounters: Embodied Others in Post-Coloniality* (London; New York: Routledge, 2000) and Ahmed, *The Cultural Politics of Emotion* (London: Routledge, 2013). Lisa Blackman's work, situated at the intersection of sociology, media studies, and body studies, has also been highly influential in developing theories of embodiment. See, for instance, Blackman, *Hearing Voices: Embodiment and Experience* (London; New York: Free Association Books, 2001); Blackman, *The Body: The Key Concepts* (Oxford; New York: Berg, 2008); and Blackman, *Immaterial Bodies: Affect, Embodiment, Mediation* (Los Angeles: Sage, 2012). The journal *Body & Society*, which Blackman edits, has been an important site of cultural studies approaches to embodiment.

closely related, particularly through their connection to the body. Just as embodiment assembles inchoate experience into a meaningful order, form entails an ordering of elements. Like the body, form can be an outward figure. Indeed, the term's etymology encompasses these two aspects, meaning both a visible shape that strongly resembles the body and an organizational principle.[18] At the same time, the body is also the material form that can be objectified, and which is subjected to political rule. Embodied form unites the absence signified by the Chauvet hands with the presence that makes the image – an image whose appearance announces aesthetics as the foundation of political existence. Reading the Chauvet hands as a representation can only point to the absent body that produced it. A focus on form reveals the embodied aesthetic process that led to its creation. Embodied form thus endows formal methods with political potential, while also bringing the question of aesthetic form into explorations of the body's representation.

To talk about form is to invoke the role of literary specificity, a concept that seems to distinguish form from 'worldly' concerns like the body and politics. Historically, this is the case with formalist approaches that sought to identify the uniqueness of literary language, something I will explore at more length shortly. Conceptually, too, formalist notions of aesthetic autonomy have largely separated the work of art or literature from political and historical contexts. What endows literature with its distinct identity – its difference from other types of language, whether scientific or colloquial – is its figurative ability to shape language over and above its propositional, discursive, or thematic content.[19] Both a newspaper article and a novel might tell a similar story, but the novel's organization of language and its deployment of poetic figures like allegory produces something in excess of the journalist's statements of fact. Literature shapes the same words found in the newspaper article into a form that communicates something beyond itself. This excess – often termed the sublime, the ineffable, or the transcendent – sets it apart from other domains, such as the political. The gap between the figurative shaping of language and the thing that escapes this process once

---

18 I take this definition from Raymond Williams' etymology of "form" in Williams, *Keywords: A Vocabulary of Culture and Society* (New York; Oxford: Oxford University Press, 1985), 138–39.

19 See Derek Attridge, *The Singularity of Literature* (London: Routledge, 2004), 10–11. For classical discussions on the specificity of literature, see many of the essays in René Wellek, *Theory of Literature* (San Diego, CA: Harcourt Brace Jovanovich, 1984) and René Wellek, *Concepts of Criticism* (New Haven, CT: Yale University Press, 1975). For more recent explorations that seek to elucidate the specificity of literature in relationship to 'theory,' see Michael Clark, ed., *Revenge of the Aesthetic: The Place of Literature in Theory Today* (Berkeley, CA: University of California Press, 2000).

again brings us back to the way writing seems to elide the body, to the hand that produces a sign of its own absence, a figure for its own de-figuration. Traditional conceptions of aesthetic autonomy separate literature from both embodiment and the political, making figurative language an unlikely site for an exploration of the political potential of embodied form.

But, as we have seen, embodiment, form, and politics are intertwined, and literary and poetic methods that are usually the purview of autonomous formalisms can reveal this intimate connection through the act of figuration. *Formal Matters* charts how many of the poetic and rhetorical tropes that have been so important for twentieth- and twenty-first century literary criticism have embodied foundations. Figures and devices like aporia, catachresis, and form itself are grounded in the body. They are figures for embodiment that simultaneously reveal the body's figurative function – the way it shapes and produces literary form. Embodiment organizes literature but literature also allows us to grasp embodiment's organizational function. The body, as the fundamental ground of language and experience, provides the site and subject of formal experimentation. Embodiment, I argue, endows literature with its specificity. The embodied foundation of figurative language thus also has political implications because it provides a speculative site for investigating the relationship between bodies and political speech and representation. This is evident in the figure of prosopopoeia, or the act of speaking on behalf of an absent person, or in catachresis, which disrupts the referential relationship between language and representation on which political configurations often depend. Elucidating the relationship between literature, the body, and the political requires us to dig deeper into the flesh and sinews of literary language rather than turn outwards towards primarily historical, social, or psychological contexts.

To illustrate how embodied form works, let me return to the Chauvet hands. The hands unite all of writing's fundamental aspects: the breath that blows paint evokes the orality of speech, the hand pressed against the wall embodies a writing tool, and the surface of the cave resembles an inscribed page. This 'handwriting' creates a sign that invites us to 'read' this process, while also gesturing to the absent presence that created it. The Chauvet hands deictically point to the specific spatial and temporal context in which they were created, and they act like a trace of physical presence. In other words, they comprise both elements of the index, what Mary Ann Doane has called the "dialectic of the empty and the full," in which the index as trace "harbors a fullness [. . .] that is always supplemental to meaning or intention," while the index as deixis "implies an emptiness, a hollowness that can only be filled in specific, contingent, always mutating situations."[20] The index conceives of representation in terms of an existential or physical connection, even as this materiality exceeds the trace, like a footprint.[21] The Chauvet hands take this indexicality one step further. They are indexes of indexes: signs of hands that point deictically (like an index finger) to the excess trace of the living hand that 'handmade' them. By materializing the body's absence, they provide a literal sign of the disembodiment of representation.

There is another way of understanding the Chauvet hands, however. This consists in thinking about them in terms of a figure that is central to my theory of embodied form: chiasmus. Deriving from the Greek letter χ (*chi*), the chiasmus is a rhetorical and poetic figure composed of two inverted clauses that are balanced against each other to express congruent but inverted ideas (an AB:BA pattern). This is encapsulated in John F. Kennedy's well-known chiasmus, "ask not what your country can do for you, but what you can do for your country." The reversal of clauses places the individual within the syntactical perimeter created by the mirroring of "country," making individual agency, duty, and action part of the fabric, but also distinct from, the body politic produced by the device's syntactical unity. Chiasmus is most easily recognizable as a device that organizes clauses, as in the example I just cited. But it can also structure wider formal and rhetorical patterns, such as the chiastic form of reverse series of questions found in Homeric epics.[22] By inverting the link between opposite terms, chiasmus enables "the agreement of a thing at variance with itself."[23] Chiasmus is thus a device "through which differences are installed, preserved, and overcome in one grounding unity of totality."[24]

The figure is also closely related to the way the body organizes perception and engages with its physical environment. Chiasmus is the name given to the intersection of the left and right optic nerves, which produces humans' binocular vision. Its cruciform shape also reflects the human body's four-limbed symmetry and proportions, as in the

---

20 Mary Ann Doane, "Indexicality: Trace and Sign: Introduction," *Differences* 18, no. 1 (January 1, 2007): 1–6, 2.
21 W. J. T. Mitchell, "Representation," in *Critical Terms for Literary Study*, ed. Frank Lentricchia and Thomas McLaughlin, 2nd ed. (Chicago: University of Chicago Press, 1995), 14.
22 John W. Welch, *Chiasmus in Antiquity: Structures, Analyses, Exegesis* (Provo, UT: Neal A. Maxwell Institute for Religious Scholarship, 1998), 11. These two kinds of chiasmus are called "grammatical" and "structural" chiasmus, see Edmund Thomas, "Chiasmus in Art and Text," *Greece & Rome* 60, no. 1 (2013): 50–88, 52.
23 Rodolphe Gasché, "Reading Chiasms: An Introduction," in *Readings in Interpretation: Hölderlin, Hegel, Heidegger*, by Andrzej Warminski (Minneapolis, MN: University of Minnesota Press, 1987), xvii.
24 Gasché, "Reading Chiasms," xviii.

spread-eagle posture of Leonardo da Vinci's Vitruvian man.²⁵ This sense of symmetry in turn implicates the body's position and movement in space, and the experience of equilibrium.²⁶ Just as X intersects at the Vitruvian man's navel, so too does chiasmus balance two sides of a fulcrum. These patterns are not naturally occurring, but rather evidence of how humans organize perception around bodily experience, finding figures that express embodiment.²⁷ The chiasmus is thus also a metaphor – crossing between the visual and the verbal – that enables humans to perceive of their body in terms of a formal unity. At the same time, this unity is the mediating term between language and the reality.

Maurice Merleau-Ponty, a thinker to whom I will return throughout this book, theorizes the formal and embodied dimensions of chiasmus. He uses the image of two hands touching to argue that the body and the world are made of one perceptual field or "flesh" that intertwines them in a chiastic relationship. Perception is haptic as well as visual, touch is inseparable from being touched, and sight from being seen. This constant reversibility produces a perceptual "thickness" that fills the space between the subjective body and the objective world – the brief hiatus between when one hand touches and the other feels.²⁸ Or, to bring this back to the image of the Chauvet hands, this overcomes the index's dichotomy as both the deictic sign pointing to the body's spatiotemporal absence and an excessive presence that the trace cannot fully capture. The chiasmus enables us to grasp the body's subjective and objective dimensions as a formal unity without neutralizing these internal differences.

This can be the case even where the figure of chiasmus is absent, since its absence already implicates its counterpart term. To give you an example of how this works when analyzing literature, I will briefly explore another image of hands in John Keats' fragmentary poem "This Living Hand":

> This living hand, now warm and capable
> Of earnest grasping, would, if it were cold
> And in the icy silence of the tomb,

---

25 See Jamin R. Pelkey, *The Semiotics of X: Chiasmus, Cognition and Extreme Body Memory* (London; New York: Bloomsbury, 2017), 15.
26 Pelkey, *The Semiotics of X*, 18.
27 See Robert Hariman, "What Is a Chiasmus? Or, Why the Abyss Stares Back," in *Chiasmus and Culture*, ed. Boris Wiseman and Anthony Paul (New York: Berghahn Books, 2014), 47.
28 Maurice Merleau-Ponty, *The Visible and the Invisible: Followed by Working Notes*, ed. Claude Lefort, trans. Alphonso Lingis (Evanston, IL: Northwestern University Press, 1975), 133–36. I explore Merleau-Ponty's notion of the chiasmus in more depth in "The Corporeal Urn."

> So haunt thy days and chill thy dreaming nights
> That thou would wish thine own heart dry of blood,
> So in my veins red life might stream again,
> And thou be conscience-calmed – see here it is –
> I hold it towards you.[29]

In a similar manner to the Chauvet hands, Keats' poem is an index of indexes – its representation of "this living hand" implies a physical connection to the writing body, even as the index points deictically ("see here it is") to the body's absence. The poem's fragmentary form also gives shape to the way representation fractures the body. The lyrical voice is embodied in "this living hand," which composes the fragment we are reading, even as the free-floating signifier severs itself from the lyrical subject's body. We might even read the hand as replacing the body of the lyrical 'I' with an index of its once excessive presence, "warm and capable of grasping," that now gestures to the emptiness of "the tomb."

Writing cuts itself off from its organ of production so that when the lyrical subject proffers the hand at the end ("I hold it towards you") it has already withdrawn its physical presence, haunting the space of writing as an uncanny specter of its own effacement. This is a poem about writing – about writing as embodied process, of a 'hand' writing – that is also at the same time an index of the body's absence.[30]

If we read the poem chiastically, however, a different body emerges.[31] There is no neat AB:BA expression at the immediate level of syntax. Rather, chiasmus shapes a wider pattern that draws us back to the embodied origin of language. Chiasmus emerges in the movement between pairs of sensations ("warm" and "cold"), times ("now" and haunted "days" and "dreaming nights"), spaces (the immediate context of "*this* living hand" and the deferred "icy silence of the tomb"), images

---

29 John Keats, "This Living Hand," in *The Complete Poems*, ed. John Barnard (London: Penguin, 2003), 459. The poem was written around 1819, but was not discovered until after Keats' death, a haunting trace of Keats' once-living presence, embodied in the ghostly hand that writes.

30 Andrew Bennett, "Language and the Body," in *The Cambridge Companion to the Body in Literature*, ed. David Hillman and Ulrika Maude (Cambridge: Cambridge University Press, 2015), 83. Bennett provides a beautiful reading of "This Living Hand" and the problematic of rendering the body in language, noting that "what is held towards you in the haunting suspense of this space of writing is precisely and solely writing, a hand – a hand, writing."

31 Shahidha Kazi Bari "Feeling Friendship: Reading Keats's 'This Living Hand' and the Sonnets on the Elgin Marbles," in *The Hand of the Interpreter: Essays on Meaning After Theory*, ed. G. F. Mitrano and Eric Jarosinski (Berlin: Peter Lang, 2009), 115. Bari notes the chiastic dimension of Keats' poem in relation to the question of embodiment, arguing it "carefully delineates the chiastic relationship of immaterial text to phenomenal body," but that ultimately "the inscribing hand is itself spectralised by the very act of writing that reduces it to trace."

("thine heart dry of blood" and "my veins red life"), abstract concepts (life and death), forms of perception (sight and touch), states of presence and absence, and voices (the lyrical 'I,' embodied in the severed hand that holds itself out to the reader). The vacillation between these antinomies produces a friction, a kind of "thickness," to reprise Merleau-Ponty's term, that fills in the gap between the opposite poles.

Indeed, this palpability emerges through the movement between two types of perception: the hand immediately present to vision ("see here it is") and the "grasping" hand held out in an invitation of touch. If the first "living hand," signified by the deixis of "this," points to an immediate context that cannot be recovered, the final hand, named only as an abstract "it," proffers an excessive presence, seeming to extend beyond the page. Yet within the movement between these two hands, the poem's form takes shape and is animated by the circulatory movement of a "red life" that "might stream again" through the "veins" of language. The two hands – as deixis and trace – provide the index's two leaves, yet they also supply the reversable clauses that construct a chiastic unity, imparting a structural cohesion that belies both the body and the poem's fragmentary forms. In a similar manner to the paint that prehistoric man blows over the surface of his hand, chiasmus breathes embodied experience into language by enabling the agreement of things that seem most at variance to themselves: the writing body and its representation. Chiasmus enables us to grasp literature's embodied dimension, whether at the surface level of lexis or syntax, or in its 'deep' tissue, the flesh and bones of structure, style, and form. To read the chiasmus in this way reveals a whole range of bodily experiences that would not be visible were we to only search for representations of bodies – for indexes of indexes.

If we read "this living hand" as a representation, even a representation intensely aware of its own process of (embodied) composition, we miss how the hand allows us to grasp its presence in other forms. These forms may only be apparent in their absence, such as the conceptually implied but syntactically absent chiasmus. Thus, the poem gives form to chiasmus beyond the direct expression of this figure, while the figure also gives form to the body – the hand – beyond the immediate appearance of representation. To put it more forcefully, the chiasmus is an embodied form. Its twisting movement incarnates the meaning of the Greek term *trope*, meaning to turn. In the friction between seeing and touching, left hand and right, absence and presence, body and representation, chiasmus produces the form of this sensation. To introduce an idea that is central to this book's argument, the figure *projects* embodiment, much like the lyrical subject holds the hand "towards you." This projection is not less real because it is aesthetic. Throughout this book, I argue that the aestheticization of the body through poetic figures produces, projects, and gives form to embodied experiences that would be imperceptible at the level of theme, discourse, or representation. The aesthetic projection is another form of embodiment – another way of organizing the senses and perception into a cohesive whole.

This formalist attention to the body's shape in literature – and literature's formation of embodiment – is inextricably tied to politics. I earlier noted the close etymological connection between form and the body: they both signify outward shapes or appearances and organizing principles. This etymology also closely ties form and the body to political models like the body politic – a literal aggregate of bodies as well as a conceptual form. The body's aesthetic dimension is yet another way of bringing form and politics together. Since the body is the foundation of aesthetic experience and perception, it is also what forms the political realm. Hannah Arendt, for instance, has argued that the five senses underpin individuals' perception of the world; what is real is what appears.[32] She conceives of the world as a stage – or one might say, a cave – where individuals are seen, heard, and disclose their individuality.[33] The human instinct to speak, hear, feel, perceive, and appear anticipates formalized political organizations and continually mediates political participation. Preventing individuals from appearing and acting in the common world equally deprives them of the right to being. Jacques Rancière develops a similar understanding of the relation between aesthetic perception and politics in his notion of the "distribution of the sensible," which is the "delimitation of spaces and times, of the visible and the invisible, of speech and noise, that simultaneously determines the place and the stakes of politics as a form of experience."[34] This distribution makes the body the basis for political action, since embodiment produces the aesthetic modes of judgment and behavior that dictate who exerts control in a community and who is excluded, whose voices communicate gravitas and whose are perceived as shrill, for instance.

Thus, embodiment underlies aesthetics, form, and politics. The body is there in the senses; it is the conceptual shape that underpins political

---

32 Hannah Arendt, *The Life of the Mind* (New York: Harcourt, 1978), 19.
33 Hannah Arendt, "Preface," in Arendt, *Men in Dark Times* (San Diego, CA: Harvest Books, 1970), viii.
34 Jacques Rancière, *The Politics of Aesthetics* (New York: Continuum, 2004), 13. Embodied experience, in the form of sensory perception, underlies virtually all of Rancière's thinking on the relationship between aesthetics and politics. Yet the connection between embodiment and political formations remains largely implicit, rather than representing a specific avenue of theorization.

entities like the body politic, the social body, or the nation-state; it is the figures that populate, produce, and are regulated by the political sphere;[35] it is the source of orality, aurality, and vocality that announces the subject's political existence; it is a visible or invisible presence; and it is the very entity that in being both subject and object models the political tension between the individual and the group that is at the basis of all political systems.

Yet literary criticism largely separates bodies and form, associating form with political configurations that absorb, squeeze out, or silence different bodies. The discursive body has helped elude these homogenizing effects. But in turning the body into an effect of language, literary criticism has overlooked embodiment's ability to shape the social and political forces that frequently objectify bodies. Returning to the embodied foundation of formal devices, such as chiasmus, is one way of reinvesting form with political potential. Chiasmus is, of course, an important part of political rhetoric (think back to Kennedy's chiasmus), or the art of persuasion. But its rhetorical form is convincing because it not only mirrors but also creates a form that is congruent to the body's organization of perception and language. (I shall come back to the notion of congruent forms at more length later in the next chapter, entitled "The Corporeal Urn.") The chiasmus helps reevaluate binaries, such as the body's subjective and objective dimensions, and it recasts the body's escape from signification. It demonstrates the crisscrossing of the individual body and the body politic – their consistent but not entirely coincidental forms. The chiasmus implies a reciprocity that goes beyond representation's indexical function in which one thing stands in for another. Perception always implicates its inverse process; seeing is inseparable from being seen, touching from being touched, much like the sensation of two hands clasping or looking at oneself in the mirror. While the chiasmus brings together these two poles in a formal unity, it does not resolve or eliminate differences. This is a key element in fights over 'identity politics,' a term that can itself be understood in terms of a chiasmus, in which appeals to recognize the oppression of difference mirror claims that appeals to recognize difference are a form of oppression. Chiasmus enables the negotiation of these opposite poles without the oppression of a total form. What might it mean, for instance, to be able to communicate with others in a genderless language without giving up or codifying one's gendered identity? Or to perceive

---

35 Jacques Rancière argues that the "order of the police" organizes bodies according to the distribution of the sensible, in Rancière, *Disagreement: Politics and Philosophy* (Minneapolis, MN: University of Minnesota Press, 1999), 21–42.

race in terms of formal, aesthetic configurations rather than discursive constructs or a biological essence? Formal devices like chiasmus, as well as others I explore in the following pages, including prosopopoeia, catachresis, metalepsis, and aporia, provide speculative sites through which to explore these political questions. *Formal Matters* returns to the embodied form of poetic and rhetorical devices to explore literature's potential to reorder, reimagine, and even warn us against other political forms.

This book thus wagers that we do not need to discard form to talk about bodies or politics. Indeed, it argues that it is only possible to talk about bodies and politics if we bring aesthetic form into the equation. A large part of the blame for form's politically suspect reputation falls upon the shoulders of early- and mid-century formalist movements, exemplified by the New Criticism. Many of these formalisms eschewed political critiques of form, even when such groups' gendered, racial, and geographic configurations betrayed conservative ideological orientations.[36] In this context, notions of organic or autonomous form helped constellate literary and aesthetic institutions – not least, literary criticism itself – that kept difference out. One of the consequences of this rejection of form's political dimension was an almost complete disregard for the relationship between the body and form. Yet embodiment shapes the very conceptual limits of formalism, from the privileging of aesthetic perception and appeals to organic unity to the notion of poetry as "the world's body."[37] Indeed, formalism's elision of the body from form enabled the separation of form from politics, perpetuating a model in which the elite white male body remained the implicit ground of literary representation and criticism.

The critique of oppressive ideological, social, and political forms has thus largely been borne by postmodernism, a "fetishized signifier" I use here to bring together a range of interconnected critical approaches

---

36 The New Critics were all white men, largely from the American South. In this sense, the formation of literary criticism's institutions around formalism implicitly excluded those deemed different. The New Critics' "roots were Southern agrarian and their sense of manners Mandarin," as Charles Altieri describes them, even if their methods and approaches became part of a democratization of literary studies in American higher education. See Altieri, "The New Criticism," in *The Edinburgh Encyclopedia of Modern Criticism and Theory*, ed. Julian Wolfreys (Edinburgh: Edinburgh University Press, 2002), 437. The language used to criticize the New Critics reflects the group's problematic ideological composition. For instance, Frank Lentricchia employs a bodily register of essence and trauma to characterize the movement as attempting to "essentialize literary language by making it a unique kind of language," and as leaving "scars" in literary studies, in Lentricchia, *After the New Criticism* (Chicago: University of Chicago Press, 1994), xiii.

37 John Crowe Ransom, *The World's Body* (Baton Rouge, LA: Louisiana State University Press, 1938).

that generally began to emerge during the second half of the twentieth century, including poststructuralism, deconstruction, feminist theory, and postcolonial studies.[38] While heterogeneous and internally diverse, these fields shifted away from a focus on form towards the order of discourse, not least because representation has a more explicitly political dimension. For a range of postmodernist thinkers, many of whom I will explore later in this chapter, form and related concepts like materiality harbor a metaphysics of presence, origin, and essence. This brings us back to my original formulation of the difference between form and representation, and their connection to the body. The earlier valorization of form occluded the body. Postmodernism's emphasis on representation, on the other hand, brought the body to the fore as a site of political power and violence. The notion of the 'discursive body' – or a body constituted in and through representation – helped refute both metaphysical conceptions of form and essentialist theories of the body. Yet in framing the body's relationship with language primarily in terms of representation, a correspondence that is necessarily separated from the material entity it depicts, postmodernism has situated embodiment beyond expression. The body escapes signification, resists representation, and exceeds language. At the moment that postmodernism emancipates the body from essentialism it becomes marked by depletion, silence, resistance, and gaps.

Whereas the formalists' elision of the body separated form from politics, postmodernism's refusal of form has paralyzed our understanding of the body's political potential. In recent years, an energetic new engagement with form, sometimes called the 'new formalism,' has sought to correct elements of the quarrel between politics and formalism, also understood in terms of a specific attention to the aesthetic. Caroline Levine, for instance, rejects the distinction between form as unifying and representation as the production of difference. She argues that form is "all shapes and configurations, all ordering principles, all patterns of repetition and difference."[39] Rather than ossifying unequal or monolithic structures, this definition has "the potential to unsettle conventional, rigid social and conceptual forms."[40] Anna Kornbluh

---

38 This characterization of postmodernism is from Christopher Breu, *Insistence of the Material: Literature in the Age of Biopolitics* (Minneapolis, MN: University of Minnesota Press, 2014), 2. He also maps the emergence of postmodernism onto the cultural turn, with its various Marxist/materialist and cultural studies developments. For more on the connection between postmodernism and the cultural turn see Fredric Jameson, *The Cultural Turn: Selected Writings on the Postmodern, 1983–1998* (London; New York: Verso, 1998).
39 Caroline Levine, *Forms: Whole, Rhythm, Hierarchy, Network* (Princeton, NJ: Princeton University Press, 2015), 3.
40 C. Levine, *Forms*, 47.

incorporates this alignment of literary and political forms into a project that "affirms the order made by forms and the forms made by order." Politically emancipatory critical projects have been largely dominated by what she calls "destituent theory," which advocates for dissembling governing structures, as in poststructuralism's critique of representation. Against the powerful "lure of formlessness," she proposes that "form is composed relationality," which contains its own agency, "underscoring that life itself essentially depends upon composed relations, institutions, states."[41] The new formalism has reinvigorated the political potentialities of form and the aesthetic. Despite these constructive engagements with the continuities between political and literary or aesthetic forms, they nevertheless largely repeat the (old) formalism's error by eliding the fundamental relationship between form and the body. In doing so, they marginalize one of the most powerful forms of political organization: embodiment.[42]

If the body is the primary site of both form and politics, then postmodernism's resistance to form is unable to provide a full account of the body's relation to literature or to politics, understood in formalist terms as the 'world.' At the same time, formalism's resistance to engaging with the embodied foundation of its master concept ultimately undermines form's aesthetic and affective power – a power that harbors political potential. Embodiment bridges the divide between politics and form

---

41 Kornbluh, *The Order of Forms*, 4. Kornbluh cites Giorgio Agamben as the consummate "destituent" thinker, but she includes in this category a whole range of approaches that focus on undoing or dismantling forms, including "Nietzschean genealogy, Benjaminian materialism, Foucauldian historicism, feminism, and deconstruction," and the critical approaches that derived from them, in Kornbluh, *The Order of Forms*, 1.

42 This book contributes to, and intervenes in, what has been called the 'new formalism,' though this field of study is not actually that new. In "The Heresy of Paraphrase," Cleanth Brooks already notes that the term "new formalists" has been used as a denigrating "epithet," by, presumably, the "old" ones, in C. Brooks, *The Well Wrought Urn: Studies in the Structure of Poetry* (New York: Houghton Mifflin Harcourt, 1947), 196. Ellen Rooney gives an excellent overview of the tussle over form in literary and cultural studies, as well as a way out of the impasse, in Rooney, "Form and Contentment," *MLQ: Modern Language Quarterly* 61, no. 1 (March 1, 2000): 17–40. For an excellent example of "an historically informed formalist criticism" in relation to Romanticist poetry see Susan J. Wolfson, *Formal Charges: The Shaping of Poetry in British Romanticism* (Stanford, CA: Stanford University Press, 1997), 1. A wide range of formalisms are represented in Susan J. Wolfson and Marshall Brown, eds., *Reading for Form* (Seattle, WA: University of Washington Press, 2006). Recent examples of formalist approaches that address some of the affective and embodied dimensions of aesthetics and which have influenced my approach include Charles Altieri, *The Particulars of Rapture: An Aesthetics of the Affects* (Ithaca, NY: Cornell University Press, 2003) and Eugenie Brinkema, *The Forms of the Affects* (Durham, NC: Duke University Press, 2014). In particular, I draw on Brinkema's exploration of the "formal dimension of affect" in Brinkema, *The Forms of the Affects*, xv, to develop my notion that embodiment is the matter of form.

by providing the aesthetic foundation from which both emerge. This book thus shifts from seeing politics as primarily acting upon embodied subjects towards understanding the way embodiment determines political forms. In doing so, it will help find alternative ways of accounting for the experience of bodies that are excluded from normative models of representation.

Against the Unrepresentable

Postmodernist thought has become intractably entangled in the framework and limits of representation even as it questions its possibility.[43] The unsayable or the unthinkable are not properties particular to the body per se but to the act of interpretation – to the *problem* of reading, interpreting, and writing.[44] Instead of accepting Jean-François Lyotard's assertion that "matter is the failure of thought," we should admit that we have failed to think matter.[45] As the social theorist Nikolas Rose argues, "nowhere was 'the discursive turn' more problematic than when debates over 'the body' seemed to deny any powers to the bloody thing itself."[46] Anything we are unable to explain about the body is a lacuna in our critical faculties rather than the body per se.

A similar failure to account for the body's materiality frames approaches that insist language fails to capture that which it seeks to describe. Of course, works of art and literature do not easily give up their meanings. This is why we consider them 'Art.' But a work's resistance to meaning does not necessarily mean that it encodes something fundamentally unrepresentable. As the American pragmatist philosopher John Dewey aptly states: "Without internal tension there would be a fluid rush to a straightaway mark; there would be nothing that could be called development and fulfillment."[47] Criticism should bring literary form's constitutive characteristics into a relationship of reciprocity,

---

43 See Andrew Gibson, *Towards a Postmodern Theory of Narrative* (Edinburgh: Edinburgh University Press, 1996), 71. He writes that postmodern culture "remains deeply wedded to representation, even as it seeks to question and disentangle itself from representation."
44 I am indebted here to Brinkema's assertion that "the return to affect on the part of critics from wildly divergent disciplinary backgrounds is, in most cases, a naïve move that leaves intact the very ideological, aesthetic, and theoretical problems it claimed to confront," in Brinkema, *The Form of the Affects*, xiv. In other words, like embodiment, affect's seemingly fundamental resistance to language is taken as evidence that it cannot be talked about.
45 Jean-François Lyotard, *The Inhuman: Reflections on Time*, trans. Geoffrey Bennington and Rachel Bowlby (Stanford, CA: Stanford University Press, 1991), 38.
46 Nikolas Rose, "The Human Sciences in a Biological Age," *Theory, Culture & Society* 30, no. 1 (January 2013): 3–34, 4.
47 John Dewey, *Art as Experience* (New York: Perigee Books, 1934), 143.

what Dewey characterizes as a "problem" that is essential to all forms of intellectual work.[48] The critical fallacy is to confuse interpretive failure or difficulty with aesthetic incompleteness – to take the resistance of texts towards offering up their meaning as a sign of aesthetic lack. Rather than converting aesthetic resistance into a solution through interpretation, postmodernist criticism takes the problem as an inexpressible aporia that enables it to sidestep the hard, intellectual work of thinking through that aporia as a failure of criticism rather than aesthetics (or the body). Anything that cannot be directly stated or represented becomes unrepresentable.

Against the unrepresentable, I draw on philosophical and literary models that argue art *expresses* an experience or an event.[49] It does so not merely through the signs, symbols, or representations of semiotic systems but also through the reciprocal relationships that dynamically connect the myriad parts of aesthetic form, as in the figure of the chiasmus. Form thus shifts the focus away from the impossibility of a representation fully capturing the idea it seeks to render, to the multiple substances and patterns in which elements of what remains unexpressed in representation can be given fuller form. My concept of embodied form challenges the dogma of the unrepresentable and offers an alternative approach to destituency and formlessness. At the same time, it resists a naïve revival of earlier formalisms by foregrounding the body's formal relation to politics.

In order to make these connections, this book will operate on several different but intertwined levels that are all related to the terms of debates with which I engage. My argument is based first and foremost on the insistence that the aesthetic is not a rarefied field that exists beyond the realm of politics or political experience, precisely because aesthetics emerges from embodiment. In this sense, embodiment is the ground of not only aesthetic perception, but also of language – the medium that humans use to communicate (to *represent*) experience. Throughout this book, I demonstrate how poetic language is inseparable from the body, not least through linguistic tropes that point to their own embodied origins. Language is embodied – and the body figures itself in language – in ways that undermine the purported separation of the body and representation. This approach also helps reinvigorate the formalist analysis of literature, demonstrating how literary specificity can have political valences.

---

48 Dewey, *Art as Experience*, 143.
49 See Dewey, *Art as Experience* and Susanne K. Langer, *Problems of Art* (New York: The Scribner Library, 1957). I will discuss Langer at length in the following chapter.

My second avenue of inquiry concerns the relationship between this universal, ahistorical understanding of embodiment – as the ground of perception and being-in-the-world – and the concrete bodies shaped by historically conditioned understandings of race, gender, and sexuality. There can be no human subjectivity without embodiment, yet particular subjects have been devalued, excluded, and violently subjected based on theories of difference, such as race, that are inseparable from the body. One of *Formal Matters'* goals is to demonstrate how form can register and give shape to the embodied experience of subjects who are often excluded from normative realms of politics, interrupting established modes of representation without at the same time hollowing out embodiment.

Last, in order to fully connect embodiment's ahistorical and real, but also historically-conditioned and specific dimensions, the book provides an ongoing conceptual analysis of the relationship between form and representation – those two poles that have often mapped onto an autonomous formalism or ideological postmodernism. I foreground how embodiment shapes perceptual forms beyond indexical or referential types of representation. However, I also demonstrate how representation need not entail an alienation. Representation can endow embodiment with linguistic weight, making it *more* perceptible not less. The book thus charts a new path with regards to representation and the body, departing from the postmodernist and poststructuralist emphasis on limits without enacting a naïve return to 'pure' form. Each element of the book's argument provides an essential component of the conceptual form that is at the basis of all literary criticism: the *body* of criticism. In turn, *Formal Matters* realizes this intellectual 'body of criticism' in the embodied shape of its intellectual enquiry. The book is structured like a chiasmus. This chiastic structure balances two very different approaches to the body and literature. The first, highly abstract and formally autonomous, is represented by the work of Anne F. Garréta and Samuel Beckett. The second explores the material consequences of the failure of representation in Primo Levi. These two approaches to form, representation, and the body are connected through my analysis of the materiality of absence in Maurice Blanchot, which acts as the book's fulcrum. The book's own embodied form provides a unified entity that can account for both form and representation, aesthetics and politics, embodiment and bodies. By bringing together formalism and postmodernism, the book provides a conceptual and historical analysis of the relationship between form and representation, while attending to bodies in both their universal and concrete existences. To return to the image of hands that opened this book, formalism and postmodernism are the two hands of literary criticism on the body that can only be fully realized when they are touching each other.

The rest of this chapter provides a brief intellectual history of two concurrent though not entirely convergent shifts: from phenomenological to poststructuralist conceptions of the body and from formalist to postmodernist modes of literary criticism. While these literary and philosophical strands are distinct, they crisscross – much like the figure of the chiasmus – in ways that are important for understanding the body's relationship to literature and literary criticism. I then identify several conceptual nodes at which these two historical trends intersect in the figure of the abject and the fragmented body, 'formless' figures for postmodernism's entrapment in the unrepresentable. Finally, drawing these strands together, I explore how formlessness – understood in terms of both language and the body – has been used as a destituent force to resist the determinative effects of representation. This model treats representation as a form of violence, emptying embodiment of political agency. Embodied form, by contrast, provides an alternative to either "the representation of violence" or "the violence of representation."[50]

Criticism of the Body

This section explores changes in critical approaches to the body in the twentieth and twenty-first centuries. These shifts have often been grouped under umbrella terms like the linguistic and corporeal turns. The former, strongly influenced by poststructuralism, broadly posited that language, representation, and discourse construct social reality, subjects, and identities. The latter sought to account for the way different types of sociality and culture overlap with the body's lived materiality and experience. Like formalism and postmodernism, these various 'turns' are not internally consistent. But they do help us trace the permutations the body and embodiment have undergone in intellectual history. Rather than providing a broad overview, I focus on the work of several thinkers who have influenced the two main approaches to the body that emerged from these 'turns.' These are Maurice Merleau-Ponty and his notion of the lived body and Michel Foucault, who theorizes its discursive counterpart, the body constituted through language or representation. I identify productive overlaps and conjunctures in the way philosophy

---

[50] Debarati Sanyal, *The Violence of Modernity: Baudelaire, Irony, and the Politics of Form* (Baltimore, MD: Johns Hopkins University Press, 2006), 28. This quotation comes from a chapter subtitle in Sanyal's book that explores how the body acts as both an aesthetic and historical site of violence in Baudelaire's poetry.

has approached the body during this period, instead of insisting upon ruptures. This is particularly evident in the third area I address: feminist theory. Feminist philosophers demonstrate the need to bring together phenomenological and poststructuralist approaches to embodiment in order to account for the body's agency and experience, as well as the way the body is subjected to systems of power and domination.

Merleau-Ponty and the lived body

As I noted earlier, the term embodiment – the body's lived experience – came to prominence during the 1990s. Much of this scholarship drew on the work of Maurice Merleau-Ponty, including his concepts of the lived body, being-in-the-world, and flesh, a perceptual substance uniting the embodied subject with the world. These aspects of his thinking foil the division between subject and object, thus challenging the dualistic nature of representation. Throughout different stages in his thinking, Merleau-Ponty retains this close connection between consciousness and material being. In *The Structure of Behavior* (1942), for instance, he introduces the notion of being-in-the-world to refer to the way a subject organizes experience into meaningful and comprehensible configurations. Perception is not consciousness of an already constituted world; it forms the world. The perceptual world is only given meaning, however, through a subject's behavior, understood in terms of gesture, posture, and comportment or bearing.[51] The perceiving subject is inherently embodied and the world is firmly grounded in the concrete and the material realm of perception.

He more explicitly takes up the question of the lived body in his subsequent work, *Phenomenology of Perception* (1945), in which he argues that the body is the locus of perception and experience. Pursuant to his objective to analyze the relationship between subjectivity, the body, and the world, Merleau-Ponty examines specific experiential examples where the body does not fully appear to the subject, even though the subject experiences it as whole, as in the sensation of the phantom limb or the certainty that the back of one's head exists even though one cannot actually see it.[52] This demonstrates the fallibility of conceiving

---

51 Merleau-Ponty writes: "the gestures of behavior, the intentions which it [an organism] traces in the space around the animal, are not directed to the true world or pure being, but to being-for-the-animal, that is, to a certain milieu characteristic of the species" or "a certain manner of treating the world, of 'being-in-the-world' or of 'existing,'" in Merleau-Ponty, *The Structure of Behavior*, trans. Alden L. Fisher (Boston, MA: Beacon Press, 1967), 125–26, 129.
52 Maurice Merleau-Ponty, *Phenomenology of Perception*, trans. Colin Smith (London: Routledge, 2002), 92–93.

of the body objectively and returns it to the 'lived' world. The body is the locus of perception, and it cannot even simply be thought of as a 'body' without recalling consciousness.[53] Before our body is 'given back' to us as an object by discourse and before we reflect on it as such, it is first and foremost the condition of our existence. Subjects construct the objective world by removing themselves from the "spontaneity" of being-in-the-world, for "each momentary situation must cease to be, for him, the totality of being." This move from the constant stimulation of being-in-the-world to an ordered, yet meaningful plane of existence resembles how form arranges different aesthetic elements into a comprehensible whole. The body is the living dimension of this process, for "the union of soul and body is not an amalgamation between two mutually external terms, subject and object, brought about by arbitrary decree. It is enacted at every instant in the movement of existence."[54] The image of two hands touching illustrates the constant vacillation between the body's subjective and objective dimensions, between the way the subject experiences the world through the body and the senses, and how the world gives the subject back this body as an image or object that can be grasped in its particularity.

Throughout different stages in his thinking, Merleau-Ponty evokes the image of two hands touching to illustrate the constant vacillation between the body's subjective and objective dimensions and how the subject experiences the world through the body and the senses. This is particularly the case in the fourth chapter of his final, unfinished work *The Visible and the Invisible* (1964), which contains a highly influential meditation on the chiasmus. In "The Intertwining – The Chiasm," Merleau-Ponty moves away from a focus on perception as a primarily visual phenomena to explore other forms of the body's engagement with the world through 'invisible' forms of perception.[55] "Flesh" accounts for both the body's materiality and the objective experience left over by subjective perception – the gap that occurs when the touching hand (which is also, at the same time, touched) cannot be both subject and object at the same time.[56] As I noted in my earlier analysis of Keats' "This Living Hand," the notion of flesh has important repercussions for the structure of representation that *Formal Matters* critiques. In contrast to the embodied subject's visual perception, which installs a representational gap between the body and the world, flesh implies a

---

53 Maurice Merleau-Ponty, *The Primacy of Perception*, trans. Arleen B. Dallery et al. (Evanston, IL: Northwestern University Press, 1964), 6.
54 Merleau-Ponty, *Phenomenology of Perception*, 100.
55 Merleau-Ponty, *The Visible and the Invisible*, 130–31.
56 Merleau-Ponty, *Phenomenology of Perception*, 105–108.

constant contact. Where the impression of distance emerges, this is the effect of an enfolding rather than a gap or fissure. The "hiatus between my right hand touched and my right hand touching" does not point to "an ontological void" or nothingness. Rather "it is spanned by the total being of my body, and by that of the world; it is the zero of pressure between two solids that makes them adhere to one another."[57] These blank spots or 'stutters' in existence signal a moment of exchange and intertwining instead of an absence.

Flesh thus incarnates the body's two dimensions as "leaves" or a "double belongingness," producing a perceptual "thickness" instead of a limit.[58] Put in another way, the chiastic reversibility of subject and object produces flesh's substance, a shared perceptual field. For Merleau-Ponty, this chiastic exchange and reversibility is also the condition of language, because this quality of the flesh contains "everything required for there to be speech from the one to the other, speech about the world."[59] The body is at the origin of language, because it is expressive.[60] The rhetorical and representational forms that thus emerge from the body are inherently intertwined, as in the poetic figure of chiasmus.

Phenomenology in general, and Merleau-Ponty in particular, provided fertile ground for thinking the body in twentieth- and twenty-first century philosophy and critical theory. His work has been foundational for contemporary approaches to embodiment, what Csordas terms "the existential ground of culture," including such things as society, race, gender, and difference,[61] while his notion of flesh helps us understand the inherently bodily condition of form. His work also contained conceptual gaps that leave it open to critique. Phenomenology favored the study of the phenomena of existence (perception, consciousness, the body, and direct objects of experience) over metaphysical categories like truth, value, and epistemology. It was nevertheless a radically subject-centered philosophy that privileged autonomous individual experience and sought to isolate pure objects of perception. This focus on individual perception tended to leave aside the body's relationship to politics, power, or ideology. The lived body, a material presence that functioned as the locus of perception, retained attachments to metaphysical concepts like truth, essence, presence, origin, and wholeness

---

57 Merleau-Ponty, *The Visible and the Invisible*, 148.
58 Merleau-Ponty, *The Visible and the Invisible*, 135.
59 Merleau-Ponty, *The Visible and the Invisible*, 155.
60 Vincent Descombes, *Modern French Philosophy* (Cambridge: Cambridge University Press, 1980), 74.
61 Thomas J. Csordas, "Embodiment as a Paradigm for Anthropology," *Ethos* 18, no. 1 (March 1, 1990): 5–47, 5.

– concepts that also haunt contemporary formalist approaches to literature.

Michel Foucault and the discursive body

Whereas phenomenology emphasized how the lived body forms the locus of perception and, by extension, constructs the world of objects, poststructuralist approaches argued that language and discourse construct social realities. Poststructuralism did not 'replace' phenomenology, which continued to be practiced by an important if minority group of thinkers.[62] But the broad shift from phenomenology to poststructuralism resulted in two important changes. First, the body's lived experience and its problematics of presence are translated into a textual metaphor. The 'body as text' will become prominent in literary criticism on the body. Second, the notion of a subject produced in and through language, as opposed to an autonomous self who forms the locus of perception and expression, comes to form the main strand of analytical enquiry. Together, these produce the model of the discursive body. The work of one thinker in particular, Michel Foucault, helped instigate this paradigm shift. He critiqued phenomenology's focus on the sovereign individual and argued that the body was shaped and disciplined by relations of power.[63] Power produces the order of discourse and knowledge about particular bodies. Rather than referring to mimesis or a pre-existing material realm, representation produces knowledge about particular bodies – criminals, the 'insane,' homosexuals – that encodes them as different.[64]

Tracing how the body changes shape through the work of Michel Foucault thus offers a productive understanding of the relationship

---

62 For examples of phenomenology during this period see Paul Ricoeur, *Oneself as Another*, trans. Katherine Blamey (Chicago: University of Chicago Press, 1995) and Paul Ricœur, *The Course of Recognition*, trans. David Pellauer (Cambridge, MA: Harvard University Press, 2005); Mikel Dufrenne, *The Phenomenology of Aesthetic Experience*, trans. Edward S. Casey (Evanston, IL: Northwestern University Press, 1973); and Michel Henry, *Philosophy and Phenomenology of the Body*, trans. Girard Etzkorn (The Hague: Martinus Nijhoff, 1975). Emmanuel Lévinas was also deeply influenced by phenomenology, although more by Heideggerian strands. Nevertheless, his work on "the face," touch, and the senses signifies the importance of the body in his thinking. See, for example, Lévinas, *Totality and Infinity: An Essay on Exteriority*, trans. Alphonso Lingis (The Hague: Martinus Nijhoff, 1979).

63 Foucault writes that "man is an invention of recent date. And one perhaps nearing its end," in Foucault, *The Order of Things* (London; New York: Routledge, 2002), 422. On the body shaped by power see Michel Foucault, *Discipline and Punish: The Birth of the Prison* (New York: Vintage Books, 1995), 72.

64 The concept of discourse and its relationship to power evolves over the course of Foucault's thinking, but he always conceives of it as productive. Discourse and representation produce knowledge about subjects.

between lived and discursive bodies. The discursive body develops across Foucault's thinking, but its first permutation appears in *Discipline and Punish* (1975) as the "docile body,"[65] or a body caught up in a political economy of power relations that "mark it, train it, torture it, force it to carry out tasks, to perform ceremonies, to emit signs."[66] This "docile body" is quite different from phenomenology's lived body; it is inscribed and shaped by techniques of power, from the standardized timetable to the classroom,[67] which mold the body's natural reflects in such a way that the exercise of power appears transparent. Foucault names this mutually constitutive nexus "power/knowledge." Power in this sense is not monolithic and 'top-down,' but productive – it creates systems of knowledge and representations, as well as subjects and bodies.[68]

The docile body provides little indication of how subjects *experience* these embodied relations of power. Gradually, however, Foucault develops a more existential account of the body through his notion of "biopower" in the three volume *The History of Sexuality* (1976–1984).[69] This concept locates the body as the source of certain processes of subjectification, rather than merely the signifying site of power and knowledge. Bodies in this sense are not just subjected to discourses, but exercise power upon themselves through particular "techniques of the self," such as sexual practices. Rather than signifying an innate type of desire, institutions, disciplines, and fields of knowledge (like psychiatry) connect a subject's intimate experience of the body to wider social and political structures, producing a 'truth' effect that obscures the mechanics of social power.[70] While later feminist theorists would find fault with

---

65 Foucault's interest in the relationship between language and the body is evident quite early in his writing. See, for instance, his essay on George's Bataille's *The Story of the Eye*, in which he interprets the story not with regards to Bataille's interest in base materiality and the corporeal experience of sexuality, but in terms of language and silence, which comes to mark the modern subject's limits. Michel Foucault, "A Preface to Transgression," in *Language, Counter-Memory, Practice: Selected Essays and Interviews*, trans. Donald. F. Bouchard and Sherry Simon (Ithaca, NY: Cornell University Press, 1977).
66 Foucault, *Discipline and Punish*, 25.
67 Foucault, *Discipline and Punish*, 150–152.
68 Foucault writes that "power and knowledge directly imply one another; that there is no power relation without the correlative constitution of a field of knowledge, nor any knowledge that does not presuppose and constitute at the same time power relations," in *Discipline and Punish*, 27. Equally, one cannot possess power; it is only realized in its exercise.
69 The three volumes are Michel Foucault, *The History of Sexuality, Vol. 1: An Introduction*, trans. Robert Hurley (New York: Vintage, 1990); Foucault, *The History of Sexuality, Vol. 2: The Use of Pleasure*, trans. Robert Hurley (New York: Vintage Books, 1990); and Foucault, *The History of Sexuality, Vol. 3: The Care of the Self*, trans. Robert Hurley (New York: Vintage, 1990).
70 Foucault, *The Use of Pleasure*, 5.

Foucault's failure to account for sexual and gender difference, the notion that power, "as one of the finer and more successful threads that bind knowledge-power to bodies," is incarnated in one of humanity's most intimate experiences was essential for understanding how individuals and groups are tied "ever more firmly to the biopolitical control of their bodies."[71] By describing how a subject incarnates practices and techniques of power, and experiences them as intimate forms of desire, Foucault's later work began to approach an understanding of power that could account for the lived experience of the subject. Yet despite moving beyond the docile, mute body of *Discipline and Punish*, the absence of the lived body makes it difficult to talk about embodied experience. The body's matter remains inexpressive and immutable even as the practices that are enacted upon it change.

We must retain Foucault and poststructuralism's insistence that the lived body is embedded in political forms that subjectify individuals, often violently. This historicist approach influenced constructivist theories of the body in a range of disciplines, including sociology, history, anthropology, and literary criticism, helping critique essentialist beliefs about sex, race, and other forms of bodily difference. Yet, in many social constructivist approaches to the body, discourse becomes another form of determinism, while the body's physical materiality is placed outside of systems of signification, inaccessible to language and thus unable to be harnessed politically. As Diana Fuss argues in her analysis of the essentialism's centrality to constructionism, "it is difficult to see how constructionism can *be* constructionism without a fundamental dependency upon essentialism." Essentialism circumscribes poststructuralism's limits to the extent that refuting it becomes essential to its constructionist project.[72] It remains up to subsequent thinkers, in particular feminist philosophers, to restore the link between the lived experience of the material body and discursive systems in ways that do not return it to an essential form or a disembodied text.

Feminism and the gendered body

The feminist philosophy that emerged in light of the 'linguistic turn' clearly demonstrates how we cannot conceive of the twentieth-century body in terms of breaks, but rather as returns, folds, and revisions. Feminist philosophers like Butler, Elisabeth Grosz, and Braidotti brought

---

71 Elizabeth Grosz, *Volatile Bodies: Toward a Corporeal Feminism* (Bloomington, IN: Indiana University Press, 1994), 155.
72 Diana Fuss, *Essentially Speaking: Feminism, Nature, and Difference* (New York: Routledge, 1989), 4.

together older phenomenological models of embodied experience, particularly from Merleau-Ponty, with Foucauldian and poststructuralist understandings of the discursive, non-essentialist body.[73] They reintroduced the importance of embodied experience and critiqued the implicitly male subject of poststructuralism. In other words, they demonstrated the inseparability of the lived body and representation, and they linked these to the question of agency.

The Foucauldian emphasis of the way power and discourse shape materiality helped critique essentialism, enabling thinkers to describe the gendered or racialized body without recourse to biology. Nevertheless, the necessity of understanding the body as a material, agential locus of experience and to acknowledge sexual difference and gendered hierarchies led many feminist thinkers to criticize Foucault's passive, docile body. In fact, Butler and Grosz take issue with the socially constructed dimension of the sexual body, because it implies that a material body "pre-exists" discourse, according it a problematic neutrality and stability.[74] If the body is inscribed by discourse, as Butler contends, it "invariably suggests that there is a [material] body that is in some sense there, pregiven, existentially available to become the site of its own ostensible construction."[75] Poststructuralism's discursive body ignores the question of sexual difference and gendered experience, assuming an implicitly masculine model.[76]

Feminist thinkers thus turned to other sources in order to critique the universal humanist subject and account for the embodiment of difference and different embodiments. In particular, Merleau-Ponty's work on embodiment, the lived body, and perception becomes an important element in what Grosz calls "feminism's major contribution to the production and structure of knowledges," that is, "its necessary reliance on lived experience."[77] Subjective and embodied experience, in other

---

73 See Judith Butler, "Sexual Ideology and Phenomenological Description: A Feminist Critique of Merleau-Ponty's *Phenomenology of Perception*," in *The Thinking Muse: Feminism and Modern French Philosophy*, ed. Jeffner Allen and Iris Marion Young (Bloomington, IN: Indiana University Press, 1989); Grosz, *Volatile Bodies*; and Rosi Braidotti, *Nomadic Subjects*.
74 Grosz, *Volatile Bodies*, 155.
75 Judith Butler, "Foucault and the Paradox of Bodily Inscriptions," *The Journal of Philosophy*, 86 (1989): 601–07, 601.
76 Nevertheless, Butler never refutes the importance of discourse in subjectification, later using discourse as the basis of the lived 'performativity' of gender in *Bodies That Matter*, stating that, "to claim that discourse is formative is not to claim that it originates, causes, or exhaustively composes that which it concedes; rather, it is to claim that there is no reference to a pure body which is not at the same time a further formation of that body," in Butler, *Bodies That Matter: On the Discursive Limits of "Sex"* (New York: Routledge, 1993), 10.
77 Grosz, *Volatile Bodies*, 94.

words, plays a central role in constructing social, cultural, and political realities. As with the implicitly male subject of Foucauldian discourse, however, Merleau-Ponty ignores the question of gender, resulting in a "universal subject" that is "presumed to characterize all genders," while simultaneously consecrating "masculine identity as the model for the human subject."[78]

Merleau-Ponty's value for feminism, as Butler states it, lies "in the works of philosophical feminism to come,"[79] which will move beyond his account of embodied experience in order to understand the lived specificity of bodily subjects. This is particularly the case regarding questions of agency and materiality, which have been taken up most productively in feminist materialist and posthumanist approaches.[80] As Stacy Alaimo argues, "what has been notably excluded from the 'primacy of the cultural' and the turn toward the linguistic and the discursive is the 'stuff' of matter."[81] *Formal Matters* seeks to not only understand the 'stuff' of matter, but to bring it into dialogue with older conceptions of literary form to think about the way embodied experience can take shape beyond poststructuralist concepts of representation, which still occlude the lived experience of certain subjects. This will, in turn, provide not only a different account of the body's relationship to language and representational systems, but will also reinvigorate formalist methods with poststructuralist and postmodernist critiques of power.

The Body of Criticism

In the previous section, I explored how our understanding of the body and embodiment has shifted across the twentieth and twenty-first centuries. These changes sometimes implicitly touched upon the relationship between form and representation, as in the chiastic figure of flesh or

---

78 Butler, "Paradox of Bodily Inscriptions," 98.
79 Butler, "Paradox of Bodily Inscriptions," 99.
80 For an example of 'classical' posthumanist feminism see Donna Haraway, *Simians, Cyborgs and Women: The Reinvention of Nature* (London: Free Association Books, 1991). On new materialisms, see, amongst others, Stacy Alaimo, *Bodily Natures: Science, Environment, and the Material Self* (Bloomington, IN: Indiana University Press, 2010); the essays collected in Stacy Alaimo and Susan J. Hekman, eds., *Material Feminisms* (Bloomington, IN: Indiana University Press, 2008); and many of the essays in Diana Coole and Samantha Frost, eds., *New Materialisms: Ontology, Agency, and Politics* (Durham, NC: Duke University Press, 2010).
81 Stacy Alaimo and Susan J. Hekman, "Trans-Corporeal Feminisms and the Ethical Space of Nature," in *Material Feminisms*, ed. Stacy Alaimo and Susan J. Hekman (Bloomington, IN: Indiana University Press, 2008), 242.

the body as text. In this section, I will trace concurrent shifts in literary criticism from formalism to postmodernism that also implicate the body. Both formalism and postmodernism are fetish terms, and there is no definitive break between them. The terms encapsulate concerns across a range of related movements and methods.[82] Nevertheless, tracing these different historical constellations will illuminate how literary critical concepts of both form and representation have at different points elided the material body – and thus help us return embodiment to literature.

Formalism

'Formalism' has never been a homogenous movement, and some 'formalists' are barely concerned with form (just as there are plenty of postmodernist critics who are deeply invested in it).[83] Various formalist schools were historically, geographically, and theoretically diverse. Nevertheless, we can broadly situate formalism's heyday in the first half of the twentieth century, and most formalist scholars insist on the specificity of literary and poetic form, arguing that the aesthetic cannot be reduced to authorial psychology, historical context, or political ideology. (In some cases, formalism's overt rejection of language's ideological dimension can be construed as a deeply conservative act.)[84] Formalism also developed at the same time as the philosophical field of phenomenology. Though there is little direct influence, phenomenology's focus on the autonomy of both bodies and objects of perception parallels the formalist methodology of eschewing contextual or ideological interpretations.[85] We can likewise trace some similar intellectual

---

82 Fredric Jameson identifies a shift away from the "technical discourse of professional philosophy" of the first half of the twentieth century towards what he somewhat warily calls "theory" or "theoretical discourse," which traffics between philosophy, political science, and history, and which is "among the manifestations of postmodernism," in Jameson, *The Cultural Turn*, 3.
83 René Wellek makes a good point when he says that of all the early- to mid-twentieth century formalists, Cleanth Brooks may be the only one truly interested in rejecting dichotomies of form (such as form and content) and advocating for an organicist understanding. See Wellek, *Concepts of Criticism*, 62. For examples that interpret formalism (largely the New Criticism) as conservative see Lentricchia, *After the New Criticism* and Terry Eagleton, *Literary Theory: An Introduction* (Minneapolis, MN: University of Minnesota Press, 2008).
84 Lentricchia, *After the New Criticism* and Eagleton, *Literary Theory*.
85 Elements of phenomenology are nevertheless evident in the Russian Formalists' notion of estrangement and in 'reader-response' theory, which privileges a reader's subjective response to texts. See Georgy Chernavin and Anna Yampolskaya, "'Estrangement' in Aesthetics and Beyond: Russian Formalism and Phenomenological Method," *Continental Philosophy Review* 52, no. 1 (March 2019): 91–113 and Wolfgang Iser, *The Act of Reading: A Theory of Aesthetic Response* (Baltimore, MD: Johns Hopkins University Press, 1994).

concerns across these historically concurrent philosophical and literary fields. Phenomenology insisted on the autonomy of both bodies and objects of perception, and this parallels formalist methodologies that privileged aesthetic autonomy. But just as Merleau-Ponty's figure of the chiasmus and the notion of the lived body provide a potential ground for new political relations, so too does formalism's focus on the power of aesthetic experience and the internal relations of form.

The two most influential formalist movements of this period, Russian Formalism and the New Criticism, treated literary and poetic language as distinct from other types of information, whether philosophical, sociological, or historical. The Russian Formalists sought to identify both literature's universal features and specific representational devices that differentiated it from everyday language, or language concerned with communicating information.[86] One of Russian Formalism's most well-known thinkers, Viktor Shklovsky, argued that literature "defamiliarizes" the world, casting it in a new light that would be imperceptible in any other form of discourse.[87] The New Critics rejected context as a heuristic of literary meaning. They developed close reading as the method most appropriate for understanding the unique value of literary language, namely that it differed from ordinary discourse (poetic language was denotative rather than connotative) and was thus able to offer access to a different kind of truth. Poetic language, including allegory, metaphor, and allusion as well as irony and paradox, treat objects in both their literal and secondary meanings. Literary form's ability to encompass both meanings communicates a universal truth – one that is not available through forms of language that only work at the connotative level.[88] A third movement, less well known in the Anglo-

---

[86] In reality, Russian 'Formalism' was never an official or even formalized movement. The term is a convenient shorthand for several loose groupings of thinkers, including Roman Jakobson, Boris Eikhenbaum, Viktor Shklovsky, and Yuri Tynyanov, who did not represent a cohesive approach to the study of literature. Nevertheless, as with the New Critics, it is possible to identify certain broad trends that differentiate Russian Formalism from approaches that privilege psychological, biographical, or historical methods. For historical and critical overviews of the movement see Avi Erlich, *Russian Formalism: History – Doctrine* (The Hague: Mouton Publishing, 1955) and Peter Steiner, *Russian Formalism: A Metapoetics* (Ithaca, NY: Cornell University Press, 1984). Alastair Renfrew details how "formalism" and "formalist" were always contested terms in this context, in Renfrew, *Towards a New Material Aesthetics: Bakhtin, Genre and the Fates of Literary Theory* (London: Legenda, 2006).

[87] The notion of "defamiliarization" is from Viktor Shklovsky, "Art, as Device," trans. Alexandra Berlina, *Poetics Today* 36, no. 3 (September 2015): 151–74.

[88] The term 'the New Criticism' was popularized by the book of the same name by John Crowe Ransom, who also founded the *Kenyon Review*. Critics that have been associated with it include Ransom, Allen Tate, and Yvor Winters, as well as Cleanth Brooks, William K. Wimsatt, and Monroe Beardsley later on. Important influences include T. S. Eliot and I.

American academy, is the Oulipo, or *Ouvroir de littérature potentielle* (Workshop for a Potential Literature). Like the Russian Formalists, the Oulipians have been both critics and writing practitioners, and have applied mathematical and scientific concepts to their writing. For the Oulipo, literature acts as a laboratory to test out new literary forms that have the potential to ramify beyond the page.[89]

The body and embodied experience were closely tied to many of these movements' conceptions of form and of aesthetic perception. Shklovsky, for instance, relates his technique of defamiliarization to bodily experience and perception.[90] Formalist methods like close reading, a mode of concentrated attention to the aesthetic effects of language, also depend on bodily experience. Close reading relies on the way embodiment organizes and focuses the flux of perception into a cohesive meaning. (Cleanth Brooks argues that the poet's task is "to unify experience,"[91] requiring a form of reading that reveals this unity.) This phenomenological approach begins by focusing intently on the object of perception – the poem, novel, or painting – and subsequently deriving general characteristics about these forms, such as their ability to transmit universal truths about beauty, life, or the individual. The body is both most present and most ignored in the master concept of form. It is the primary figure of unification, bringing together subject and object, specific experience and universal existence, organizing principle and formal matter, interior and exterior, intrinsic and extrinsic. It is, in other words, the basis of the "bounded container" without which formalism melts into formlessness.[92] Yet, formalism's myopic focus on aesthetic autonomy blinded it to form's bodily contours and to the way poetic language emerges from embodiment. *Formal Matters* thus develops a mode of close reading that attends not only to the movements of language but to

---

A. Richards. For a good overview of the history and composition of the New Critics, as well as their misunderstood methods, see René Wellek, "The New Criticism: Pro and Contra," *Critical Inquiry* 4, no. 4 (1978): 611–24 and Mark Jancovich, *The Cultural Politics of the New Criticism* (Cambridge; New York: Cambridge University Press, 1993).

89 Warren Motte, "Shapes of Things," *L'Esprit Créateur* 48, no. 2 (2008): 5–17, 10. In terms of both chronology and method, the Oulipo bridges formalism and postmodernism. For instance, one of the most Oulipian texts is Italo Calvino's *If on a winter's night a traveler*, which is also considered a quintessentially postmodern texts in terms of its ludic self-referentiality. For a good overview of the Oulipo and their influence see Dennis Duncan, *The Oulipo and Modern Thought* (Oxford: Oxford University Press, 2019).

90 On embodiment and "defamiliarization" or "estrangement" in Shklovsky's thinking see Douglas Robinson, *Estrangement and the Somatics of Literature: Tolstoy, Shklovsky, Brecht* (Baltimore, MD: Johns Hopkins University Press, 2008).

91 C. Brooks, *The Well Wrought Urn*, 212.

92 C. Levine, *Forms*, 27.

the body's presence in form. Embodiment is the very ground of poetic and aesthetic form.

Postmodernism

If formalists largely elide embodiment from their conception of form, postmodernism foregrounds the importance of the body, but rejects theories of form.[93] Similarly, just as poststructuralist and constructivist approaches to the body began to eclipse phenomenology, postmodernist literary criticism, with its focus on ideological critique and the power of representation, began to supplant formalism. Against the implicitly subject-centered existentialism of phenomenology, theory increasingly questioned humanism, or the belief in the individual as rational and autonomous rather than conditioned by his (and it was always his) environment. Similarly, formalism's insistence on the autonomy of the aesthetic seemed ill-equipped to account for literature and art's engagement with political movements emerging within the academy and wider society, such as women's liberation and the post-May 1968 generation of thinkers.

In contrast to formalism's aestheticism, postmodernism is more closely related to semiotics, or the study of signs and systems of signification. This focus on signs and the structures that organize them into larger discourses necessitated a shift towards representation. Although both form and representation have a close relationship to politics, representation has a more explicitly ideological dimension. Because representations will always stand in for something else, a focus on literature as a representation necessitates engaging with the thing – the social, cultural, and political world – the text represents. To approach an aesthetic object through representation means it cannot be divorced from the world it depicts but is rather embedded in social and historical worlds. Thus, if formalists sought to identify the unique qualities of poetic language and from there to derive universal, ahistorical principles of literature, postmodernism insisted that literature – like all other forms of discourse – is of a specifically historical nature.[94] The major interpretive development to emerge

---

93 Much postmodernist literary criticism does not do away with form, of course (a move that would, in any case, be impossible), but rather argues it is shaped by social and political forces. See, for instance, Terry Eagleton, *Criticism and Ideology: A Study in Marxist Literary Theory* (London: Verso, 1978). Fredric Jameson is also deeply concerned with form as ideology, arguing "that form is immanently and intrinsically an ideology in its own right," in Jameson, *The Political Unconscious: Narrative as a Socially Symbolic Act* (Ithaca, NY: Cornell University Press, 1982), 127.

94 Lentricchia, *After the New Criticism*, xiv. Lentricchia differentiates between the teleological or universal historical theories that influenced the New Critics and the historical

from postmodernism was the marrying of close reading with historical materialist approaches that sought to remove the veil of ideology, or what has often been called "symptomatic reading."[95] Deconstruction, too, relies on a mode of intense close reading that focuses on gaps, inconsistencies, latencies, and aporias rather than wholeness and unity.[96] Eschewing a direct focus on the object of perception, postmodernism sought to uncover the historical and ideological processes that led to – and are embodied in – the aesthetic object.

The linguistic turn's shift from form to representation pushed literary studies to gradually abandon an attachment to aesthetic specificity and autonomy. Fields like the New Historicism, for instance, treated literature as one discourse among many. Indeed, it is partly the turn away from form that, perhaps ironically, brings the body to the fore much more in postmodernism than in formalism.[97] If the concrete body is the untheorized ground of poetic language in formalism – a constant but never explicit presence that need not be made fully visible – then for postmodernism, the body helps trace out the material limits of discourse. As postmodernism turned away from the universal subject and

approaches influenced by Hayden White's argument that historical methodology shapes historical perspective.
95 The term originally comes from Louis Althusser to describe a mode of interpretation that focuses on a text's latent meaning, in Althusser, *Reading Capital*, trans. Etienne Balibar (New York: Pantheon Books, 1971), 32. Eve Kosofsky Sedgewick has also termed this type of analysis "paranoid reading," deriving from what Paul Ricoeur calls the "hermeneutics of suspicion." See Kosofsky Sedgwick, *Touching Feeling* (Durham, NC: Duke University Press, 2003), Chap. 4 and Paul Ricoeur, *Freud and Philosophy: An Essay on Interpretation*, trans. Denis Savage (New Haven, CT: Yale University Press, 1970), 32.
96 See Christopher Norris, *Contest of Faculties: Philosophy and Theory after Deconstruction* (New York; London: Routledge, 2009), 220–21.
97 The scholarship on literature, language, and the body is vast, but touchstone texts include Elaine Scarry, *The Body in Pain: The Making and Unmaking of the World* (Oxford: Oxford University Press, 1987) and Elaine Scarry, *Resisting Representation* (Oxford: Oxford University Press, 1994); Peter Brooks, *Body Work: Objects of Desire in Modern Narrative* (Cambridge, MA: Harvard University Press, 1993); Cathy Caruth, *Unclaimed Experience: Trauma, Narrative, and History* (Baltimore, MD: Johns Hopkins University Press, 1996); Katie Conboy and Nadia Medina, eds., *Writing on the Body: Female Embodiment and Feminist Theory* (New York: Columbia University Press, 1997); Arthur W. Frank, *The Wounded Storyteller: Body, Illness, and Ethics* (Chicago: University of Chicago Press, 1997); Christine Froula, *Modernism's Body: Sex, Culture, and Joyce* (New York: Columbia University Press, 1996); and Lori Hope Lefkovitz, ed., *Textual Bodies: Changing Boundaries of Literary Representation* (Albany, NY: SUNY Press, 1997). More recent scholarship often engages with 'embodiment,' including William A. Cohen, *Embodied: Victorian Literature and the Senses* (Minneapolis, MN: University of Minnesota Press, 2009); Breu, *Insistence of the Material*; Guillemette Bolens, *The Style of Gestures: Embodiment and Cognition in Literary Narrative*, trans. Alain Berthoz (Baltimore, MD: Johns Hopkins University Press, 2012); and David Hillman and Ulrika Maude, eds., *The Cambridge Companion to the Body in Literature* (Cambridge: Cambridge University Press, 2015).

transcendental, abstract truths, it desired "to make contact with some ground, with the physical stripped of metaphysical pretensions."[98] Yet in doing away with form, postmodernist approaches have placed the materiality of the body beyond representation. In their introduction to the New Historicism, for instance, Catherine Gallagher and Stephen Greenblatt argue that the materiality of the human body "functions as a kind of 'spoiler,' always baffling or exceeding the ways in which it is represented."[99] While representation allowed postmodernist thinkers to critique the discursive structures of power and knowledge that produce subjects, the focus on discourse also turned embodiment and the material body into textuality, what Patricia Waugh has called postmodernism's "flesh-eating proclivities."[100] To read for this body, one must read for its absence. The postmodernist metaphor of "writing the body," Waugh argues, merely extends "the Platonist/Cartesian evacuation and elimination of the affective body."[101] In one of the seminal studies of the body in literature, for instance, Peter Brooks argues that the impossibility of capturing the body in language is a function of "the representation of the body in signs [which] endeavors to make the body present, but always within the context of its absence, since use of the linguistic sign implies the absence of the thing for which it stands."[102] Language can only render the body's negative image, a form of dematerialization – or of matter turned into text – that haunts postmodernist approaches to literature and the body.

To approach the body as a function of form, however, expands the conceptual tools at our disposal for tracing both embodiment's influence on literature and its manifestation in aspects of literature that exceed the representational or mimetic.[103] At the same time, it is necessary to conceive of new reading practices that do not reproduce the logic of representation, which dictates that the meaning of a text lies in what it does not overtly express. As long as we are reading for what a text cannot say, the body will forever resist interpretation, exceed signification, escape

---

98 Cecile Lindsay, "Lyotard and the Postmodern Body," *L'Esprit Créateur* 31, no. 1 (1991): 33–47, 33.
99 Catherine Gallagher and Stephen Greenblatt, *Practicing New Historicism* (Chicago: University of Chicago Press, 2000), 15.
100 Patricia Waugh, "Writing the Body: Modernism and Postmodernism," in *The Body and the Arts*, ed. Corinne J. Saunders, Ulrika Maude, and Jane Macnaughton (Basingstoke; New York: Palgrave Macmillan, 2009), 133.
101 Waugh, "Writing the Body," 136.
102 P. Brooks, *Body Work*, 7–8.
103 Whereas Waugh turns (back to) modernist aesthetics as a way of bringing "the body back into language, thought, and expression," in Waugh, "Writing the Body," 136, I attend more closely to the concept of form as itself an organizing principle of embodiment.

representation. Yet while form may offer the most fruitful way accessing embodied experiences that surpass representation, traditional formalist methods have consistently missed the body's presence because they do not see the body as an essential component of aesthetic form. My method thus puts into dialogue postmodernism's political concerns with form's organization of aesthetic elements into a cohesive (though not total) figure. Doing so will help us read for the body as a unified whole that may not be readily recognizable on a representational or thematic register.[104] Representations are but one element – one body part – of the whole. Embodied form enables us to grasp modes of attachment, affordance, and connection in the body's organization of poetic language.

Violence and the Formless Body

Let me now turn to several specific examples through which we can grasp how the shift from form to representation and from the body's presence to its dematerialization are intertwined in the figure of the unrepresentable body. This will lead onto my critique of postmodernism, which frames the relationship between the body and representation as a form of violence. Postmodernism's critique of form is part of a larger questioning of master narratives, universal institutions, and metaphysics, those seemingly opaque or oppressive structures of thought. One of the nodes in which we can trace this shift takes place in Jacques Derrida's "Structure, Sign, and Play," often cited as one of the foundational texts of poststructuralism and deconstruction.[105] Derrida's target in this essay

---

104 Cleanth Brooks distinguishes between scientific and poetic methods of analyzing experience. Whereas the scientist breaks experience "up into parts" and distinguishes "part from part," the poet's task is "to unify experience," in C. Brooks, *The Well Wrought Urn*, 213. For the New Critics, then, close reading is the only practice proper to literary criticism. Other contextual approaches may be useful, but they "describe the process of composition, not the structure of the thing composed," in C. Brooks, "The Formalist Critics," *The Kenyon Review* 13, no. 1 (1951): 72–81, 74.

105 Derrida originally wrote "La structure, le signe et le jeu dans le discours des sciences humaines" (Structure, Sign, and Play in the Discourse of the Human Sciences) for a conference at Johns Hopkins University in 1966, in which Paul de Man, Roland Barthes, Jacques Lacan, and Tzvetan Todorov also participated. It was later collected in *L'Ecriture et la différance* (1967, *Writing and Difference*), before being translated and published in a collected volume dedicated to the conference, entitled *The Structuralist Controversy: The Languages of Criticism and the Sciences of Man* (1970) and later English translations of *Writing and Difference*. François Cusset calls this conference "a founding moment" of poststructuralism, in Cusset, *French Theory: How Foucault, Derrida, Deleuze, & Co. Transformed the Intellectual Life of the United States*, trans. Jeff Fort (Minneapolis: University of Minnesota Press, 2008), 32. Although poststructuralism and deconstruction refuse metaphysical concepts like 'origin,' it is tempting to treat 1966 as their birth point.

is structuralism, but his use of structure is often itself synonymous with form. (We can also note certain similarities between structuralism and formalism, both in terms of their close historical emergence and their similar focus on universal concepts, structures, and patterns.) The essay's final paragraphs open up interpretive pathways that diverge radically from earlier reading models, like the New Criticism.[106] Yet it is also clear that deconstruction and other postmodernist approaches are indebted to these earlier formalisms (in fact, opponents of deconstruction often equated it with the New Critics' narrow preoccupation with the text).[107]

In the essay, Derrida argues that Western philosophical and metaphysical conceptions of "structure" are synonymous with "center." In turn, "center" stands in for a range of metaphysical first principles that designate origin, wholeness, essence, substance, consciousness, and presence. (He uses Greek terms like *eidos, telos,* and *ousia.*)[108] This defers the need to understand "the structurality of structure"[109] – that is, the epistemological limits of Western metaphysics – by "giving it a center" or a "point of origin." He links this critique to the question of form: "By orienting and organizing the coherence of the system, the center of a structure permits the play of its elements inside the total form [*la forme totale*]. And even today the notion of a structure lacking any center represents the unthinkable itself."[110] The center is thus both unique to the structure and something universal that exists outside of it. The center determines the structure's organization because it "escapes structurality." This substitution of "center for center" constitutes, for Derrida, the fundamental project of Western metaphysics, which is "the determination of Being as *presence* in all senses of the word," or the projection of a unitary subject.[111]

> In addition to the Johns Hopkins conference, which was originally intended to embed *structuralism* in the American academy, the same year saw the publication of Jacques Lacan's *Écrits* and Michel Foucault's *The Order of Things*. For a non-hagiographic discussion of this conference that carefully places it within the context of poststructuralism and other types of postmodern 'theory' see Jean-Michel Rabaté, *The Future of Theory* (Oxford, UK: Blackwell Publishers, 2002), 36–46.

106 Norris argues that "the closing paragraphs of 'Structure, Sign and Play' were adapted to catch the current mood of critics chafing under the rigid dispensation of 'old' New Critical precept," in Norris, *Contest of Faculties*, 137. Norris is critical of the way the subsequent reception of Derrida's essay emphasized its "joyously post-New-Critical interpretive license" in a way that superseded Derrida's serious engagement with the history of metaphysics.
107 See Norris, *Contest of Faculties*, 70–71 for an overview of these debates.
108 Jacques Derrida, *Writing and Difference*, trans. Alan Bass (London: Routledge, 2009), 353.
109 Derrida, *Writing and Difference*, 351–52.
110 Derrida, *Writing and Difference*, 352.
111 Derrida, *Writing and Difference*, 353.

Derrida identifies a strand of thinking in which a formless form – a form without any central organizing function – is unpresentable to thought itself. We can recognize a parallel to this autonomous, fully contained, and yet also transcendental form in early- to mid-century formalisms. Derrida's deconstructive project seeks to demonstrate that it is impossible to transcend such structures – that there is no natural center, presence, or being. He turns away from the language of form and structure, tainted by a metaphysics of wholeness, to "discourse," a "system in which the central signified, the original or transcendental signified, is never absolutely present outside a system of differences."[112] This "system of differences" (or *différance*) revises the Saussurean notion that linguistic signs only convey meaning through their difference from other signs. *Différance* signals how language can never fully capture the thing it seeks to represent. Meaning is constantly deferred along a chain of signifiers, and this displacement undermines the dualisms essential to a self that pre-exists discourse. In a later interview with Julia Kristeva, he calls this "the presence of something present (for example, in the form of the identity of the subject who is present for all his operations.)" *Différance* signifies that "the conscious and speaking subject [. . .] is not present, nor above all present to itself before *différance*"; the subject "is constituted only in being divided from itself."[113] Derrida does not explicitly evoke the body either here or in "Structure, Sign, and Play." But terms like presence, origin, and center recall formal organicism and physical materiality – those things that are immediately present to thought.[114] However, the inverse of this is a form that cannot be reduced to a metaphysical presence, but that is nevertheless fully presentable as a material presence. In this way, the material body becomes unrepresentable.

---

112 Derrida, *Writing and Difference*, 354.
113 Jacques Derrida, *Positions*, trans. Alan Bass (Chicago: University of Chicago Press, 1998), 29. This reflection takes place in the interview with Julia Kristeva, "Semiology and Grammatology."
114 Indeed, the organizers of the Johns Hopkins conference, Richard Macksey and Eugenio Donato, capture the "common denominator" that brings together the many contributions to the conference, in the opening remarks to the accompany volume, *The Structuralist Controversy*. A quote by Gilles Deleuze succinctly condenses the "bloodless" impulses of poststructuralism, which is animated by "a cold and concerted destruction of the subject, a lively distaste for notions of origin, of lost origin, of recovered origin, a dismantling of unifying pseudo-syntheses of consciousness, a denunciation of all the mystifications of history performed in the name of progress, of consciousness, and of the future of reason." This is quoted in Macksey and Donato, "The Space Between – 1971," in *The Structuralist Controversy: The Languages of Criticism and the Sciences of Man*, ed. Richard Macksey and Eugenio Donato (Baltimore, MD: Johns Hopkins University Press, 1970), x.

Derrida's putative object of criticism in "Structure, Sign, and Play" is structuralism, specifically Claude Lévi-Strauss' anthropology. But the essay evokes a critical spirit of infinite play that also distances itself from the kind of rigid interpretive modes found in the New Criticism (even as it remains indebted to close reading). Formalists institutionalized the interpretive practice on which many postmodernist approaches to literature draw, but, as François Cusset argues, "they never laid a foundation for *the critique of critical reason* that" Derrida deployed "in an effort to reveal the rationalist illusions of ordinary reading – in relation to the totality of the text, its autonomy, its semantic articulation."[115] This became the project of the New Criticism's reluctant heirs, such as Paul de Man, as well its most trenchant critics, such as the New Historicism.

Derrida's essay also puts forward one of the major characteristics of postmodernist critique, namely the idea that there is no way outside of such boundaries, even as the boundary itself posits something unrepresentable. For postmodernism, the unrepresentable signifies the limits of critique, and critique can thus never be a metaphysical project that exceeds itself or constitutes itself as origin, end, and authority. Using a similar register to Derrida, Jean-François Lyotard describes the postmodern as:

> that which in the modern invokes the unpresentable in presentation itself, that which refuses the consolation of correct forms, refuses the consensus of taste permitting a common experience of nostalgia for the impossible, and inquires into new presentations – not to take pleasure in them, but to better produce the feeling that there is something unpresentable.[116]

Like Derrida, Lyotard associates form with Platonic *eidos*, or transcendental universal forms as opposed to material things. Postmodern critique refuses the belief in a "transparent and communicable experience," or in language's referential capacity to communicate this experience.[117] To acknowledge an experience that is unpresentable to thought also refuses formal unity or a coincidence between representation and thought. This approach is useful to the extent that it allows postmodernism to critique the limits of its own theoretical project, or to posit its theoretical project as a critique of limits and the (im)possibility of moving beyond them. Yet what is evident in both Derrida and Lyotard's conception of what

---

115 Cusset, *French Theory*, 52. Italics in original.
116 Jean-François Lyotard, *The Postmodern Explained: Correspondence 1982–1985*, trans. Don Barry et al. (Minneapolis, MN: University of Minnesota Press, 1992), 15.
117 Lyotard, *The Postmodern Explained*, 16. See also Derrida's essay on Michel Foucault, "Cogito and the History of Madness," collected in *Writing and Difference*, for a discussion of how any attempt to depart from the tradition of philosophical reason only reinscribes concepts and methods from this tradition.

is representable is a suspicion of presence, being, or subject. These all remain too close to humanist concepts of an authentic self.

Postmodernist theories about the abject and fragmented body, which dissolve the subject's boundaries, encapsulate this unrepresentable materiality. The abject is most closely associated with the highly influential psychoanalytic and feminist theorist Julia Kristeva, who argues that abjection is the horror of witnessing the body's inextricable materiality, which "draws me toward the place where meaning collapses" and that is "edged with the sublime."[118] The abject threatens the distinction between subject and object, self and other, producing a sense of disgust embodied in the reaction to such things as corpses, vomit, shit, blood, and other bodily excretions that signal at once the body's rejection and incorporation. Fundamentally, however, it is "not lack of cleanliness or health that causes abjection but what disturbs identity, system, order. What does not respect borders, positions, rules." It recalls the boundary established as the subject enters the symbolic order, or the order of language and representation, society, institutions, norms, traditions, and rules (of politics, in other words), which entails a repression of bodily materiality, what must be "permanently thrust aside in order to live."[119] It is a reminder of those fundamental elements of embodied existence that escape representation and whose return threatens the fragile boundaries of not only the self but also the social order as a whole. The abject is "a terror that dissembles,"[120] a kind of *formlessness*. It disturbs those seemingly impenetrable forms of order that materialize in concrete institutions like the law – the institutionalization of political power – by creating something unrepresentable.

The abject represents one example of the postmodern body. Another is the fragmented body. Indeed, the close connection between the fragmented and the abject body is demonstrated in Lyotard's figure of the libidinal body, a "so-called body" whose "surfaces" are "spread out." Through objects that dismember and deconstruct – "scissors," "scalpels and tweezers" – Lyotard meticulously (one might say, sadistically) dissects and exposes the body in a process of almost sexual violence that "expose[s] the labia majora" as well as other organs of reproduction and digestion. Eventually the body is spread and fully exposed.[121] This body's grotesque flaying exposes how representation wreaks violence on

---

118 Julia Kristeva, *Powers of Horror: An Essay on Abjection*, trans. Leon S. Roudiez (New York: Columbia University Press, 1982), 2.
119 Kristeva, *Powers of Horror*, 3.
120 Kristeva, *Powers of Horror*, 4.
121 Jean-François Lyotard, *Libidinal Economy*, trans. Iain Hamilton Grant (Bloomington, IN: Indiana University Press, 1993), 1.

the material body. As Cecile Lindsay writes of this passage, Lyotard's use of figurative language seeks to reveal the rhetorical nature of all discourse, and thus the way in which "language cannot really represent the libidinal body because that body never was and will never be present as an object to be represented."[122]

Lyotard's exteriorization of the body through figurative language is once again part of an anti-metaphysical project that refuses an organic or Cartesian body. In undoing distinctions like inside and outside, Lyotard seeks to disconnect the body from identity, and all of the institutions that govern and oppress subjects.[123] This results in a body of different parts, a fragmented body, although Lyotard refuses the term, "because there has only ever been fragments [*des morceaux*] of bodies and there will never be a body, this wandering collection being the very affirmation of the non-body."[124]

Lyotard's simultaneous invocation and rejection of the body indicates that there is an ambivalence in many postmodernist approaches to the abject, the fragmented, or the unrepresentable. On the one hand, these concepts disrupt the symbolic or social order, which is also the realm of power and control. They can thus signal an emancipatory project of subverting oppressive political systems. On the other hand, precisely because they disrupt order, they can be harnessed for horrific political ends. Unsurprisingly, discussions of the abject and the sublime often invoke the Holocaust. For Kristeva, Auschwitz is the ultimate abjection. It is symbolized by discarded heaps of children's shoes – themselves objects that stand in for their absent subjects.[125] For Lyotard, Auschwitz is a sort of horrific sublime that exceeds understanding: it is a "silence imposed on knowledge" or "the sign that something remains to be phrased which is not."[126] He associates this type of terror with a "nostalgia for the all and the one, for a reconciliation of the concept and the sensible, for a transparent and communicable experience."[127] He employs the same bellicose language of terror when he calls for a "war on totality" to destroy the possibility of seemingly total forms.[128]

---

122 Lindsay, "Lyotard and the Postmodern Body," 35. She provides a highly sophisticated analysis of the relation between the postmodern and the body in Lyotard's thought.
123 See Lindsay, "Lyotard and the Postmodern Body," 37.
124 Jean-François Lyotard, *Dérive à partir de Marx et Freud* (Paris: Galilée, 1994), 14. My translation.
125 Kristeva, *Powers of Horror*, 4.
126 Jean-François Lyotard, *The Differend: Phrases in Dispute*, trans. Georges Van Den Abbeele (Manchester: Manchester University Press, 1988), 56, 57.
127 Lyotard, *The Postmodern Explained*, 16.
128 Lyotard, *The Postmodern Explained*, 16.

Lyotard's call for a "war on totality" and the evocation of Auschwitz as the horror that reduces the body to pure materiality returns us to the political stakes of placing the body beyond representation. The corporeal is what exists before discourse, the symbolic order, or representation. The abject acknowledges the body's corporeal existence. Indeed, it reduces the body, at least momentarily, to pure corporeal existence, and it places embodied experience outside of political control. At the same time, it makes this corporeality the condition of violence. Before I turn to exploring an alternative relationship between representation and embodiment, I want to dwell upon the intersection between violence and the body in postmodernist thought.

Both Kristeva and Lyotard's descriptions of the body conceive of representation as a form of violence – a view that still holds remarkable sway in literary criticism. As Foucault writes, "we must conceive discourse as a violence which we do to things, or in any case as a practice which we impose on them."[129] The limits and boundaries of truth are subject to a constant "policing" that designates what can be thought at a particular historical juncture.[130] Discourse's disciplinary function produces certain bodies, sometimes violently but always with force. Butler takes up this notion of the violent erection of boundaries when she argues that the "marking off" or creation of a boundary "will have some normative force and, indeed, some violence, for it can construct only through erasing."[131] The construction of discursive categories, whether of gender, sexuality, race, or class, thus always entails a form of violence. Teresa de Lauretis also echoes Foucault and Butler's concerns, insisting on the connection between violence's "semiotic" and "social" valences. She argues that "some order of language, some kind of discursive representation is at work not only in the concept of 'violence' but in the social practices of violence as well."[132] De Lauretis contrasts this "rhetoric of violence," in which representation imposes certain forms of truth and being, to the "violence of rhetoric," which she associates with the "violence of the letter" in Derrida's work, or the erasure of femininity by turning it into a purely textuality figure.[133]

For thinkers like Foucault, Butler, de Lauretis, and Derrida, violence results not only from the breakdown of order but also, importantly,

---

129 Foucault, "The Order of Discourse," 67.
130 Foucault, "The Order of Discourse," 61.
131 Butler, *Bodies That Matter*, 11.
132 Teresa de Lauretis, "The Violence of Rhetoric: Considerations on Representation and Gender," *Semiotica* 54, no. 1–2 (1985): 11–31, 32.
133 Quoted in de Lauretis, "The Violence of Rhetoric," 32.

through its imposition.[134] Violence is a structural principle that shapes the norms governing our embodied experiences, whether through the legal ability to use a pronoun that makes one's bodily identity livable or in the policing of black bodies that subject them to the constant threat of annihilation. Yet power is not monolithic or unidirectional. Its productive dimension means it can also be turned back against dominant structures, either as a form of critique or as a mode of political resistance. Against the violent force of discourse, rhetoric, and representation, postmodernist thinkers have wielded what Beatrice Hanssen has called "counterviolence": "a symbolic, figurative, discursive force, wielded as a counterprinciple," which "is meant to undo metaphysical, institutional sedimentations of force, especially the violence exercised by instrumental reason, with its logic *and* practices of exclusion."[135] In postmodernist critique, these forms of counterviolence have most often been waged at the level of discourse, for instance in the critique of Western philosophy's metaphysical foundations. They have also targeted how discourse reifies metaphysical categories, as in Butler's notion that "matter" is not a pre-existent substance but is constituted through "*a process of materialization that stabilizes over time to produce the effect of boundary, fixity, and surface we call matter.*"[136] These counterdiscourses have both revealed the patterns of power and dominance that shape ontological and epistemological categories, and offered ways of undoing and deconstructing such categories.

As my analysis of the relationship between the unrepresentable body and the celebration of formlessness have indicated above, postmodernist modes of counterviolence have often been enacted through the interconnection of these two figures. Taken together, the abject or fragmented body and the undoing of governing forms have helped dismantle the primary target of postmodernist criticism: a sovereign subject housed in a unified body and metaphysical principles like presence, origin, unity, and wholeness. The fragmented container of the body shatters the fantasy of the autonomous, sovereign subject that in turn subverts the totalizing, unified effects of form, understood in terms of boundaries, categories, practices, or norms. The fragmented body resists both political and

---

134 For instance, Agamben has celebrated a kind of formlessless as a way of eluding and undoing the structures of power: "If to constituent power there correspond revolutions, revolts, and new constitutions, namely, a violence that puts in place and constitutes a new law, for *destituent potential* it is necessary to think entirely different strategies," quoted in Kornbluh, *The Order of Forms*, 2. Kornbluh has termed this impulse "anarcho-vitalism," or a drive towards formlessness.
135 Beatrice Hanssen, *Critique of Violence: Between Poststructuralism and Critical Theory* (London; New York: Routledge, 2000), 14.
136 Butler, *Bodies That Matter*, 9. Italics in original.

aesthetic determination, while also embodying the effects of discursive construction. Similarly, the critique of form emerged from a desire to undo the metaphysical foundations of thought that emphasized wholeness and totality. Formal unity and embodied integrity, in other words, are not only naïve fantasies but dangerous forms of metaphysical thinking that seduce through the utopian promise of totality – a seduction that, as we see in Kristeva and Lyotard's evocation of the Holocaust, leads to those impenetrable forms whose objective is to annihilate difference, namely the concentration camp and the gulag. Resistance resides in fragmentation and undoing.

But is violence necessary for resistance? In her astute critique of the relationship between power and violence in critical theory and poststructuralism, Hanssen asks whether counterviolence and other "subversive technologies stifle or instead enable the possibility of transformative change, violence-free communication or ethico-political action?"[137] As Hanssen notes, "the conceptual vicissitudes of violence," once meaning "the use of physical force," have been "stretched beyond its former clearly demarcated boundaries" to include "such phenomenologically elusive categories as psychological, symbolic, structural, epistemic, hermeneutical, and aesthetic violence."[138] The rhetoric of violence flattens the brute, material force that is enacted upon bodies into a linguistic effect. A trite example of this is the invocation of 'thoughts and prayers' as a replacement for political action against structural violence, whether for victims of rape or school shootings. The flip side of this is the retreat to excuses that it was 'only rhetoric' when words provoke actual violence. Yet the counterdiscourse of the unrepresentable body undermines resistance; it fragments the seat of agency, placing the embodied experience of those most vulnerable to political violence outside of our perceptual sphere. This does not emancipate the body from representation. It makes it more susceptible to violence wielded by those who enjoy full political representation and whose experience implicitly shapes our governing forms.[139] Judith Butler, for instance, later identifies a paradox at the center of postmodernist debates about the subject:

> How can it be that the subject, taken to be the condition for and instrument of agency, is at the same time the effect of subordination, understood as the deprivation of agency? If subordination is the condition of possibility

---

137 Hanssen, *Critique of Violence*, 14.
138 Hanssen, *Critique of Violence*, 9.
139 See Scarry, *The Body in Pain* for a highly influential discussion of the body's ineffability and how this affects political representation.

for agency, how might agency be thought in opposition to the forces of subordination?[140]

Resistance becomes realizable only as a counterforce – a *reaction* – rather than as a progressive project of building and (re)construction.

In *Formal Matters*, I extend Hanssen's question about whether the conflation of power and violence has foreclosed other possible modes of resistance, and, if so, where these modes of resistance might be located. If poststructuralism and postmodernism have cast form as a type of violence, and have sought to make the body unrepresentable in order to resist the violence of form, can the unifying effects of form and the formal unification of the body ever be counterdiscourses of resistance? Form does always entail order, structure, patterns, shapes, 'discipline,' and, to a certain extent, norms. Yet this need not end in violence or radical exclusion. When brought into relationship with embodiment's agency and volition, form holds out the potential to arrange, make manifest, and give shape to modes of resistance – to create affective and aesthetic attachments – that do not necessarily require violence or that use violence as a rhetorical tool.

Form affords ways of reinstating an embodied agency in language that need not reinforce the autonomous, universal subject. Rather than seeing the production of the subject as an inherently violent and exclusionary process, we might understand it – in formal terms – as a way of bringing together a wide range of paradoxical and even competing forces and affects. The body-as-form provides a container for these differences, without the need to assimilate or homogenize them. The answer, then, is not to place embodiment beyond representation or to fragment the body so that it cannot become an object of power. Rather, it is to change the nature of political forms so that they can accommodate materiality without transforming it either into brute materiality or metaphysical presence. Literature, as one of the most fundamental types of 'form-making,' will help test out the stakes of changing intransigent forms, as well as the possibilities and benefits of imagining new, even unthinkable ones (something that, as the Holocaust shows, can be far from desirable.)

---

140 Judith Butler, *The Psychic Life of Power: Theories in Subjection* (Stanford, CA: Stanford University Press, 1997), 10. Indeed, much of Butler's later work is in many ways an attempt to understand why individuals would, in her words, turn around at the sound of the policeman's voice and allow themselves to be constructed as a social subject, in Butler, *The Psychic Life of Power*, 5.

Embodiment's Corpus

This intertwined conceptual and historical framework has shaped the book's corpus, which focuses on twentieth-century European literature. While literary explorations of embodiment certainly predate the twentieth century, this book focuses on work produced during a period dominated by two rival critical approaches to literature, the first insisting on the primacy of form, the second on the importance of representation. It is also a period where radically new concepts of the body emerged, at the same time that the body came under extreme political pressure, most significantly in the form of the concentration camp. In this sense, I treat twentieth-century literature as both an "aesthetic regime"[141] and a historical period. To read this aesthetic and historical period through the concept of embodied form allows the body's universal and historical dimensions to emerge in tandem with each other. It provides a fuller understanding of the point where form ends, representation begins, and where, perhaps, the boundaries between them become more indistinct.

To explore these concerns, this book turns to four twentieth-century European writers whose works give form to embodied experience where representation – both aesthetic and political – fails to figure. The work of Anne F. Garréta (France), Samuel Beckett (Ireland), Maurice Blanchot (France), and Primo Levi (Italy) redistributes embodiment in literary form in order to offer alternative compositions of the body not reduced to characteristics of race, gender, sexuality, or disability. The body, as the fundamental ground of language and experience, provides the site and subject of this experimentation. These diverse authors, distinct in terms of language, region, time period, genre, theme, subject, mode, and style, are thus united by a highly modernist impulse to produce new literary forms that self-consciously theorize form itself.[142] As Stephen Ross argues, the close relationship between formal experimentation and theoretical production in modernism has been lost with the turn to historicist, materialist, and other approaches that treat literary language as one discourse amongst many.[143] As we have seen, this same turn to discourse and representation elides the body. Returning the body to form – and returning form to theory – will help bridge this divide.

---

141 Rancière, *The Politics of Aesthetics*, 23.
142 See Stephen Ross, "Introduction: The Missing Link," in *Modernism and Theory: A Critical Debate*, ed. Stephen Ross (New York: Routledge, 2009), 2–3. See also Rabaté, *The Future of Theory*, 134.
143 Ross, "Introduction: The Missing Link," 14.

Formal Matter's arc traces abstract concepts of form as they gradually gain a more concrete reality in relation to political contexts in which the relationship between the body and representation carries life or death consequences. The book's structure is chiastic, balancing conceptual forms of embodiment on one side, with concrete representations of the body on the other, as they come into violent contact with the Holocaust. The first chapter, "The Corporeal Urn," provides a fuller analysis of embodied form in relation to institutions of criticism, phenomenology, rhetoric, and aesthetics. It explores how a series of formal figures and interpretive devices enable us to read for embodied form beyond representations of specific bodies. These devices include the notion of 'logical forms' – or figures that project embodied experience – as well as poetic tropes like chiasmus, prosopopoeia, catachresis, metalepsis, and aporia. Through these different figures and formal constellations, I demonstrate how a return to older formalist methods reinvigorates our understanding of the body and its relationship to politics.

After establishing the conceptual ground of embodied form, the second chapter, "*La Pensée incarnée*: Embodying the Unrepresentable in Anne Garréta's *Sphinx*," explores how abstract aesthetic forms can disrupt and redistribute characteristics like gender and race that the normative force of discourse has naturalized. The French author and academic Anne F. Garréta (1962–) has only recently become known to English-speaking audiences through the translation of several of her novels. Her radical literary experiments with form combine with her deep knowledge of queer and feminist theory to produce texts that critique postmodernist assumptions about literature's referential function. The chapter analyzes her first novel, *Sphinx* (1986), which her English translator asserts is the first 'genderless' novel. Garréta eschews any gendered description of the two main characters, a difficult project given that it means avoiding the use of most pronouns, as well as corresponding adjectives and some verbs, which require gender agreement in French. Since gender is a discursive construct, *Sphinx*'s 'genderless' language would logically dictate that it lacks both a body and form. The genderless body in the novel sharply contrasts, however, with the overdetermination of the black body, which reduces the protagonist's love interest to a racialized object. The book thus exemplifies the postmodernist binary of a body that either escapes or is reduced to representation. But shifting attention to the valences of form allows a different body to emerge, while also deconstructing both discursive and biological categories of race. Through an exploration of logical figures like the sphinx and the way prosopopoeia performs embodiment, I demonstrate how the body is given form beyond representation in ways that speculatively offer new political relations.

Having explored how gender and race – types of representation that have a material influence on both embodied experience and political rights – can be deconstructed as formal configurations, the third chapter produces two highly formalist figures from embodied materiality: figure and ground. "'All life is figure and ground': Samuel Beckett and the Politics of Embodied Form" explores a range of works by Beckett, a writer who exemplifies the failure of language and the fracturing of the body, what has often been called his "aesthetics of failure." Against this emphasis on failure, lack, and withdrawal, I explore how dismembered body parts and organs are figures for the embodied foundations of speech and language. In turn, I argue that his texts produce form as a ground through which different conceptions of the body emerge that would be unintelligible when read through representation. Metalepsis ties together embodiment's 'push and pull' movements. It is the trope for extension and elision, but it also simultaneously draws in and accumulates language into an embodied form. Whereas deaf, blind, mute, and dismembered bodies are often excluded from the literal grounds of representation – speaking, acting, and appearing – the approach I develop in this chapter demonstrates how seemingly fractured bodies produce literary forms that make this embodied experience graspable, even as it is distributed in unexpected ways. Yet metalepsis does not install a falsely holistic or unified body. Rather, I argue that Beckett's broken, stuttering, and tortured bodies demonstrate the dangers of turning form over to violence and totality.

The first half of the book thus traces how abstract concepts of form can disrupt naturalized, physical categories like sex, gender, and race, while also acknowledging the dangers of separating form from material contexts of power and violence. This chiastic crisscrossing between race/gender and figure/ground anticipates the book's fourth chapter, "The Unbearable Lightness of Being: Chiasmus, Embodiment, and Interpretation in Maurice Blanchot," which takes up the challenge of writing criticism with an embodied form. Blanchot is a philosopher who has long been read in terms of the negativity, neutrality, and withdrawal of language and the subject. By contrast, I read the experience of lightness in his short final *récit*, *The Instant of My Death* (1994, *L'Instant de ma mort*), as producing a form of thought that embodies absence in the figure of the chiasmus. Indeed, this chapter functions as the fulcrum for *Formal Matter*'s chiastic structure, making this book's form a key element in demonstrating how embodiment organizes form, interpretation, and thought. On one side is poised my analysis of Garréta and Beckett's formalist autonomy. On the other side hangs my exploration of the stakes and possibilities of representing embodiment in Primo

Levi's Holocaust testimonies. The deconstruction of race and gender – immaterial categories that have concrete material consequences – in Garréta and Beckett are necessary for understanding Levi's engagement with embodiment, which challenges the reduction of Jews to base corporeality. In turn, the historical specificity of Levi's writing casts another light on the formal allusiveness of race and gender in the previous chapters. Levi does not turn away from the demands of representation. Rather, his work demonstrates how embodiment is necessary for representation – both literary and political – to take form.

The final chapter, then, "The Hunger Artist: Testimony, Representation, and Embodiment in Primo Levi," explicitly interrogates the relationship between the body and representation. The Holocaust exterminated the overwhelming majority of witnesses, and consequently, postmodernist theorists have often treated it as the unrepresentable event *par excellence*. These philosophical questions have gone hand in hand with aesthetic debates about how to appropriately represent the Shoah. Yet the supposed unrepresentability of the Holocaust marginalizes the embodied experience of its victims, placing their suffering beyond understanding. This chapter intervenes in these debates through an analysis of embodiment in Levi's testimonial literature, including *If This Is a Man* (1947, *Se questo è un uomo*), *The Truce* (1963, *La tregua*), and *The Drowned and the Saved* (1986, *I sommersi e i salvati*). Only recently has scholarship touched upon the importance of the body in Levi's fictional writing; generally, scholars have associated Levi with a tradition of humanism that emphasizes how the autonomous, rational human subject can overcome the bounds of bodily materiality. By contrast, this chapter argues that embodiment underpins Levi's testimonial writing. In turn, it shows that not only is embodiment a fundamental element of testimonial form, but that testimony makes embodiment representable. Even when undergoing unthinkable trauma, the body retains a material integrity that imbues Levi's testimony with the vitality of phenomenological experience, particularly through the process of writing itself. Drawing on Rancière's critique of the unrepresentable, I demonstrate how Levi's paratactic redistribution of embodiment and the object and animal world offers more opportunities for representing embodiment, not less.

This chapter thus comes full circle to the debates about the relationship between representation and the body posed at the beginning of this book. Levi's work helps us trace out an alternative approach to representation that does not inherently do violence to the body, or place a limit on representation, even when the body has been subject to the most violent forms of political representation. But this new understanding of the body's relationship to representation is only possible once form has disrupted and redistributed the racialized, gendered, sexed, and otherwise differentiated body. My analysis of Levi demonstrates how abstract concepts of form can illuminate the violence and trauma of the Holocaust precisely because of form's attachment to, rather than autonomy from, political representation.

Finally, in the "Afterword," I revisit the political dimension of embodied form, and the embodied form of politics, through the work of Hannah Arendt. Using her notion of "common sense" as the sense of the body politic, I argue that literary form helps integrate the embodied experience of those who do not figure within normative realms of representation into wider political forms. Against the destituency of both poststructuralism and totalitarianism, Arendt insists upon the need to construct shared forms of sensory perception that exceed the individual, subjective experiences of the body. Poetic language and form provide the expressive 'bridge' between embodiment and politics.

In grouping these writers together, I navigate a divergent path between the body and literature in the second half of the twentieth century and demonstrate the book's scope by tracing the way it operates in radically different contexts. In other words, I trace *formal* relations between these writers; and their work demonstrates the ubiquity of embodied form. This formal, rather than historical, arrangement nevertheless frames an exploration of the way power and identity have shaped the modern body, including race, gender, and sexuality. These works consistently disrupt pre-existing associations of what bodies should look like and how they should act in the world. They thus have political implications. By retraining our attention to elements of embodied experience that may escape the realm of representation – but that are nevertheless composed in autonomous aesthetic spaces – these works attune us to the presence of bodies and embodied experiences normally denied access to the political realm of appearances, whether women and sexual minorities under patriarchal systems in Garréta; Jews during the Holocaust, a key concern in Levi; the disabled, vulnerable bodies of Beckett; or simply the seemingly absent body itself in Blanchot. Embodied form offers an alternative to the once emancipatory but now normative models of postmodernism, political representation, and identity. At a time when politics increasingly debases bodies and language, the book will reinvest matter with meaning.

In doing so, this book also uncovers the bodily forms that underpin literary criticism as a practice. *Formal Matter's* chiastic structure demonstrates how embodiment implicitly shapes intellectual enquiry. To insist that literary criticism should have a body – and that this body is not fragmented, shattered, or subverted – positions this book against the current critical paradigm, which remains immured in injunctions against representation. In order to think beyond the limits of representation – or of representation as a limit – this book seeks to recover a strain of aesthetic criticism that foregrounds the unity of textual form. But the book does not turn away from the ethical demands of accounting for the body's relation to power that discursive approaches have made an imperative. Embodiment refocuses the notion of the literary by bringing attention to the way experience is constructed into a meaningful whole. A reengagement with aesthetic autonomy and bodily cohesion might seem terribly anachronistic in the age of digital transformations, virtual reality, artificial intelligence, and posthumanism. But this book sets its sights on reinvesting language, representation, and form with meaning by attending to the power structures that allow certain bodies to make meaning in the first place. My wager is that understanding the relation between embodied and literary form will not only allow us to understand texts better, it will, by providing us more forms, mediums, and methods for expressing it, enable a richer *embodied experience* too.

Chapter 1

The Corporeal Urn

Form and embodiment are inseparable. Without a thorough investigation of the body's relation to literary form we fail to fully understand either one. By bringing together formalist methods with the body's political dimension, *Formal Matters* moves beyond exploring how literature represents bodies or how the body constitutes a literary theme. I tie an attention to aesthetic form with bodily experience via the notion of 'embodied form.' This helps account for both the political treatment of the body – what appears through representation – and embodiment's agential capacity to shape, rather than merely to reflect, the political sphere. One of this book's major arguments is that postmodernism's discourse of the failure of representation has become an unhelpful master narrative that renders bodily experience fundamentally unknowable, and it thus relegates it to a realm outside of political representation. Postmodernism has privileged the subjection, fragmentation, and objectification of the body over lines of enquiry that reclaim embodied agency. By contrast, *Formal Matters* is driven by two impulses. First, it constructs a path beyond the impasse that language cannot fully capture the body and, conversely, that the body fundamentally escapes representation. Second, it provides a formalist methodology that is able to account for embodied experience where it appears most attenuated and eclipsed. In contrast to the postmodern insistence that language cannot fully capture the object it seeks to represent, I argue that embodiment is not what escapes but what *constitutes* form. It is thus able to mold the political realm in ways that have not yet been fully acknowledged.

The need to challenge the master narrative of unrepresentability has never been more urgent. The fetishism of the virtual, the posthuman, and the cyborg have increasingly relegated bodily materiality to an inconvenience – an obstacle to immortality and boundless knowledge. At the same time, the politics surrounding mass displacement and containment frequently objectify racialized and gendered bodies, turning them into anonymous sites of biopolitical control. Embodied materiality either vanishes or turns into brute biological matter.

How can we return vitality to form without subjugating either the body or literature to politics? *Formal Matters* takes up this challenge by recovering older concepts of form that were once the preserve of formalist literary criticism and aesthetics. It puts these fields into dialogue with phenomenology and postmodernism's attention to ideology to theorize how power relations materially shape bodily forms and the way bodies reconfigure the political realm. In the "Introduction," I argued that embodiment is an organizing principle. It provides literary texts with a bodily form, and it shapes wider thought patterns. These broad movements of thought include literary criticism. In this chapter, I explore how the body's form shapes literary criticism's contours, concepts, and modes, and I tie this to a deeper analysis of the figures of embodied form.

To begin with, then, I demonstrate how the body organizes critical approaches as disparate as formalism, which elides the body, and postmodernism, which places it beyond representation. I will now turn to two scholars, Cleanth Brooks and Mary Poovey, who exemplify the approaches of their respective schools, the New Criticism and the New Historicism, to demonstrate how embodiment underpins critical interpretation.[1] The difference between the two schools can be formulated as a division between content and form, on the one hand, and context and representation on the other. But reframing their interventions in terms of embodied form moves beyond this false distinction. Embodiment underpins the New Critics' conception of form, while the question of form equally enables the postmodernist and historicist discursive body.

The figure I use to illustrate this metaphor in the New Criticism is the urn. If the figure of the lamp illuminates the Romanticist project,[2] no image better captures the New Criticism's model of form than the urn. It is central to Cleanth Brooks' famous essay, "The Language of Paradox," which explores poetic form as an enclosed vessel. The urn is the embodiment of the poem, the hermetically-sealed container whose contents cannot be contaminated by worldly pollutants (even though they were once of the world), but within which all manner of paradox, tension,

---

1 I am building on Caroline Levine's analysis of how the "bounded container" – signified by the urn in Brooks and the social body in Poovey – construct the conceptual boundaries of their thought. I move beyond Levine's comparison, however, by insisting on the embodied foundation of the bounded container. See C. Levine, *Forms*, 27–37.
2 The now famous distinction between the mirror, which represents the mimetic literary tradition, and the lamp, representing the shift to Romanticism, comes from Meyer Howard Abrams, *The Mirror and the Lamp: Romantic Theory and the Critical Tradition* (Oxford: Oxford University Press, 1953).

irony, and dramatic conflict interact to produce a unified whole. The urn makes its first appearance in Brooks' essay in a citation of Thomas Gray's "Elegy Written in a Country Churchyard":

> Can storied urn or animated bust
> Back to its mansion call the fleeting breath?
> Can Honour's voice provoke the silent dust?
> Or Flatt'ry sooth the dull cold ear of Death?[3]

Let us linger a moment on the urn. It is shapely, curvaceous. It often contains actual human remains – "the silent dust" – continuing to give form to "the fleeting breath" of a body that no longer exists. This form is ideal: it is both unblemished and materializes the mental image of abstract ideas, including loss, death, and absence. It provides an object invested with the power of affective modes like mourning and grief. But in its sealed existence, the urn is not dynamic or "animated"; it can no longer act upon the world. It falls deaf upon "the dull cold ear of Death." Like the bodily remains it is designed to hold, its separation from lived experience is ultimately signified by the empty space that it encloses to make a whole.

The urn is an example of what Levine calls a "bounded container."[4] But the body is the most fundamental bounded container. It seems impossible to be both inside and outside the body at the same time. Susan Stewart describes the body as presenting "the paradox of container and contained at once."[5] The position one takes in relation to the container signals a particular approach to literary form. Stand outside of it and you probably favor context-oriented or ideological approaches. Duck inside and you are no doubt a formalist. But both historicist and formalist approaches mobilize the container to account for form, whether social or poetic.

The body as bounded container is not confined to formalism. It underpins a range of political and social forms, from the *esprit de corps* to the body politic. An excellent example of the way the body shapes the parameters of critical enquiry is Mary Poovey's *Making a Social Body: British Cultural Formation, 1830–1864*, which details the emergence of mass culture in nineteenth-century Britain through the figure of a bodily container, the "social body" of the title. Like the time period Poovey uses as a framework, the social body provides a conceptual form that enables her to make compelling arguments about the historical

---

3 C. Brooks, *The Well Wrought Urn*, 8.
4 C. Levine, *Forms*, 27.
5 Susan Stewart, *On Longing: Narratives of the Miniature, the Gigantic, the Souvenir, the Collection* (Durham, NC: Duke University Press, 1993), 104.

phenomena she observes through aesthetic and non-aesthetic objects, which she accords equal discursive weight. She ties these to the historical formation of epistemological categories like genres, disciplines, and discourses.[6] Poovey's social body is of a more immediately recognizable corporeal shape than Brooks' urn. It provides a metaphor, image, and model for a society composed of different segments that can be united to form an "organic whole," or, conversely, isolated in order to treat elements that threaten social cohesion, like poverty. The concept of a "*social body* therefore promised full membership in a whole [. . .] to a part identified as needing both discipline and care."[7] While the model here is explicitly social (and metaphorical), it is a body in terms of both its shape and its susceptibility to disease. Again, this bodily form has a dual function. It embodies the ideal: the abstract concept of a unified polis that has never and will never truly exist. It also signifies a dangerous separation that enabled British elites to construct a population in need of discipline and control. As an ideal of formal unity, the discourse of the social body helped create a new mass culture of homogenization that sought to erase dangerous forms of difference.[8] Whereas Brooks celebrates the unity of form, then, Poovey is suspicious of the ideological ends to which formal unity can be employed, even as she harnesses a specific form to conceptualize and join up a complex range of historical discourses and processes.[9]

What is striking about both Brooks and Poovey's analyses is the distinctly bodily shape of the aesthetic and social forms on which they rely. Embodiment is not only about the kinds of representation – urns, social bodies – that appear in both texts and scholarly interpretation; it is what shapes aesthetic objects and cultural formations *and* their interpretation. Nor does embodiment necessarily entail the experience of individual bodies, neither of which are central to their arguments. Rather, embodiment underlies Brooks and Poovey's production of form. What else are they doing when evoking urns and social bodies but constructing these forms? We do not need to tether embodiment to the sort of authentic or essential selves that postmodernism has so rightly critiqued. Just as chiasmus is an embodied figure of thought, embodiment shapes critical enquiry, and this shaping principle emerges in the bodily forms that interpretive labor produces, like the urn or the social body. Embodiment is discursive to the extent that the critic produces the body as a know-

---

6 Mary Poovey, *Making a Social Body: British Cultural Formation, 1830–1864* (Chicago: University of Chicago Press, 1995), 3.
7 Poovey, *Making a Social Body*, 8. Italics in original.
8 Poovey, *Making a Social Body*. 2.
9 C. Levine, *Forms*, 28.

able object, while bodies, identities, and communities are literary and aesthetic configurations.

Embodied Form

In my reading of the 'corporeal urn,' I have already demonstrated several principles of what I call embodied form. The first of these is the notion that embodiment is an *organizational principle*. Embodiment composes the chaos of sensory experience into comprehensible categories of similarity, difference, specificity, and generality. By sorting perceptual experience into coherent patterns, the body is closely related to aesthetic objects. Embodied form accounts for the body's fundamental capacity to organize perception and action into meaningful patterns of experience; it unifies object and subject and thus bridges the gap between representation and the body. The second principle that I develop is what I call, following the work of the philosopher Susanne K. Langer, a 'logical form.' The urn is the body's logical form. It provides a congruent rather than mimetic figure that projects embodiment. Other logical forms are poetic and literary tropes. Even the term 'trope' – from the Greek *tropos*, meaning to twist or to turn – is a logical form, in the sense that it condenses the body's expressive movement into the basis of figuration. Throughout this book, I will turn to a number of logical forms and embodied tropes to read embodiment beyond representation or theme. The third principle implicit in my reading of the corporeal urn is how interpretation forms embodiment. In bringing the urn's bodily shape into focus, I have not merely excavated an underlying or pre-existing form. Rather, I have produced one. In order to fully understand the valences of embodied form, let us now explore each of these concepts in turn. It will subsequently become apparent that embodied form is not predicated on identifying bodily representations of difference – for instance, exploring how literature represents women – but on a series of formal figures. Thus, I demonstrate how critics and readers bring these bodies into being.

Logical forms

Literature and the body are not, of course, composed of the same materials, so how can the aesthetic be both bodily and poetic at the same time? And how do we read for embodied form without getting hung up on representations of the body? The notion that literary form expresses embodiment offers a counterpoint to approaching literature in terms of how it represents or thematizes the body. Early- and mid-century philosophers of art and aesthetic experience, like John Dewey and Susanne K. Langer, often argued that aesthetic objects provide the direct experience of feeling.[10] Langer, for instance, argues that an artwork is "an expressive form created for our perception through sense or imagination, and what it expresses is human feeling."[11] For these thinkers, aesthetic forms are living, vital, and organic. Art objects do not imitate life but provide a corresponding – or what Langer calls "logical" – form. A novel does not have a body in the way that its human reader does; it lacks skin, organs, limbs, and a central nervous system. Yet something in a book's narrative structure or form organizes experience in a way that closely resembles how embodiment orders the inchoate flux of somatic sensations, perception, and impressions into a meaningful whole. In this sense, literary form and embodiment – like a mold used to cast an object and the cast object itself – are congruent but not identical. The principle that unites these two logical forms is one of inverse, rather than direct, correspondence.[12]

Thus, one of the central principles of my theory of embodied form is that aesthetic form *projects* embodiment, and it does so by providing a logical form for the body. Art condenses human experience into a figurative form. In order to be convincing, such forms must be able to perform aspects of the living processes of organic forms, such as change, the interdependence of parts to organic whole, the rhythms of life (breath, heartbeat, oxidation), and dialectic processes of reproduction, growth, and decay. Works of art cannot literally reproduce the biological operations that sustain the most basic lifeforms, nor the higher-level responses that develop in more complex organisms, like emotion and perception, nor the translation of these instinctive reactions into human's "symbolic responses," such as memory and reason. But that does not necessarily entail a mimetic failure. Instead, artistic form extends the body rather than merely copying it.[13] While literature is not created from life's physical forms, its structure exemplifies the body's organizing functions.

It may seem obvious to say that literature projects embodied experience. This is surely also what enables literature to represent the body. However, representation connotes an imitation, whereas expression

---

10 There are important overlaps between Dewey and Langer's thinking, particularly in relation to their sense of art's form as living and organic. Dewey is considered a pragmatist philosopher, however, while Langer did not associate herself with a particular school of thought, even though her work engages with both pragmatism and phenomenology.
11 Langer, *Problems of Art*, 15
12 Langer, *Problems of Art*, 16–19.
13 Langer, *Problems of Art*, 53.

directly relates to the source of human feeling. Langer defines feeling as *"everything that can be felt*, from physical sensation, pain and comfort, excitement and repose, to the most complex emotions, intellectual tensions, or the steady feeling-tones of a conscious human life."[14] An expressive form articulates the variety of human feeling through a network of parts, points, or elements that produce a unified whole.[15] Representations of the body will be part of this expressive form, but embodied experience cannot be reduced to them. Rather, a whole range of formal elements express embodiment; these include rhetorical figures like chiasmus, rhythmical structures that reproduce the sensation of breath, and tempos and temporalities of birth and decay. If we approach the relation between embodiment and literature through the principle of representation, then these elements may be imperceptible or disconnected. In the absence of an identifiable principle of congruence, literary criticism is unable to recognize the body and literature's logical forms, which can thus only be expressed as an absence or lack. I reframe the relationship between embodiment and literature through the principle of expression, and this demonstrates how they are logical forms.

To illustrate how literature projects embodiment through logical forms, I will briefly offer a pertinent non-literary example. Like the Earth, the whole body cannot be grasped simultaneously. Whether one's body or someone else's, part of the body, like the Earth, will always be blocked from view by precisely the same body that one seeks to see in its entirety. Yet, humans have developed a method for grasping the entirety of a celestial sphere like our Earth: maps. Maps are based on the principle of projection, that is, the representation of a three-dimensional entity on a one-dimensional plane. Different projections of maps exist, but they nevertheless express the same logical form. Take two map projections, the Mercator map, which most of us have encountered in textbooks, and the Gall-Peters projection. The Mercator map is a cylindrical projection of the Earth's surface. Its linear scale, which helped navigators sail in straight lines, distorts objects far from the equator, such that North America and Europe take up a disproportionate amount of space relative to their actual surface areas. The Gall-Peters projection, by contrast, is a rectangular projection that represents the size of the geographical areas in their correct proportions but only by distorting their shapes into elongated forms.[16] Neither map is a 'truer' representation of the Earth, rather they are both projections of the same geographical relations –

---

14 Langer, *Problems of Art*, 15. Italics in original.
15 Langer, *Problems of Art*, 20.
16 Each map was used for different political ends, of course. For a humorous representation of the way the Galls-Peter projection defamiliarizes how the Mercator map has naturalized

organized according to political and social imperatives – that enable the viewer to grasp those relations in different but analogous ways. The map cannot literally reproduce the Earth's three-dimensional shape (although, of course, a globe can, albeit it on a much smaller scale). It *projects* the sphere.[17] This projection enables the two maps to each express the same logical form in different ways.

We can use the same principle for the relation between literature and embodiment. Just as we cannot see the Earth as a spherical object, neither can we see the body in its entirety or simultaneity. This is not only related to the surface of the body, but also to the full range of experiential phenomena the body undergoes at any given time. This immediate, inchoate experience is often the most difficult to capture in language (and why it is often described as 'ineffable'). Such experiences may be proprioception (the body's implicit awareness of itself in relation to space and movement) or the formless affects that emerge before any cognitive 'naming' like anger, melancholy, or fear. But this changes if we think about expressive forms in terms of projection. Thus, while literature cannot directly reproduce the body, by coalescing a range of different formal elements, literature *projects* the body's logical form. The opposite is true too. Through embodiment, life's fundamental processes find a logical expression.

Literary works, I argue, are able to express embodied experience through their very form rather than their propositional, discursive, or representational content. The work of art or literature furnishes the direct experience of a sensation, not merely an indexical sign. In other words, the artwork provides the experience that it describes.[18] We can extend this understanding to embodied form: the poem (or the text) does not simply represent the body, it provides an *experience of* the body. Its formal unity – as shapely as the body itself – projects the unity of embodied experience. Embodied form moves beyond 'the body'; it expresses embodied experience as a structure of feeling. Embodiment thus becomes a quality of the text – a tone, mood, texture, rhythm, movement, or structure – rather than a theme or representation. Language may never be able to *literally* represent the body, but by working through analogies it can produce a whole that effectively transmits the body's unity in a way that is not graspable within the constant flow of sensations that makes up the vast majority of our embodied experience – what Cleanth

---

the Global North's horizon of geographical perception see Season 2, Episode 16 of *The West Wing*.
17 Langer, *Problems of Art*, 20.
18 Langer, *Problems of Art*, 45. See also C. Brooks, *The Well Wrought Urn*, 213 and Dewey, *Art as Experience*.

Brooks calls "a compression and precision otherwise unobtainable."[19] Embodied form enables a better understanding of how form's different parts interconnect in order to make a unified organic system that projects and expresses forms of life. But it also helps us experience *embodiment* better, to become attuned to the different ways bodily experience is expressed in different forms.

Chiasmus, prosopopoeia, and catachresis

As I noted in the "Introduction," the chiasmus is one of the most important logical forms that appears in *Formal Matters*. It is a rhetorical and poetic figure composed of two inverted clauses that are balanced against each other to express congruent but inverted ideas (an AB:BA pattern). Its structure also reflects the human body's symmetry and its perception of movement and space.[20] Merleau-Ponty explores the figure of the chiasmus as a form of embodiment, and his notion of the chiasmus provides a counterpoint to Dewey and Langer's philosophy of art. Whereas Langer's notion of "living" forms accords an expressive, somatic agency to aesthetic objects, Merleau-Ponty argues that the body and the world are made of one perceptual field – or "flesh" – that chiastically intertwines them in an overarching sensate structure. The chiasmus is exemplified by a figure with which you will now be familiar: two hands touching. As I noted in the "Introduction," Merleau-Ponty invokes this image to illustrate how the body is simultaneously subject and object.[21] The haptic dimension of two hands touching designates how "flesh" is a form of perception based on touch rather than vision. Flesh fills the space between the subjective body and the objective world, between the one perceiving and the one perceived; it is a "thickness"[22] and an "element."[23] Thus the perception of the body, "the visible," which appears to end in representations, does not point to a realm of pure experience that exists beyond perception and which can only be accessed obliquely through representation. Instead, the visible is "a quality pregnant with texture, the surface of a depth, a cross section

---

19 C. Brooks, *The Well Wrought Urn*, 10.
20 Mark Turner notes that "the metaphoric projection onto contraries of a linear bilaterally symmetric scale is an extremely basic tool of human understanding and invention, and it is ineradicably metaphoric. It has a tremendous general scope, but it is not a mere formal abstraction. Instead, it is grounded in our embodied understanding of the symmetry of our bodies and our environments" in Turner, *Reading Minds: The Study of English in the Age of Cognitive Science* (Princeton, NJ: Princeton University Press, 2021), 80.
21 Merleau-Ponty, *The Visible and the Invisible*, 133–34.
22 Merleau-Ponty, *The Visible and the Invisible*, 135.
23 Merleau-Ponty, *The Visible and the Invisible*, 139.

upon a massive being, a grain or corpuscle."[24] In this sense, we can understand representation as a *fold*; it is the secretion of embodiment into a recognizable identity or representation. The chiasmus projects the body's form into a series of interconnecting inversions that produce the very fabric of the text. Literature makes manifest life's fundamental forms.

Chiasmus is closely related to another poetic figure: prosopopoeia, or endowing absent or dead people, supernatural beings, inanimate objects, and abstract ideas with a voice and action.[25] Prosopopoeia comes from the Greek *prosopon poeien*, or to make a face. As Paul de Man details, the act of giving a voice to an absent entity – it is often used to voice the presence of a dead person in the lyric form – is implicit in the term's etymology: "voice assumes mouth, eye, and finally face, a chain that is manifest in the etymology of the trope's name, *prosopon poien*, to confer a mask or a face (*prosopon*)."[26] Prosopopoeia is a bodily figure figured through its absence. But by embodying something abstract in a human form, prosopopoeia is also, I argue, a figure of embodiment.[27] Like chiasmus, it produces a thickness or element where once there was disconnection or absence. Acts of seeing, speaking, and breathing closely tie prosopopoeia to the senses and sense relations; by inhaling life into an absent or dead presence, they produce vivid language and form. This intense depiction of emotions and characters creates pathos, which names both the technique of provoking an emotional response and the emotional reaction the device creates in a reader or audience. Prosopopoeia projects the experience of its process. It produces the experience it seeks to depict through reading or viewing. It thus offers an interesting site for understanding the relationship between language and the body beyond representation, as well as the way poetic or literary

---

24 Merleau-Ponty, *The Visible and the Invisible*, 136.
25 Writing in 1821, Paul Fontanier described prosopopoeia as the "presentation of absent, dead, or supernatural beings, or even inanimate objects with the ability to act, speak, and respond," quoted in Bernard Dupriez, *A Dictionary of Literary Devices*, trans. Albert W. Halsall (New York: Harvester Wheatsheaf, 1991), 357. Paul de Man argues the chiasmus is the corollary of prosopopoeia: in giving voice to an absent presence, like the dead or an object, prosopopoeia also implies that the thing being addressed is expected to reply, in de Man, "Autobiography as De-Facement," *MLN* 94, no. 5 (1979): 919–30, 927. See also Michael Riffaterre, "Prosopopeia," *Yale French Studies*, no. 69 (1985): 107–23, 112.
26 De Man, "Autobiography as De-Facement," 926.
27 De Man and Riffaterre both note the importance of the senses to prosopopoeia, and the body and its various accouterments – clothing and so on – all feature heavily in their analyses of the figure. However, de Man and Riffaterre both dismiss the centrality of the senses, seeing it as an effect, rather than a central principle, of prosopopoeia's act of giving a voice. This returns us to earlier points I have made about the way that postmodernist criticism overlooks how embodied experience shapes the form of interpretation.

form is able to produce representational experience. Paradoxically, by providing a voice to an absent figure – by embodying something abstract – prosopopoeia enables us to trace how embodiment can be present even when it seems most attenuated.

Like the embodied foundation of chiasmus, prosopopoeia's 'face making' is always already embodied. Both prosopopoeia and chiasmus involve the interpenetration of the subject and the object. Their mutually embodied, aesthetic functions endow them with the ability to bridge the division between subjectivity and objectivity. Chiasmus and prosopopoeia posit an alternative relationship of the body to representation, which in turn becomes manifest at the level of language and form. Whereas metaphor, by pointing to something it literally cannot be, belongs to language's referential function,[28] prosopopoeia can never be referential. Metaphor presumes the inability to literally represent something but prosopopoeia literally gives form to an absence. For this reason, Michael Riffaterre has called prosopopoeia, the "figure of figurality." It is the attempt to figure in language the process of figuration. It is thus the very index of literariness,[29] and its literariness – its figuration of the figure – it is often evoked through texts that self-consciously point to the act of producing embodied form.

If prosopopoeia's 'face-making' function produces embodied presence, then the related trope of catachresis disrupts the relationship between the body and referential language. Catachreses are terms created for concepts that have no proper name, such as 'foot of a mountain' or 'legs of a table.' Just as prosopopoeia is the literal figure of making a face, the relationship between the figurative and literal underpins catachresis' relationship to the body. As Alessandra Raengo aptly puts it, "catachreses are literally false [. . .] but figuratively true."[30] The supports of a table may function in a similar manner to legs, but they are not the same anatomically. Catachresis maintains the appearance of figurality, while using figurative meaning as if it was literal. For this reason, it also has the potential to alienate us from language, by demonstrating how the seemingly literal term is figurative. It is not surprising, then, that many common catachreses use body parts to describe material or inanimate objects. Naming objects through body parts embodies the incompleteness of a system of meaning that cannot provide a proper referent. The body's disaggregated elements incarnate the severance of

---

28 See Jonathan Culler, *The Pursuit of Signs: Semiotics, Literature, Deconstruction*, Routledge Classics (London: Routledge, 2002), 213–214.
29 Riffaterre, "Prosopopoeia," 110.
30 Alessandra Raengo, *On the Sleeve of the Visual* (Hanover, NH: Dartmouth College Press, 2013), 54–55.

the material thing and the signifier. Catachrestic figures often project the rhetorical origins of the word, which derive from the Greek for 'abuse,' but have come to mean a semantic error or misuse. The 'abuse' of language at the foundation of catachresis thus necessarily always produces an amputated meaning. The image of a severed limb applies the figurative sense of amputation as it was literal, while still maintaining a sense of literal *figurality*. Or catachresis acts like a prosthesis, filling in a gap in language with the approximation of a bodily form. While it could be argued that catachresis demonstrates the insufficiency of language, particularly towards the body, I argue that – like prosopopoeia – it is *productive*. It generates new, often disconcerting meanings that draw attention to representation's alienating function.

Metalepsis and aporia

Formal Matters explores two further tropes that work in a different manner to chiasmus, prosopopoeia, and catachresis. While these latter tropes produce, perform, and project embodiment, metalepsis and aporia figure absence as a form of embodiment. In theories of narratology inspired by the work of Gérard Genette, metalepsis describes the breakdown between different diegetic levels, akin to breaking the fourth wall in theatre.[31] In classical literary criticism and rhetoric, however, it has a slightly different meaning. Deriving from the Greek term *metalambanô* (to exchange, to take in in a new way), metalepsis enfolds a number of meanings, including to "receive instead or later," to "translate," to "render," and to "transfer from the literal to the spiritual level."[32] Metalepsis entails a kind of metonymy of metonymy, a series of rhetorical substitutions. This can take place at the level of syntax (exchanging one word for another and then again for another) or on a broader scale through the allusion to previous figures within texts or through intertextuality. This sense of referring back to previous figural schemas led the Renaissance critic George Puttenham to call metalepsis the trope of the "far-fetched"[33] – a use that is evident in Christopher Marlow's famous description of Helen of Troy as "the face that launched a thousand ships." The physical distance implied by the movement of the ships is reinforced by the metaleptic allusion to the metaphor of beauty embodied by Helen's face, and her face's disproportionate power also points to the

---

31 See Gérard Genette, *Narrative Discourse: An Essay in Method*, trans. Jane Lewin (Ithaca, NY: Cornell University Press, 1980).
32 John Hollander, *The Figure of Echo: A Mode of Allusion in Milton and After* (Berkeley; Los Angeles, CA: University of California Press, 1981), 134–35.
33 Cited in Hollander, *The Figure of Echo*, 114.

way metalepsis attributes a present effect to a distant cause. But it is also a mediating figure, providing the intermediary term between different figurative states. At the same time, it omits the central figure of Helen, thus both compressing meaning and extending the figure to prolong it. The rhetorical act of 'fetching from afar' – of extending or leaping across linking terms – creates an exaggerated, distorted meaning. Metalepsis provides the trope for its own in-between or mediating function. For this reason, critics have often called it "the trope of the trope," a "master trope," or a "meta-trope" that passes along and incorporates a chain of other tropes.[34] But whereas other tropes are often deployed in the pursuit of a more and more precise or substantive figuration, metalepsis entails ellipsis, seeming "both elusive and allusive at once."[35] For this reason, it requires an active reading stance. If the reader is able to move beyond commonplace linguistic assumptions and grasp the figurative sense then the trope succeeds; if the reader falls short and cannot make this leap, the trope fails.[36]

Like prosopopoeia, the spatial and temporal elements of metalepsis involve a phenomenal dimension. Yet as a second or third order figure, that is, a figure that refers to yet another figure or that demands a leap of the imagination because it omits a central term, metalepsis cannot properly 'figure' the body in the same manner as prosopopoeia, which projects embodied presence. In a similar manner to catachresis, metalepsis suggests a kind of figurative failure; it signals an inability to properly name what it seeks to describe. But whereas the catachrestic 'abuse' of language is so literal it is no longer obvious (anyone can see that mountains do not have actual feet but the foot of a mountain has nevertheless become a commonplace), in metalepsis the failure requires the reader to actively seek out and identify the moment of transference. If the reader is able to grasp the implied connection between the direct expression and its indirect correspondence, then the figure produces a sense of figurative complexity. Meaning is withheld and then belatedly granted. However, the figure fails if it does not provide the reader with enough information to fill in the missing term (a common feature). Metalepsis thus gives form to those moments where figures fail to figure themselves, such as mixed metaphors or partial metonymies. It is the trope for figural failure

---

34 Hollander calls it a "meta-trope" in Hollander, *The Figure of Echo*, 114. Harold Bloom calls it the "trope-of-tropes" in Bloom, *A Map of Misreading* (Oxford: Oxford University Press, 2003), 94.
35 Hollander, *The Figure of Echo*, 116.
36 Brian Cummings, "Metalepsis: The Boundaries of Metaphor," in *Renaissance Figures of Speech*, ed. Sylvia Adamson, Gavin Alexander, and Katrin Ettenhuber (Cambridge: Cambridge University Press, 2011), 220–21.

as well as the possibilities of figural success. To bring this into dialogue with embodied form, if we read for metalepsis we can fill in the body's fragmented form, or at least identify the (missing) middle term. The failure to represent the body, then, is not an aesthetic failure but a failure of *reading*. As the figure for failed figurality, metalepsis helps us grasp where literary representation appears to elide embodiment, or where interpretation does not 'stretch' to look for it.

More well-known than metalepsis is aporia, a common concept in postmodernist theories that point to the limits of language, representation, and the body, as in Giorgio Agamben's notion of the "aporia of Auschwitz," which arises from the bodily absence of the "true" witnesses, those who, precisely because they experienced the totality of the Holocaust, cannot testify to it.[37] When employed in this way, however, aporia effaces its own origins as a rhetorical figure for doubt, reifying it into a limit on representation, in particular the embodied act of speech on which testimony depends. The postmodernist use of aporia separates it from its embodied origins, making the body's presence an inexpressible doubt. Like all the other figures I have explored, however, in its original use aporia had a close relationship with the body.

In ancient philosophy, aporia, deriving from the Greek *a-poros*, meaning 'un-passable' or 'untraversable,' was used to describe puzzlement, expressed in almost physical terms. Platonic metaphors describe aporia as a state of speechlessness, of feeling "numb in mind and tongue." This sense of shock or stupefaction extends to the body's orientation in space, in the description of aporia as "an unstable, vertiginous state," of feeling "shaken" or "tempest-tossed." These earthquake-like images highlight the way aporia throws down impediments, preventing one from reaching "a much-desired place."[38] The original rhetorical figure for doubt connects to both the embodied origins of speech and the body's relationship to its physical environment – to *topos*, meaning 'place' in Greek; the desire to know becomes an almost physical quest to traverse the wild landscape across which multiple obstacles are strewn. It retains this sense of the body's location and projection in space in Renaissance rhetoric on testimony, alongside other tropes that project embodied presence like prosopopoeia.[39] Poststructuralism and deconstruction foreground aporia's spatial dimension, but generally overlook

---

37 Giorgio Agamben, *Remnants of Auschwitz: The Witness and the Archive*, trans. Daniel Heller-Roazen (New York: Zone Books, 2002), 32.
38 George Karamanolis and Vasilis Politis gloss these different metaphors in Karamanolis and Politis, "Introduction," in *The Aporetic Tradition in Ancient Philosophy*, ed. George Karamanolis and Vasilis Politis (New York: Cambridge University Press, 2018), 1.
39 See R. W. Serjeantson, "Testimony: The Artless Proof," in *Renaissance Figures of Speech*,

its connection to embodiment, since the body signifies the irrecoverable site of an original, authentic experience that cannot be communicated in language. J. Hillis Miller characterizes aporia as "the blind alleys in thought to which repetition leads,"[40] turning blindness into a quality of space rather than the body. This echoes Derrida's characterization of aporia as the "blind spots" in metaphysical arguments, which occur when certain forms of logic come up against the limits of their own reasoning. This similarly occludes embodiment, turning it into something unable to 'see' – or, presumably, *speak* – its embodied form.[41]

If the other tropes I explored above demonstrate how embodiment is at the foundation of poetic and rhetorical language, aporia provides the ground for the figuration of embodiment. Prosopopoeia and catachresis have a direct relationship to embodiment, either performing, projecting, or disrupting it and its relation to referential language. Aporia, on the other hand, supplies the material realm of language in which the body moves. Aporia is the terrain of linguistic form that subjects struggle through in a physical quest to understand and speak to (to testify to) their embodied experience. Aporia is thus the trope of the unspeakable. Rather than conceiving of the unspeakable as an inherent property of language or the body, aporia points to its *rhetorical* dimension, that is, how the unspeakable is a figure that already imposes boundaries on what can and cannot be expressed. Conceiving of aporia as a physical, material terrain helps move past the 'im-passe,' in a manner that is difficult if we separate aporia from its material, physical origins.

Embodiment as interpretation

My reading of the 'corporeal urn' demonstrated how interpretation produces forms. Whereas a method devoted to identifying representations of bodies presumes that such bodies pre-exist interpretation, I argue that embodiment is *formed through* interpretation. This aspect of my argument specifically implicates the role of the critic. The literary critic brings embodiment and form together in ways that make it perceptible – and thus able to be *felt* – to others, beyond description or excavation. The literary critic is a co-producer of aesthetic meaning.

The New Critics also developed a number of principles for the way

---

ed. Sylvia Adamson, Gavin Alexander, and Katrin Ettenhuber (Cambridge: Cambridge University Press, 2011).
40 J. Hillis Miller, "Line," in *The J. Hillis Miller Reader*, ed. Julian Wolfreys (Stanford, CA: Stanford University Press, 2005), 248.
41 See Niall Lucy, *A Derrida Dictionary* (Malden, MA; Oxford: Blackwell Publishers, 2004), 1 for a characterization of Derrida's use of aporia.

critics should approach texts and teach others to read them. If poems do not make statements about reality, but rather produce an experience, the formalist is duty bound to bring the reader as close as possible to that experience. The critic cannot elucidate the poem's experience by making statements about it. One must develop a vocabulary and a set of concepts appropriate to the aesthetic object that speak to aesthetic experience. But the critic's role is also where I will depart from the New Critics. If Cleanth Brooks quite rightly refused to see form as "the transparent pane of glass through which the stuff of poetry is reflected, directly and immediately,"[42] he nevertheless accorded the critic a fairly "neutral" position. The critic's task is to describe and evaluate the aesthetic object.[43] All of the energy of this enterprise must be devoted to assisting the reader to engage more attentively with the work, but it nevertheless eschews "interpretation" per se.[44] This sentiment is echoed in recent calls for "surface" or "descriptive" reading, which argue that a text can 'speak for itself' and the critic should make minimal interventions, least of all ones that seek to expose ideological or political subtexts. These recent calls have often valorized the 'lay' reader and their emotional reactions to books.[45] Appeals to how one 'feels' about literature are quite different from Cleanth Brooks' call for a "self-effacing" and "analytic" critic who appeals neither to his own reactions to the poem nor to a reader's.[46] The New Critics cannot be accused of taking texts at face value or of appealing to the tastes and reading habits of the book club reader. Still, both positions elide criticism's ethical or political dimension.

A strategy from cultural and social anthropology, a field that has been strongly influenced by phenomenology, helps illuminate the literary critic's active role. Beginning in the 1980s, anthropology underwent a 'literary turn.' Against the classical view that anthropologists provide detached, scientific cultural observations, thinkers like Clifford Geertz argued that ethnography has a distinctly literary character.[47] Even when presented as objective truth, anthropological narratives use specific

---

42 C. Brooks, *The Well Wrought Urn*, 223.
43 C. Brooks, "The Formalist Critics," 74.
44 Nicholas Gaskill, "The Close and the Concrete: Aesthetic Formalism in Context," *New Literary History* 47, no. 4 (2016): 505–24, 513. Gaskill provides an excellent analysis of the New Critics' understanding of interpretation.
45 Stephen Best and Sharon Marcus, "Surface Reading: An Introduction," *Representations* 108, no. 1 (2009): 1–21. See also Rita Felski, *The Limits of Critique* (Chicago: University of Chicago Press, 2015).
46 C. Brooks, "The Formalist Critics," 76.
47 Clifford Geertz, *Works and Lives: The Anthropologist as Author* (Stanford, CA: Stanford University Press, 1988).

representational strategies and figurative tropes; they draw on generic conventions and bear the markings of authorial identities. For instance, the detached, abstract voice found in classical anthropology can be understood as a type of omniscient narration whose truth-effect derives from its rhetorical staging.[48] In this way, anthropology sought to not only critique the production of knowledge as a form of representation but to also produce aesthetic and literary methods for making sense of cultural and social structures.[49] Leading on from this, Stephen Tyler has argued that ethnography should "evoke" rather than try to provide an empirical representation.[50]

These self-reflexive and aesthetic practices have been brought into fruitful dialogue with anthropology's engagement with embodiment and the body. This is evident in ethnographic practices that require practitioners to theorize how their own embodied experiences have contributed to the production of knowledge about other embodied subjects and their cultures. Aaron Turner argues that this requires not only a post-fact reflection on how the anthropologist experienced a particular culture, but an understanding of the anthropologist as a fully embodied subject whose physicality shapes the cultural knowledge produced through observation.[51] An embodied ethnographic practice demonstrates the potential of literary approaches that self-reflexively theorize the production of embodiment as having a specifically formal or literary character. In turn, it demonstrates how such cultural representations are grounded in embodied experience. These approaches echo the classical phenomenological proposition that "existence precedes essence,"[52] or the principle that there is no essential being that pre-exists human consciousness, action, and appearance. Cultural anthropology's critique of representation and its self-reflexive methods deriving from the observer's own embodied experience provide a point of departure for thinking about how literary criticism can shift away from identifying specific bodies to understanding how interpretation produces embodiment and

---

48 Nigel Rapport, *The Prose and the Passion: Anthropology, Literature, and the Writing of E. M. Forster* (Manchester: Manchester University Press, 1994), 8.
49 The 'literary turn' in anthropology is mirrored by the 'anthropological turn' in literary studies. For an overview of the interaction of these different fields see E. Valentine Daniel and Jeffrey M. Peck, eds., *Culture/Contexture: Explorations in Anthropology and Literary Studies* (Berkeley, CA: University of California Press, 1996).
50 Stephen Tyler, *The Unspeakable: Discourse, Dialogue, and Rhetoric in the Postmodern World* (Madison, WI: University of Wisconsin Press, 1987), 205–208.
51 Aaron Turner, "Embodied Ethnography. Doing Culture," *Social Anthropology* 8, no. 1 (January, 2007): 51–60, 53.
52 This concept comes from Jean-Paul Sartre, *Existentialism Is a Humanism*, ed. John Kulka, trans. Carol Macomber (New Haven, CT: Yale University Press, 2007), 20.

embodied forms. Literary figures give form to embodiment, and literary interpretation is a key part of producing embodied form.

Rather than seeking a pre-existing body in the text, I argue that close reading is what produces embodied form. I want to preserve the New Criticism's detachment while accepting that the critic is not a neutral party in this game of interpretation. We need to own up to the way we are complicit in constructing certain bodies. This is all the more important when discussing the body's relation to literature, because there is scarcely an entity that elicits more emotion – that, quite literally, *embodies* emotion – than the body. This is not an appeal to how a text makes the reader 'feel,' but how a text provides an *experience* of embodiment that is not otherwise apparent or graspable – an experience that interpretation and close reading help produce. And it is necessarily the critic that facilitates and to a certain extent brings embodiment into a recognizable form, whether shaped like an urn or a social body.

Throughout this book, I will turn to moments in texts where embodied experience seems most absent or fragmented in order to demonstrate how the body can take shape in formal elements beyond representation. At the same time, I remain aware that my critical methods are bringing such bodily forms into being – I am not only tuning readers into previously overlooked elements but giving a conceptual shape to inchoate experiences that may not otherwise be understood as embodied. The book's chiastic structure itself embodies the way embodiment shapes critical inquiry. The critic's role in producing embodied forms brings me back to politics. In this model, literary criticism can help imagine how currently excluded, marginalized, or devalued forms of embodiment can reshape political arrangements to make them fit in. In turn, the concept of embodied form will help return the corporeal, somatic, and physical dimensions of form to the literary. Let us now turn to understanding how these forms work in the practice of literary criticism.

Chapter 2

La Pensée incarnée: Embodying the Unrepresentable in Anne F. Garréta's *Sphinx*

The French author Anne F. Garréta was a political formalist *avant la lettre*. She has been publishing in her native language since 1986, but translation has only recently made her work accessible to an Anglophone readership. However, she has close ties to both French and American literary and cultural milieus. She has been an academic at institutions in both countries, and as much as her oeuvre is influenced by French literary history, it is also steeped in an awareness of critical theory common in North American universities.[1] Indeed, Anglophone scholarship has tended to approach her work in terms of queer theory and 'women's writing' – and often as an extension of Garréta's own identity as a queer woman – overlooking how her writing's form resists such identificatory modes and the valorization of alterity.[2]

I start this book with an exploration of Garréta because her oeuvre encapsulates the political approach that emerges when we theorize the relationship between embodiment and form. In this chapter, I argue that the embodied form of Garréta's work subtly works against the politics of representation by reshaping the body's connection to literature beyond the mimetic, particularly in relation to gender and race. It does so by deploying poetic figures that project and redistribute embodiment.

---

1 Garréta attended the prestigious *École normal supérieure* in Paris before completing a PhD in seventeenth- and eighteenth-century French literature at New York University. She has taught at institutions including the University of Rennes II and Duke University.
2 Annabel L. Kim's *Unbecoming Language: Anti-Identitarian French Feminist Fictions* (Columbus, OH: The Ohio University Press, 2018) is an excellent exception to this tendency to read Garréta's work through the lens of Garréta's perceived biographical identity. Kim's notion of the "body of language," rather than the body *in* language, parallels my notion of embodied form. For some examples of scholarship that reads Garréta through queer or gender identity see Lucille Cairns, "Queer Paradox/Paradoxical Queer: Anne Garréta's *Pas un jour* (2002)," *Journal of Lesbian Studies* 11, no. 1–2 (August 2007): 70–87 and Gill Rye, "Uncertain Readings and Meaningful Dialogue: Language and Sexual Identity in Anne Garréta's *Sphinx* and Tahar Ben Jelloun's *L'Enfant de sable* and *La Nuit sacrée*," *Neophilologus* 84, no. 4 (2000): 531–40.

I explore this through her first novel, the audacious, difficult *Sphinx*. The novel follows the love affair between the unnamed narrator, a young, white French doctoral student in theology who falls into an unlikely career DJing, and A***, an African American cabaret dancer, who is a decade older. On one level, the novel is a conventional love story, with the narrative arc following the couple's romantic journey, which culminates in A***'s tragic death on stage. The novel takes place in recognizable places, including Paris, where it is largely set; New York City (A***'s city of origin); and Amsterdam, where the narrator writes the words that will become the memoir-like text in our hands. It is in Amsterdam, too, where the narrator is attacked and killed in a botched robbery, providing a sense of melancholic closure.

On another level, however, the novel does not operate according to the traditional generic conventions of heterosexual (or even homosexual) desire: the novel entirely avoids describing either the narrator or A*** with recourse to gender. In deconstructing the gendered foundations of language – an operation that is difficult enough in English, let alone in French, where gender is a fundamental element of grammar – *Sphinx* is a consummately postmodern novel. It anticipates Judith Butler's theory of gender performativity, or how repeated acts constitute gender as a discursive category or identity.[3] Garréta's novel goes even farther, with the absence of gender seeming to put the body beyond discourse. Embodied experience and presence continually slip through representation's grasp in an emancipatory project that theorizes the dissolution of identity categories through formal literary operations.

However, the allusiveness of gender exists in stark contrast to the novel's unambiguous and sometimes gratuitous representation of race, in particular A***'s blackness. The direct representation of race reduces the racialized body to an object that elides embodied experience, turning A*** into a silent figure who cannot speak for themself.[4] This racial overdetermination evokes the elision of particular embodied subjects from the realm of political representation, or, in turn, the way racialized identities are reduced to an outward appearance. The novel's repeated evocation of A***'s race seems even more unjustified within the novel's formal logic, given that race, like gender, is a discursive category.

---

3 Judith Butler first develops this theory in Butler, *Gender Trouble: Feminism and the Subversion of Identity* (New York: Routledge, 1990). Though I do not have the space to devote to it here, the novel also anticipates the increasing visibility of transgender identities in the years since its publication. Its erasure of gender categories and the gendered subject opens up important avenues for thinking about the way transgender identities can be expressed in language and literary form.
4 I use the gender-neutral pronouns they/them to refer to both A*** and the protagonist.

The unrepresentability of gender and the overdetermination of race capture the postmodernist tension between a body that either escapes or is reduced to representation. Yet if we shift our attention to the novel's form, it becomes apparent that embodiment takes shape otherwise. Three interrelated figures comprise this process: the logical form of the sphinx and the poetic devices of prosopopoeia and catachresis. The titular sphinx acts as a logical form that provides a congruent though not coincidental form for A***'s genderless body. Prosopopoeia – the act of 'making a face' – projects their absent presence into the figure, breathing life into a dead object. Catachresis, by contrast, disrupts the representational relationship between A***'s body and racial signifiers. In 'misnaming' A***'s skin as 'black,' catachresis redistributes overly determined racial representations into abstract formal, aesthetic configurations. Taken together, the figures give shape to a body that is fragmented at the level of representation, while disrupting and redistributing the representational fixity of the racialized body. By shifting away from the politics of representation and recasting the relationship between the body and language in terms of literary form, *Sphinx* offers a new approach to understanding how embodied experience can manifest in poetic language beyond mimesis.

To understand the centrality of form and formalism to Garréta's oeuvre it will be helpful to situate her in relationship to the Oulipo. As briefly touched upon in the "Introduction," the Oulipo was founded in 1960 as a literary movement devoted to formalist experimentation, in particular through applying mathematical formulas or constraints to literary production. Its members conceive of the Oulipo as a "laboratory" where literary rules can be tried out to produce new aesthetic forms.[5] The Oulipo's aims and interests evolved over time, moving initially from syntactical experimentation enacted at the level of individual words and sentences, such as anagrams and lipograms, to semantic exploration, which was more conceptual in nature and involved constraints, affecting not only linguistic structure but also plot, character, and narrative structure.[6] The shift towards semantic exploration produced works in which experiments with form became a key part of their thematics. For many Oulipian works, as Warren Motte argues, "form becomes theme."[7] Formal experimentation represents an explicit narrative subject of many works, while their forms comment upon this thematization through the ramifying effects of experimentation.

---

5 Duncan, *The Oulipo and Modern Thought*, 15.
6 Duncan, *The Oulipo and Modern Thought*, 25.
7 Motte, "Shapes of Things," 11.

Although *Sphinx* significantly predates Garréta's induction into the group in 2000, it is already possible to discern the exploratory function of form in the novel. The group's apoliticism and autonomous approach to literary form is at odds with the political function of literary form in Garréta's oeuvre.[8] Yet many of the group's principles are still relevant to her literary production.[9] Garréta's work also brings together syntactical and semantic experimentation. In *Sphinx*, the elision of gender necessarily takes place at the level of syntax, and yet this syntactical experimentation shapes the concept of a 'genderless' novel, one in which the production of such a language reveals the possibility of moving beyond seemingly fixed categories. The relationship between form and theme or representation is particularly pertinent to the body's role in *Sphinx*. Representations of bodies abound, yet the novel also explicitly *produces* formal figures through a thematic exploration of the relationship between embodiment and language. Equally, the creation of embodied forms sets in motion the thematization of the body as a racialized or gendered entity. In contrast to gender, which escapes signification, race is overdetermined in *Sphinx*. Gender and race thus present the two sides of the postmodernist body: one that escapes signification and is refused political representation, the other that is reduced to representation and only exists as a dematerialized identity. Garréta combines the experimental element of the Oulipo with a political project in order to turn literature into a laboratory where new social and cultural norms can be envisaged. The autonomy of literary form thus serves a political function for Garréta, as she expressed in an interview in 2000:

> fiction can be a space in which it is possible to take a distance, to disassociate from these constructions to see how they are made, what purpose they serve and to whom, to pose the question of their necessity and their utility. It is to take fiction seriously in order to put into play its power to effectuate or to affect individual beliefs.

Literature's ability to organize, shape, and refashion social categories is closely tied to its embodied form, or how it gives shape to inchoate experiences. She calls this *la pensée incarnée*, or "thought embodied."[10] Form, as it will become apparent, gives shape to both abstract thought and the material body.

---

8 While individual members of the Oulipo have publicly espoused political views, the group is not aligned with any particular ideology or political position.
9 For instance, she applied principles of the Turning Test to *Sphinx*.
10 Anne Garréta and Eva Domeneghini, "Entretien avec Anne F. Garréta" [Interview with Anne F. Garréta], October 13, 2000, http://cosmogonie.free.fr/index2.html. My translation.

Sphinx and the Riddle of Embodied Form

Upon initial reading, *Sphinx* seems a consummately postmodernist novel: its genderlessness suggests the failure of language to capture the object it seeks to represent; the novel's tone, focalized through the first-person narrator, is one of ironic detachment and desuetude; and A***'s sublime corporeality seems to exceed the possibilities of language. The narrator even studies theology's apophatic tradition, which dictates God can only be spoken about in the negative.[11] The postmodernist aporia of representation is most pronounced in relation to the body, which the novel depicts as an incomplete object or beyond the realm of expression. In the "Introduction," I argued that the unrepresentable is the central aporia of postmodernism. As a concept – or perhaps a 'non-concept' – it is connected to a range of anxieties about the violence of representation and its ultimate impossibility. The paradigm of the unrepresentable is particularly pernicious when wielded against the body because it places bodily experience beyond signification. The obverse of the unrepresentable is a body reduced to an object through representation. Both strip embodied subjects of agency.

The titular figure of *Sphinx* thus seems to incarnate postmodernism's aporetic body. Aporia derives from the Greek for impasse, difficult passage (that is, literally passing through something), or perplexity. In mythology, the sphinx, a monstrous hybrid with the body of a lion and the head of a human, bars travelers' passage, who can only pass by if they are able to answer a riddle. Yet in its actual existence, it is a mute object, retaining only the body's outward form. It is the literal and figurative gateway to the novel's suspicion of representation as it pertains to the body.[12] But the sphinx also points to another way of reading embodiment as a question of form. While it is a material object, it is carved from "living rock," and it derives from Egyptian via Greek

---

11 While this all sounds rather po-faced, Garréta is also a very funny writer, whose humor is related to both the formal and political elements of her writing. For a discussion of humor in her work see María Dolores Vivero García, "Humour, engagement et création littéraire chez Anne Garréta," *Women in French Studies* 19, no. 1 (2011): 85–93.
12 The most famous riddle of the sphinx is also about the body in time: what goes on four legs in the morning, two legs in the afternoon, and three legs at night. In Sophocles' *Oedipus Tyrannus*, Oedipus is able to answer this riddle because of his visceral experience of the body: he is a man in the afternoon of his life who already walks on three legs. See Seth Benardete, *The Argument of the Action: Essays on Greek Poetry and Philosophy* (Chicago: University of Chicago Press, 2000), 71. Thank you to Charlie Barrett for pointing this out to me.

for "living image."[13] It is thus an aesthetic figure that points to the embodied dimension of material objects.[14] It provides a logical form for the body, projecting rather than representing bodily experience. Keeping in mind the sphinx's two meanings – the aporia of representation and the materiality of form – will help navigate new ways of reading for the body.[15]

The sphinx projects the body's outer shape, but its almost disdainful silence also acts as the foil for poetic figures that perform embodiment. Performance is an important theme in the novel, signaled by the two protagonists' careers in the performance industries. The text also emphasizes the performativity of identities, particularly sexual and gendered identities, from the dissolute *padre* who first takes the narrator to the club where they will end up DJing to the cast of dancers, sex workers, and other night life characters that populate the text's cityscapes. Beyond questions of identity and representation, however, the text undermines the separation of representation and materiality through poetic and formal figures that *enact* and *project* embodiment, much in the same manner that A***'s dancer character is based on the performance of pure embodied expression.

The Unrepresentable Body

Sphinx is saturated with a tangible, vivid sense-scape of imagery, colors, odors, tastes, and touch. This sensory landscape operates at almost all times in the narrative, whether in the "sweltering, vitrified clash of light and flesh in the swaying red darkness" of nightclubs;[16] the "dirty yellow tint," "wailing women," and "syncopated beep-beep" of a grubby hospital in New York (102–103); or the tantalizing trail of the perfume "Parure" (or "Appearance") left behind by the narrator's friend as a reminder of aesthetic presence (7). Similarly, there is a continual "suc-

---

13 Susan Bauer Wise, *The History of the Ancient World* (New York: W. W. Norton), 299–302. This means it was carved in place rather than in a stone that was then moved to the chosen site.
14 See Kim, *Unbecoming Language*, 143–44 for a discussion of the sphinx as an aesthetic and material figure.
15 For an exploration of the way the figure of the sphinx helps "supersede" gender categories see Owen Heathcote, "Beyond Antoinette Fouque (*Il y a deux sexes*) and Beyond Virginie Despentes (*King Kong théories*)? Anne Garréta's Sphinxes," in *Women's Writing in the Twenty-First Century: Life as Literature*, ed. Amaleena Damlé and Gill Rye (Cardiff: University of Wales Press, 2013).
16 Anne Garréta, *Sphinx*, trans. Emma Ramadan (Dallas, TX: Deep Vellum Publishing, 2015), 5. Henceforth cited parenthetically. I have quoted from the English translation but note where I alter or comment on the translation.

cession of bodies" [*un ballet de corps*] (2) that parade through the text. This is evident in the undifferentiated "flesh" that dances to the narrator's music (28); the specific bodies of A*** and their dancer friends, who brush the narrator with "naked skin, [...] boas and feather fans" (8); and the intermingled limbs of A*** and the narrator, "sexes mixed" (55), collapsed in post-coital exhaustion. Thus, in contrast to some of the other works I explore in this book, in which embodied experience is virtually absent and those bodies that do exist seem like bloodless phantoms, *Sphinx* is a work in which embodiment saturates every level of the text, from context to representation to form.

Yet despite the continual presence of bodies and tangible sensations, embodied experience nevertheless seems to escape representation. This is most evident at the level of gender. Scrubbing language of gender is a hard-enough task in English, as evidenced by experimental fictions like Jeanette Winterson's *Written on the Body* (1992), but this is exceptionally difficult in French. In English, gender is only used to describe people or living beings (semantic gender). French, on the other hand, works through grammatical gender, meaning that all nouns are classed according to either masculine or feminine categories. Adjectives, subject and direct object pronouns like *il* [he] and *elle* [she], compound past tense verbs, and pronominal or 'reflexive' verbs must all agree with the gender case. This means that a subject's gender is revealed with almost any verb in the past tense or adjective. *Sphinx* tests out the possibilities of a world in which this binary does not structure desire or identity by removing grammar from linguistic form. In doing so, Garréta sets out to demonstrate "not only the contingency of gender, but also its inanity and insignificance as a category."[17] Given the importance of gender to the structural cohesion of French, then, Garréta cannot simply avoid or omit gender – she must *re-form* the French language.

To render the two central characters' genders inscrutable, it is necessary to employ linguistic and narrative strategies that fundamentally shape the text's tone, style, and form. The novel thus favors the imperfect and *passé simple* preterit tenses over compound past tenses like the *passé composé*. It employs impersonal moods using the infinitive or participle, and the use of the passive voice also avoids gendered pronouns. For instance, like many verbs of movement, the verb *aller* (to go) uses *être* (to be) as the auxiliary in the *passé composé*, the most common past tense in French; this, in turn, requires the past participle to agree in gender with the subject of the verb. The ungendered *I went*

---

17 In the same interview, she says that all of her literary works are formalist in order to "construct an autonomous universe to test a hypothesis," in Garréta and Domenenghini.

in English is *je suis allé(e)* in French. In other words, simply describing how the narrator or A*** go from one place to another would have required revealing their gender. To avoid this, the narrator is often dragged places or led along, or Garréta uses the imperfect tense used to describe habitual, ongoing action: watching bodies dance, writing an interminable thesis, trudging from one bar to another. Such strategies produce a sense of aimlessness, passivity, and ennui, and the arrangement of events is often unclear; different diegetic timelines bleed into each other. The *passé simple*, a past tense used only in written French, also plays an important role in the narrative. This is a common tense in literature, but its overwhelming preponderance over the *passé composé* in what is ostensibly a memoir renders the narrator's affected and formal tone a key part of their character development.[18]

It is at the level of representing the body, particularly A***'s body, that the genderlessness of Garréta's French is most evident.[19] In order to avoid describing A*** directly, which would require adjectives that agree with A***'s gender, the narrator disaggregates A***'s body into "a hand poised for a moment on my face" (40), "a vision of A***'s face near mine" (48), or "the tactile impression of skin and the shape of that flesh (54). Echoing a Shakespearian sonnet, the narrator details "what I loved above all else: those hips, narrow and broad at the same time, those legs that I never knew how to describe except, mundanely, as slim and long" (84). Or A*** is crystallized in forms that approximate bodies: a "spirit" [*forme d'esprit*] (35), a "cadaver" (85), a "ghost" (40), and a "sphinx" (58). Unable to describe A*** fully without recourse to gender, the text transforms A*** into transient fragments: "ephemeral, this body was undeniably ephemeral" (84).

The fragmentation of A***'s body is frequently framed by language that comments upon its own inability to capture the object it seeks to represent. When declaring their love to A***, the narrator alternates

---

18 See Emma Ramadan's excellent translator's note in the English edition of *Sphinx* for a discussion of the mechanics of translating Garréta's genderless French into English.
19 The elision of gender from French need not automatically put embodiment beyond representation. Nor is gender synonymous with embodiment. It is a discursive category that constructs binary differences from supposedly distinct anatomical differences. But categories like 'man/woman' or 'masculine/feminine' do not necessarily reflect peoples' embodied experience, particularly for those who do not fit into such categories. Similarly, gendered experience is often used synonymously to describe female experience, tacitly reinscribing the traditional relationship between women and the body. In *Sphinx*, the absence of linguistic, grammatical gender does appear to make its central characters' embodiment unrepresentable at a syntactical, semantic, and lexical level, the linguistic layers that gradually build up into the discursive category of gender. But Garréta's re-forming of the French language demonstrates how embodied experience that does not signify within representation or discourse can be redistributed in language through formal means.

"aimlessly between snippets of narration, the minutes of my interior monologue, syllogisms and images, passing without transition from slang to high style and from the trivial to the abstract, without ever finding the right tone or genre in which to deliver" the words (42–43). Despite the narrator's frequent code-switching, language seems to point only to a lack. At times, language collides with its own limits, explicitly representing A***'s body as unrepresentable. Describing the first time they have sex and the sense of sublimity it produces, the narrator states that "it's impossible to recapture the feeling of abandon through words" (55). Conversely, the fragmentation of A***'s body disrupts representation:

> The temporal order of events, even the simple spatial points of reference, all disappeared without my realizing it; everything is blurred in my memory. I have in my mouth, still, the taste of skin, of the sweat on that skin; against my hands, the tactile impression of skin and the shape of that flesh. (54)

The tactile, gustatory qualities of A***'s body disorder narrative diegesis and chronology.

While the insufficiency of language here seems harmless, at other moments it becomes a dangerous failing. Even the word "ephemeral," which evokes notions of insubstantial immateriality, performs a violence upon the fabric of language: "Ephemeral – a word that I heard pronounced like a murder, as an image before my eyes, floating, tearing the veil; a living and funereal abrasion coming to break on the surface of anamnesis" (84–85).[20] Language becomes an abyss into which the narrator falls.[21] The narrator's attempt to describe A*** – "the indescribable other" – only points to the futility of this effort, "so much did the meanings escape me" (86). Language turns over itself to the point of exhaustion, dramatizing postmodernism's aporia: "*Inadequate*, I would repeat the word to myself [. . .] Why give voice to the unarticulated? Because the inexpressible doesn't articulate itself in the least; it shatters into pieces before even taking form" (86). This battle with language is figured as an almost physical combat: "my jaws clamping down on my breath [..] to nip in the bud the inarticulate expressions that were surging and gnawing," while simultaneously "syncopating my breath to

---

20 The term "anamnesis" has multiple valences here beyond simply recollection. It also refers to the Platonic tradition that argues humans have an innate knowledge that must be rediscovered, as well as the Christian doctrine of transubstantiation, in which anamnesis signifies the resurrection of Christ.

21 'The Fall' is a recurrent trope in the novel, from the Biblical fall, to A***'s literal fall and resulting death, to the narrator's final fall in Amsterdam where they die in a botched robbery, in an intertextual echo of Albert Camus' *The Fall (1956, La Chute)*.

its blows" (86). Read through the lens of postmodernism, this passage and others like it seem point to the inability to fully capture the body in language, and, even more so, to the impossibility of escaping from the strictures of discursive identities like gender without giving up the corporeal.

On the one hand, the violent combat between the body, which resists signification, and language, which seeks at all costs to describe it, is the most extreme example of the postmodernist aporia in the novel. Discourse does violence to the body, fragmenting it; to resist this violence as a counterdiscourse, the body must make itself unrepresentable. At one point, A*** accuses the narrator of treating A*** only as an image or reflection (73), or A*** becomes an absent presence – a ghost or spirit whose materiality is dispatched from the symbolic order. The body's unrepresentability points to a very real failure in our ability to account for the embodied experiences of individuals like A***, who are most often associated with their bodies. On the other hand, *Sphinx* frequently acknowledges its own fictional status, reflecting upon its strategies for giving form to embodiment beyond representation. This helps undo the symbolic violence wrought upon the body. For instance, the struggle in this passage is not necessarily to describe the body in language but rather a struggle to resist the temptation of describing the body inadequately through language – to "nip in the bud" the impulse to use a language that will only prove insufficient. It is important that the site of this battle between the inexpressible body and the desire to use language is located in the body, while language describes its own inability to fully capture the body through bodily organs ("jaws") and actions ("breath," "gnawing"). In such passages, language becomes a commentary upon its own embodiment, even though this embodiment cannot be fully represented at the level of description.

The text thus frequently turns language upon itself, gnawing itself, in order to fill in the gaps of representation. It does so through formal figures that self-consciously draw attention to the way they produce form. Before I explore some formal strategies of both writing and interpretation that might allow us to 'fill in' A***'s absent presence, let me now turn to the novel's treatment of race. While gender exceeds representation, resulting in a fragmented or absent body, race is overdetermined, reducing the body to an object. Gender and race offer the binary of the postmodernist body, either exceeding representation or reducing it to a fixed object.

The Overdetermination of Race

To escape the essentialism of sex, *Sphinx* renders gender – the discursive script of sex – unrepresentable. Yet the illegibility of gender is offset by the seemingly crude treatment of race and the way it operates as a generic obstacle through which the love story between the narrator and A*** can be resolved.[22] Paradoxically, race appears more pre-determined than gender. The novel thus both comments upon and performs the dangers of the politics of representation. Why, in a language in which gender is almost inescapable, but that does not require the discursive marking of race, does Garréta fall back on such recognizable stereotypes? And why is race such a prominent part of A*** and the text's difference, when gender is not? The answer to these questions is not straightforward, and it is not possible to fully reframe the novel's treatment of race in terms of an emancipatory politics. Nevertheless, by shifting away from the referential surface of race, a formalist reading of the text demonstrates how A***'s body exceeds the normative workings of representational language; it is redistributed through the text's form in ways that can disrupt the metaphorical connections that connect specific bodies with racial identities.

Before I explore the formal redistribution of race, I will spend some time describing the overdetermination of race in the novel. Race is legible in both blackness and whiteness, but blackness signifies as a more visible symbol of difference. That is, it signifies more obviously as a sign of difference. Even when these states are emancipatory – such as A***'s familial milieu where the narrator finds some relief from the ascetic strictures of their life in France – the black body provides a more heightened access to affective life and pleasure. It is *more* bodily. The lengthy descriptions of A***'s body, too, engage in a long tradition of the fetishization of blackness, as does A***'s career as a dancer.[23]

The racial difference between A*** and the narrator is immediately remarked upon by their social circle and the wider milieu of bars and nightclubs, ranging from the seedy to the chic, that they frequent: "everywhere we went, people made remarks about our striking dissimilarity. They teased me over the contrast in the color between

---

22 See Kim's discussion of the genre of the love story normally requiring difference, in order that it can join two separate individuals, in Kim, *Unbecoming Language*, 129.
23 Kim notes that there are resemblances between A*** and Josephine Baker, another African American dancer in Paris, in Kim, *Unbecoming Language*, 134. Certainly, the performative aspect makes this script open to interpretation, just as Baker was able to harness the social script of the racialized body in order to partially determine her own cultural representation.

our skins, they stressed the difference in our mannerisms" (36). Even though A*** and the narrator also differ in terms of nationality, class, age, educational background, and native tongues, the major difference between them is explicitly framed in terms of their skin color. In other words, A*** and the narrator are confronted with the crudeness of identity politics:

> What did I get out of spending all my time with someone with whom I shared no social, intellectual, or racial community? That was precisely the question troubling them. Black skin, white skin: our looks were against us. Our intimacy went against the mandate dictating that birds of a feather flock together [*ce qui se ressemble s'assemble*]. And this impossible clash of colors [*assortiment de couleurs*] produced the general opinion that this was an unnatural union. (36)

The French more clearly emphasizes visibility ('those who resemble each other, assemble together'), whereas the English translation highlights animality, which is taken up several paragraphs later when their friends argue they come from different species.

The novel takes great pains to describe A***'s body without recourse to indexes of gender, but at certain moments it seems as if A*** cannot escape the discursive scripting of race. This tension between the elision of gender and the overdetermination of race is evident in the way the narrator perceives A*** immediately after a conversation with a mafioso barfly, who urges the narrator to pursue A*** in the face of their friends and acquaintances' resistance:

> What I was feeling for A*** needed its own embodiment [*incarnation*]; the pleasure I took in A***'s company demanded its own fulfillment. I wanted A***, it was true, and all my other desires, needs, and plans paled in comparison. Suddenly, the obsessive clamor for amorous possession took hold of me. I was surprised to find myself desiring, painfully. In a sudden rush of vertigo, I was tantalized by the idea of contact with A***'s skin. I wanted to dismiss, destroy all those who were thronging around A***, keeping this presence from me. I wanted to wrest A*** from their company, from the intrusive glances clinging to us there, and hide us both away. With an unknowingly crazed look, I was always watching this irresistible body. But my gaze was narrowing and stiffening [*le regard se crispait et se raidissait*] under the tension of carnal desire. That night, A*** was wearing a black silk shirt and white pleated leather pants that showed off a firm behind [*le modelé musculeux de ses hanches*]. A***'s hair, shaved not long ago for the show, was beginning to grow back, materializing as a light shadow. That face, thus restored to its pure nudity, appeared without interference, without anything that could deceptively modify its proportions or veil its imperfections. Its features had retained nothing of A***'s African origins [*son origine nègre*], except for a barely perceptible, sensual heaviness of the mouth. (39)

The "narrowing and stiffening" of the narrator's gaze embodies desire, fetishizing A***'s body. Even the disavowal that A***'s face retains nothing of its "African" origins operates through setting up a pre-existing racial reference, transforming their body into an exotic mask-like object expressed through A***'s "sensual heaviness." (It should be noted that the pejorative French term *nègre* is not equivalent to "African," but nor is it as offensive as the 'n-word' in English.) Indeed, later in the novel, just before A*** falls and dies on stage, A*** accuses the narrator of "never having considered, or taken into account, anything other than an image, other than my singular and therefore false, vision of A***" (72). "How do you see me anyway," A*** throws back in the narrator's face before taking the stage (73).

This commentary upon the process of representation demonstrates a degree of awareness about the construction of race as a form of difference. Yet this self-consciousness at times seems wielded as a way of justifying the use of race as a foil for gender. Thus, the *jouissance* that A***'s body represents becomes the basis for a wider treatment of blackness as affording a richer affective life. Indeed, while there are overt references to the narrator's whiteness throughout the narrative, whiteness – as an identity, appearance, or form – does not define the narrator to the same extent A*** is defined by blackness. In contrast to A***'s vivid blackness, whiteness becomes not so much blank as *bland*, or what in French would be called *fade*, a term that applies to both color and taste. For instance, in contrast to the asceticism of "white, Anglo-Saxon, Puritan America," the narrator's "America is of black origins – the music, the voices, the food. There's a term for that in the black community: soul. Soul music, soul food" (62). Just as the narrator exaggerates the racial dimension of A***'s body through the proportion of pleasure that it gives them, black culture enlivens the narrator's sensual life: "the old black mommas laughed with delight to see that I had such an appetite. A***, who was used to seeing me bored or indifferent when faced with earthly sustenance, was astonished and overjoyed. I was forgetting to repine, I was finally tasting life, savoring each bite" (63). This "soul food" revives the narrator from the strictures of asceticism in a deeply embodied process of spiritual transformation. It is difficult in these passages to ignore how the white narrator consumes black America, reanimating their attenuated body by ingesting this culture as a material source. This sense of cultural appropriation is heightened by the narrator's claim to not see racial differences:

> I felt at home there, so much did they make me feel like a part of their family, effortlessly forgetting our differences in race, color, culture, class – everything

that one might cite as possible traits of alterity. It was as if the language they were speaking and the food they were cooking had always been familiar to me. (63)

The reference to "soul food," "soul music," and "black mommas" is jarring within *Sphinx's* tone, with its echoes of Baudelairean spleen and postmodern ennui, although it is not the only example of an excessive evocation of racial alterity. It echoes the use of the term *nègre* and remarks about "North Africans in tired suits packed tightly at the bar" (translation altered, 3), which function as an index of class.[24] These markers of race stand in crude contrast to the subtle and sophisticated elision of gender from the discursive workings of French. Whereas removing gender from language undoes it as a naturalized category, the narrator notes how blackness has indelibly shaped their own language:

> my English still bears the stigmata from the time spent among an almost exclusively black community. Imperceptibly, the expressions and characteristic improprieties of their speech slipped into the tissue of the academic English I had been taught in high school. The language I speak is a monstrous hybrid, mingling Oxford and Harlem, Byron and gospel. To the point of caricature, I pronounce these African American utterances with a *rather British* accent, and sometimes swallow up to half of the syllables of a too perfectly constructed sentence. (64, italics in original)

The term "stigmata" carries a lot of weight here. While the novel subtly elides gender, race is violently marked on the 'tissue' of language; the passage suggests that race has the potential to become an intrinsic element of the narrator's body, while, in turn, this association endows language with an essential materiality. Whereas *Sphinx* demonstrates that gender is not a necessary social category by creating a language devoid of it – and by extension, of course, demonstrating that gender is not essential (lest anyone had been in doubt) – it implies language can essentialize race. The consequences of this are potentially devastating: far from undoing race, language imbues race with a materiality in the social sphere that derives from the power associated with nature, innateness, and essentialism. The transformation of language into a natural form reifies race.[25]

---

24 The English translation replaces the term *Nord Africains* with "working-class men."
25 This is a rather curious move in French, because in contrast to the central place of gender in the structure of the language – and, by extension, to its sedimentation of social roles and categories – France's universalist system does not recognize race as an official category of difference, based on the fact that race is not a biological fact. This 'colorblind' policy does not, of course, eliminate racism. My point here is that discourses around race do not circulate as widely in either the public or political spheres in France as they do in the United States (though this is changing). This may be why black American culture plays such a large

Sphinx's representation of race is problematic.²⁶ Without wanting to absolve the novel of its racial politics, particularly in relation to its thematic and representational treatment of race, I nevertheless argue that at the level of literary form, race takes on a subtly different shape that points not to its overdetermination as a fixed representation but to the manner in which form may allow us to apprehend race differently and to reorder its metaphorical associations. Race becomes an uncontained embodiment; a material affect that shapes form.

Making Figures

Having explored both the unrepresentability of the body, signified by genderless language, and the body's overdetermination through the objectification of race, I now want to propose an alternative way of reading the body through two poetic figures: prosopopoeia and catachresis. These figures demonstrate both how embodiment provides the foundation for literary form and how literary form can produce alternative conceptions of the body beyond the determination of identity. In "The Corporeal Urn," I argued that literature is able to project or perform, rather than represent, embodied experience through logical forms. A logical form provides a congruent, rather than mimetic, form for life's rhythms, movements, and patterns. Logical forms can be outward shapes, like an urn, that project the body's shape. Or they can be poetic processes or figures that enact embodied experience, such as the rhetorical balancing of inverted clauses found in chiasmus. In the novel, the sphinx provides a logical form for the body, while prosopopoeia is the poetic act that enacts embodiment. This is the act of giving voice to an absent presence, a dead person, an inanimate object, or even embodying an abstract idea.

For de Man and other deconstructionists, prosopopoeia ultimately points to the absence of the person or thing it purports to speak on

---

part in the fetishization of race in the novel. Race and blackness in the United States, especially at the time the novel was written, exerted more influence in both social and political discourses about difference. The transplantation of the narrator and A***'s love story to Harlem at one point seems to exaggerate racial difference in order to undermine gender. Yet the reasons for this move within the logic of the novel remain unclear. While the creation of a genderless language and even a genderless *genre* demonstrate how the novel is oriented towards using language, discourse, and form to imagine new modes of being, the novel's racial politics stand in marked contrast to its emancipatory formal possibilities.

26 The translation of race in the novel is also revealing for the way that it sometimes *elides* the novel's problematic racial politics, for instance translating *nègre* as "African," or eliminating the reference to North African men, which I have mentioned before.

behalf of or describe; this is a function of the way language always undoes its own meaning.[27] By contrast, I propose that we approach prosopopoeia in terms of its original rhetorical function of addressing an audience in order to produce pathos. A register of speech in classical tragedies,[28] pathos was a way of arousing a strong affective response in the audience – a response that projected and extended the performance of emotions on the stage. Pathos renders characters more vivid. But it is also a trope that *performs* embodiment. We will remember that prosopopoeia, derived from Greek, literally means 'making a face'; prosopopoeia enacts the process of producing a figure. For this reason, it has often been called the figure of figurality – or the attempt to figure in language the process of figuration[29] – a notion that echoes the status of the sphinx as a "living" rock, rendering in material form the act of making a figure.[30] Prosopopoeia is also closely tied to catachresis, a figure I will explore at more length in the next section on race. Catachresis is another form of personification in which a word is used to describe an idea without a referent, such as 'table legs' or 'foot of a mountain.' Using the word *black* to describe people with high levels of melanin in their skin is also a catachresis. While prosopopoeia transforms the literal into the figurative, catachresis uses figurative meaning as if it was literal.

The act of prosopopoeia takes place in a scene about halfway through the narrative in which the narrator first watches A*** perform a dance to the song "Sphinx."[31] Watching A*** on stage, the narrator is able to discern the enunciation of some of the song's lyrics on A***'s lips. Yet A*** remains silent. In the place of A*** speaking, the song's lyrical "I" performs the act of giving a voice to A***'s presence. The song's content contains a number of classical prosopoetic themes, including the evocation of suffering and death, the ephemerality of existence, and the conjuring of the supernatural. Its function in the narrative is also classically prosopoetic: it stages the text's status as an epitaph, performs pathos, and produces the figure of figurality, or moments when the

---

27 De Man explores prosopopoeia across a number of his essays, but in particular in "Autobiography as De-facement."
28 Although pathos has a somewhat pejorative meaning in contemporary literary theory, signaling an excessive, 'pathetic' emotional state, I use it here in relation to its original rhetorical definition.
29 Michael Riffaterre, "Prosopopeia," 110.
30 Indeed, in Riffaterre's analysis of prosopopoeia, on which I base my analysis of the figure, he analyzes a series of rocks, tombs, and headstones in French literature, such images embodying the materiality of prosopopoeia – its objective of making present an abstract absence.
31 This is an actual song released originally in English by the French singer Amanda Lear in 1978.

rhetorical and the formal coincide. The prosopopoeia figures its own process of giving voice to a presence that is, in this case, a dead person (A***), an inanimate object (the sphinx), and immaterial concept (the body):

> *I can't stand the pain*
> *and I keep looking for all the faces I had*
> *before the world began.*
> *I've only known desire and my poor soul will burn*
> *into eternal fire.*
> *And I can't even cry,*
> *a sphinx can never cry.*
> *I wish that I could be*
> *a silent sphinx eternally.*
> *I don't want any past*
> *only want things which cannot last.*
> *Phony words of love*
> *or painful truth, I've heard it all before.*
> *A conversation piece,*
> *a woman or a priest, it's all a point of view.* (57, italics in original)[32]

The song begins with the cryptic voice of the lyrical persona declaring its search for "all the faces I had/ before the world began." The act of searching for a face performs the act of prosopopoeia – 'making a face' – which is itself already a type of performative utterance. Thus, if prosopopoeia comments upon the process of creating a figure, the song performs prosopopoeia's performative dimension, literally setting out to 'make' a figure. Also, at the heart of the song is the prosopoetic contradiction of giving voice to an absent person, condensed in the antinomy of verbalizing "I wish I could be/ a silent sphinx eternally." This invocation of the sphinx does not succeed in fixing it as an identifiable representation. It is unclear what the sphinx stands for or who it is meant to symbolize. Rather, it produces the figure of figurality by connecting the immaterial idea with the material object through the lexical distribution of sensations. Some of these, such as "pain," "desire," and "burn[ing]" are explicit, others such as suffering and yearning are evoked through their absence. These are all 'pathetic' emotions that appeal to feelings of pity and compassion. Indeed, the failed pathetic fallacy (itself already a failure) of a sphinx that cannot cry produces its opposite: pathos. The rhetorical production of pathos – Greek for 'suffering' – projects the embodied emotions the sphinx cannot feel for the reader (or audience),

---

32 Garréta's French rendering of the song omits and changes elements of the original English lyrics. As far as I can tell, however, the English translation of *Sphinx* leaves the original lyrics unchanged.

bringing into the aesthetic field of perception an entity that cannot speak for itself, an uncanny or supernatural presence – the immaterial made material, the figural made literal.

The song's poetics thus oscillate between the literal and the figural, an ambivalence embodied in the figure of the sphinx as the material form of the figural. The sphinx incarnates the figurative function of speech as a literal form. The embodied underpinnings of prosopopoeia demonstrate how the figure does not substantiate an absence but rather gives form to embodied presence beyond representation. We can see this process at work in the prose paragraph that immediately follows the song, which substantiates this embodied form in a literal commentary on the figurative:

> The vision comes back to me instantly: A*** crossing the stage in the feline roving of the choreography, embodying an enigmatic, silent figure [*donner corps à une énigmatique figure de silence*] twisting to the extreme limit of dislocation in miraculous movements that were syncopated but not staccato. Even as this body fades away, a spectral figure [*une figure fantomatique*] remains, immobile; the stage is populated by incarnations, sudden gestures, hieratic poses set in a relentless progression. There was something cat-like or divine in this body that, moved by some sly, sensual pleasure, was embodying in nonchalant strides a languid damnation, an immemorial fatality made into movement. (57–58)

The song's prosopopoeia incarnates the sphinx as the figurative function of speech as a literal form. This sets off a process that turns the figurative body into a series of literal figures of speech whose proper rhetorical description coincides with their bodily shape. Whereas metaphor and metonymy use a word in an 'improper' sense, prosopopoeia's primary, concrete meaning unites rhetorical form and bodily shape. The body becomes a figure, and figures turn into bodies. Thus A***'s silent, absent, immaterial body embodies "an enigmatic figure of silence" and a "spectral figure." Similarly, the movement and gestures of the song become embodied in the image of "hieratic poses." Hieratic refers to a form of Egyptian writing, and it is also used to denote the priestly caste – a religious connotation that is echoed in the sense of "divinity," "incarnations," "damnation," and "immemorial fatality." These two meanings are brought together via the word's third definition: highly stylized and formal art, often embodied in particular poses. Thus, the "hieratic poses" literalize the "sudden gestures," turning them into formal figures, in a process that parallels how A***'s cat-like form is an "immemorial fatality" that is "made into movement [*fait geste*]" (58). As I noted earlier, the term *trope* means to twist and turn in Greek. This constant reversal between movement and stasis, voice and silence, the "syncopated but not staccato" movements of A***'s body "twisting to the extreme limit of dislocation in miraculous movements," are the exertions of language itself as it gives literal form to the figurative body.

The body here is both literal and figurative; it is the basic, concrete ground of the poetic figure. Form projects embodiment into the very structure of language. *Sphinx* turns the body into a literal figure – the figure of the figure – in order to give it a new form beyond representation, mimesis, or referentiality. By making the act of representation its own subject – rather than a vehicle we can leave behind once we have grasped the represented object – literary form incarnates, rather than points beyond, itself.

In giving voice to an absent person or an inanimate object, prosopopoeia is the literal figure of acting and appearing. It thus has political implications: it projects into what Arendt calls "the space of appearance"[33] – speech, action, and presence – a figure that would not otherwise be able to speak for itself, and in doing so it *produces* an embodied form. This 'self,' if we can call it that, is not referential, however; it does not reflect an actual gendered subject, or, as we will see in the next section, a racialized subject. The political subject is created through embodied form. Prosopopoeia thus exposes the conceit of representation, which naturalizes the act of standing for something else. *Sphinx* scrubs gendered categories through the creation of a language whose form erases grammatical gender, and it consequently demolishes the gendered subject. Prosopopoeia similarly reminds us that all speech – whether undertaken by oneself or on the part of an other – is *rhetorical*. (Rhetoric is of course far from 'empty.') In the following section, we will explore how catachresis figuratively renders the literal, which demonstrates how the symbolic and political system of race reproduces rhetorical violence. Conversely, however, understanding the formal, aesthetic, and rhetorical foundation of catachresis can undermine the referential system of language that produces race as the sign of a natural body.

Race and Catachresis

In the previous section, I explored how form can give presence to a seemingly absent body. Let me now turn to the way form can also loosen the representational fixity of the racialized body through catachresis. It does so, I argue, by severing the referential relationship between the body and the signs, symbols, and icons that naturalize race. Whereas prosopopoeia

---

33 Hannah Arendt, *The Human Condition* (Chicago: University of Chicago Press, 1958), 198.

projects an absent presence, catachresis supplements the deficiency of language to capture the object it seeks to represent by filling that gap with another term.[34] The relationship between the figurative and literal underpins catachresis' connection to the body, and it thus reflects how prosopopoeia is the literal figure of making a face. Catachreses, as I noted in "The Corporeal Urn," are "literally false [. . .] but figuratively true."[35] Terms like 'foot of the mountain' use figurative language as if it was literal, alienating language from its own figurate force. While it could be argued that catachresis demonstrates the insufficiency of language, particularly towards the body, I argue that – like prosopopoeia – it is *productive*. It generates new, often disconcerting meanings that draw attention to representation's alienating function. This is evident when de Man argues that "something monstrous lurks in the most innocent of catachreses: when one speaks of the legs of the table or the face of the mountain, catachresis is already turning into prosopopoeia and one begins to perceive a world of potential ghosts and monsters."[36] These monsters, ghosts, and other hybrid or uncanny forms, such as sphinxes, throw into relief representation's seemingly self-evident reflection of the body by producing figures that draw attention to their own incompleteness, immateriality, or deformation. Catachresis thus produces an excessive affect that cannot be contained by mimetic language.

When we use a term like 'foot of a mountain,' the catachrestic 'abuse' of language is innocuous enough. Yet when catachresis is used in the rhetorical formulation of race then the abuse of language has more serious consequences, which are masked by the term's apparent self-evidence.[37] Thus, we catachrestically use the term 'black' to describe a person with high levels of melanin in their skin, but whose skin is not literally black.[38] This catachresis suggests that the concept 'blackness'

---

34 See Paul Ricoeur, *The Rule of Metaphor: The Creation of Meaning in Language* (London: Routledge, 2006), 72.
35 Raengo, *On the Sleeve of the Visual*, 54–55. My analysis also builds on Cécile Bishop's work on how catachresis disrupts the visual markers between race and representation, in Bishop "Photography, Race and Invisibility," *Photographies* 11, no. 2-3 (September 2, 2018): 193–213.
36 Paul de Man, "The Epistemology of Metaphor," *Critical Inquiry* 5, no. 1 (1978): 13–30, 21.
37 For a discussion of the way catachresis naturalizes the abuse of language see Jonathan Culler, "Commentary," *New Literary History* 6, no. 1 (1974): 219–29, 224.
38 The same is of course true for 'white,' which catachrestically names – and naturalizes – people with lower levels of melanin and pigmentation in their skin. But whereas 'black' and 'blackness' operate as the dominate signs of racial difference, 'white' and 'whiteness' elide how the racial condition they signify has become the blank or 'neutral' background onto which other forms of difference are projected. In other words, 'white' also signifies how 'whiteness' becomes the de facto normative state.

names has no proper referent; our system of meaning cannot accommodate it.

As a color, black results from the complete absence of light. It denotes an inability to visualize and an immateriality that haunts the racial sign of 'blackness.' The catachresis of 'black' thus naturalizes the way in which 'blackness' signifies a conceptual and ontological absence – a formlessness – in Western culture.[39] Yet for this reason, catachresis also "ruptures the field of representation."[40] Another way of thinking about catachresis, then, is as a 'cut' that severs the relationship between the body and referential language. Raengo argues that catachresis has the "ability to rhetorically sever and rearrange the very texture of reality to establish a wedge between the 'thing' and its representation" and thus "to redraw the terms by which we encounter either."[41] I bring the generative and the disruptive dimensions of catachresis together to demonstrate how it can sever the seemingly self-evident referential relationship between the body and race. In turn, this can reorder the metaphorical relationship between race and the body. At the same time, this operation allows an uncontained, unidentifiable embodiment to seep into the novel's formal texture.

Sphinx and its English translation use several different terms to describe blackness. These include *nègre, noir,* "black," and "African."[42] These are all catachreses when used to describe A***, who is not literally black or African. (It is also, of course, a catachresis to describe the narrator as white.) Yet at times, Garréta does use the word *noir/* black to describe blackness in a chromatic sense, which disrupts the metaphorical relationship between blackness and the body. Let us return to a passage that I explored above, one that is problematic for its fetishization of A***'s black body. In it, the narrator describes how "A*** was wearing a black silk shirt and white pleated leather pants that showed off a firm behind" (39). The passage sets up a stereotype only to disavow it by insisting that A***'s face "had retained nothing" of its "African origins" [*origine nègre*]. To describe A***'s face in these terms, even as a disavowal of racial difference, is a catachresis in both French and English. Yet there is another operation involving terms that are otherwise used to describe race in the novel, namely black and white.

---

39 See Calvin L. Warren, *Ontological Terror: Blackness, Nihilism, and Emancipation* (Durham, NC: Duke University Press Books, 2018), 144.
40 Warren, *Ontological Terror*, 144.
41 Raengo, *On the Sleeve of the Visual*, 68.
42 The translation also uses the term "dark-skinned," which is less catachrestic, to describe the two characters at the end who kill the narrator, although this is a translation of "ces deux Noirs" (119).

Only here, they are used to describe A***'s clothing, specifically clothing constructed from materials that have a close connection to bodies. Silk derives from the cocoons of silkworm larvae, while leather is animal skin. Thus, a metonymic association emerges between A***'s skin color and texture and the clothing, which acts like a second skin or a covering carapace. While A***'s racially differentiated body is a catachresis – applying a figural sense of blackness as if it was literal – their black and white clothing, made out of literal skin, achieves the opposite. It applies a literal use of color and material as if it was figural. This figural and literal interconnection of black and white skins thus momentarily, and perhaps inadvertently, reveals the catachrestic form of race. The presentation of literal black and white skins in the prosopopoeia of making A***'s face reveals the catachrestic investment of A***'s skin color with the figurative weight of blackness.

The ambivalent mode of catachresis – at once disruptive (or 'abusive') and productive – is evident throughout *Sphinx*, particularly in the production of monstrous, hybrid, and ghostly figures for language and writing. We will remember that the narrator describes "black" language as a "stigmata" that "slipped into the tissue" of their English. The stigmata is of course a religious image of Christ's crucifixion wounds. The catachresis of evoking a "black" language is thus already an abuse that disrupts language's referential function, producing an ironic "monstrous hybrid, mingling Oxford and Harlem, Byron and gospel" (64). This notion of catachresis as a cut that generates new figures is also evident in a key passage in the novel, immediately following the prosopoetic performance of A***'s absent embodiment. Having watched A*** perform their figural dance made literal in the text's embodied figures, the narrator returns to A***'s dressing room. On the threshold of the space, the narrator encounters A***

> Immobile as if in a prayer or a confession, legs bent, forearms fixed on a high barstool supporting A***'s entire body weight. Hands dangling, wrists slack, gaze abandoned and lost in the emptiness, then focusing on me as I entered and following me to where I sat down opposite. It was like the disdainful pose of the sphinx (or the image I had of it then), the same sharp aesthetic [*l'esthétique aiguë*]. I thought this to myself and, laughing, affectionately let slip [*l'apostrophai*], "my sphinx" – as if I had said "my love." We remained face-to-face, our bodies as if petrified. A terror silted up in my throat; the desire I had felt welling up in me at the sight of those distant movements on the stage had been suspended. I could do nothing but adore. Those eyes, so black, fixed on me, subjected me to an unbearable torture. (58)

The sphinx's "disdainful pose" and "sharp aesthetic" reenact the prosopopoeia of making a face. Recall that a sphinx is a sculpture, carved from "living" rock. The tool required to cut the rock into this form resembles the writing instrument (or *stylus*) that etches or engraves, or the inscription on an epitaph, or language as a tool that creates a "stigmata."[43] Prosopopoeia thus gives way to the cut of catachresis, of which there are two in the passage. The first and most obvious is naming A*** as a sphinx. The other, less obvious, is the catachresis of describing A***'s eyes as "black." This draws attention to the way both blackness and seeing blackness as a form of racial difference become naturalized. Other senses, notably taste, are associated with race in *Sphinx*, but it is most crudely rendered through visual signs. (Think back to the disavowal of A***'s features as "African.") Yet here the transfer of blackness from A***'s facial features to their eyes performs a deliberate catachresis, and draws attention to the visual economy of blackness, while also severing the body from referential language: eyes can be no more black than skin, but they do not signify racially to the same extent.[44] The catachrestic transfer of blackness to A***'s eyes does not simply demonstrate the contingency of racial categories, it visualizes the catachrestic act as an instance of rupture.

At other points in the novel catachresis severs referents from their conventional meaning through formal processes, such as the chromatic effect of transforming A***'s figuratively black skin into a literal black surface. Here, however, catachresis acts as a figurative cut to disrupt language's seeming literalness. The wedge between the word and the referent is corporealized through the catachrestic production of a hybrid materiality.[45] The sphinx is the material figure of catachresis; it is a monstrous hybrid that gives form to the formless – the very thing that slips continually out of the grasp of mimetic or representational language. But this materiality is not limited to only the sphinx figure. A***'s embodied form haunts language when it becomes a hybrid, monstrous, or ghostly figure. The generative effect of catachresis produces an embodied excess, but not excessive in terms of something that exceeds the representational, like the sublime, but rather an excessive or abundant materiality. A***'s body becomes an uncontainable presence; it is a tone, style, affect, and range of figures that permeate the novel's form.

43 Raengo uses the notion of the *stylus* to connect photography and writing, in Raengo, *On the Sleeve of the Visual*, 68. I build on this idea to think about the way writing is a corporeal act that materially shapes embodied figures.
44 Nicholas Harrison, *Postcolonial Criticism: History, Theory, and the Work of Fiction* (Malden, MA; Cambridge: Polity, 2003), 76.
45 Catachresis, as Raengo argues, can "corporealize the unbridgeable gap between seeing and saying by fashioning objects (or scenarios or fetishes) the sit between the two," in Raengo, *On the Sleeve of the Visual*, 53.

One way catachresis achieves this is by transforming the senses into a formal texture. Just as the catachresis of assigning blackness to eyes visualizes the referential rupture between language and the body, so too are other catachreses in the novel closely tied to redistributing sensory experience beyond representation. For instance, the expansive, uncontainable aspect of A***'s body – its redistribution into other formal elements – is apparent in this passage, which foregrounds the importance of touch. It closely follows a passage in which A***'s body has been fixed as a racial object. After the narrator and A*** part ways that evening, the narrator tosses and turns in bed, haunted by

> the memory of A***'s scent, by the residual imprint, barely there, of a shoulder resting against my own this morning as we spoke. The ghost of A***'s presence against mine; a hand poised for a moment on my face, our thighs pressed together in a cramped space. I had the sensation in my flesh of contact with those limbs, no longer there; the effect lingered long after its source had disappeared, retaining the same intensity. A hallucinatory sensation, as if my body has suffered an amputation. This sensation that, even after the split [*la coupure*], the separation of our two bodies kept scalding me, kept me awake. I oscillated the entire morning between the rage of embracing only a void, and the memory, the bliss of an instant, of the past night that I was trying to hard mentally to recompose. (40)

The passage is traversed by variously incomplete or immaterial bodies. These ghosts, residual imprints, and detached limbs contrast with the vivid, intense embodied sensation of amputations, burns, and cuts that physically mutilate the body's integrity. At other points in the novel, the narrator catachrestically invests A***'s body with the symbolic and semiotic weight of blackness. But the language in this passage severs the referential relationship between the racialized body and language. It figures catachresis as a physical process of dismemberment and disconnection that cuts off the body from any proper or pre-existing referent. Catachresis – an abuse of language – is a *dis*-figuration. This disfiguration reveals two important elements. The first is language's corporeal dimension, or how the body shapes the very conditions of expression, as well as its content. The second is the way figures like catachresis deliberately fragment language. This provides the grounds for new formal modes to emerge, which may be able to recompose these elements. Form brings together different body parts rather than rendering them unrepresentable. The writing here reflects upon its own process of composing A***'s body, of producing a presence where physically one lacks. Like prosopopoeia, then, to approach catachresis in terms of its literal and figurative relationship to the body reveals the embodied foundation of poetic language and form, as well as the way form can reconfigure or redistribute embodiment in figures beyond representation.

The tactile imprint of A***'s uncontainable embodiment seeps into other affective forms that attempt to name the conceptual gap of race or blackness without recourse to pre-existent terms. Tellingly, this shift from language as referential and mimetic to form as productive takes place through the evocation of taste. In a Proustian sleight of hand, the memory of the taste of stereotypically African American dishes causes some feeling to appear "without being summoned":

> Even now, the taste of sweet potato melts into the taste of iced tea in my mouth. Is there anything more vertiginous that gustative reminiscence? For it upends completely the conventional working of memory. When I recall this meal, something [*quelque chose*] appears without being summoned, something that does not serve as a witness to anything, that does not help me to follow the thread of my memory [*du souvenir d'aucun supplément de signification*]. But this something returns – not under the guise of a phantom, of an immaterial representation of an object now vanished, of a perception swallowed up and designated to a bygone past, coming from the imagination to reincarnate itself feebly in the present. Instead, it [*quelque chose*] crystallizes, taking on an intense, fugitive form, a carnal presence – the rebirth of a sensation whose former source has long ago disappeared. A vivid hallucination, a tangible reliving that invades the mouth and spreads down the back of the throat, taking on body, flesh, and warmth [*prend corps et chair et chaleur*]: the flavor itself, still intact, of this long-gone nourishment. (63–64)

The passage immediately preceding this one catachrestically invokes "old black mommas" (these "mommas" cannot, of course, be literally black). What is at play here, however, is catachresis' generative aspect, or how it severs the referential relationship between bodies and the representational fixity of race. The narrative reflects upon the act of naming a concept, experience, or perception that has no proper referent and that is no longer a property of the body. The body itself dissolves the mimetic connection between race and language, swallowing up, digesting, absorbing, transforming, returning blackness into the "something" that catachresis sets out name. This passage unwinds the catachrestic process of naming blackness, revealing the process of figuration. Race, like embodiment, may be this "something" (in French, this *quelque chose*) that escapes signification, but that expresses itself in other more subtle forms. Embodied existence is the "something" that language cannot directly name but which crystallizes into the formal figure of "an intense, fugitive form, a carnal presence"; it projects a "sensation whose former source [. . .] long ago disappeared."

This fugitive, carnal form is an instance where language turns in on itself to reveal its standing as form. But if prosopopoeia is the figure of figurality, then catachresis might be said to be the failed figurality of race.[46] Catachresis works at the syntactical level by reassigning words in order to produce new semantic meanings for ideas without a reference. The body's decomposed fragments provide new connections between the tangible element and the disconnected sign. It is partly for this reason that A*** exists as an intangible presence (difficult to capture in referential language), disaggregated fragments, or an overdetermined racialized body. But the 'cut' of catachresis can also be productive; it redistributes embodiment in elements of literary form beyond representation. This is particularly important when it comes to race because it enables bodies that normally do not signify to appear in the political realm without being reduced to their outward appearance or identity. Put otherwise, race might become a formal property – an aesthetic appearance that does not have an innate or essential quality. If the novel demonstrates how language composes (and can thus 'decompose') gender, its at times catachrestic treatment of race suggests that embodied racial characteristic like skin color can be understood as formal configurations rather than innate biological properties. Understanding race as a mode of aesthetic appearance might counteract colorblind discourses – captured in the pat insistence that one does not 'see' color – that obscure racism's effects. (Recall the narrator's suggestion that they do not see "race, color, culture, class" precisely at the moment they are consuming it.) The formal organization of race enables us to perceive racial difference without reducing race to biology or overdetermining the racial body as a dematerialized entity.

Each of the three passages I explored in this section are notable for the different body parts that are central to the catachresis. The initial instance of catachrestically naming A*** as a sphinx takes place by displacing black onto their eyes and vocalizing the act of naming. A***'s body in the second passage is disaggregated into different limbs: hands, shoulders, legs. In the final passage, it is the mouth – as the organ of language – that struggles to express the "something" of race. If we take both these body parts and these different passages separately then it appears catachresis severs the relationship between embodiment and referential language, but does not fully recompose it. Yet the cut of catachresis also offers another way of understanding how these different body parts fit together, for each of the passages also operates through attendant sensual registers: sight and hearing, touch, and taste and smell. In severing the referential link between language and the racialized body, catachresis allows an uncontainable embodiment to seep through the

---

[46] Raengo calls catachresis a "failed figurality," in Raengo, *On the Sleeve of the Visual*, 57.

text. Sight, hearing, touch, smell, and taste: the five senses recompose the fragmented or objectified body into a whole beyond representation. Catachresis allows A*** a "body, flesh, and warmth," as described in the passage I just explored, that exceeds the limits of representation.

The Politics of Projection

In this chapter, I have sought to demonstrate how poetic, formal, and rhetorical figures give shape to embodiment, and how embodiment underpins the production of literary forms. This moves us beyond the postmodernist aporia – the sphinx's riddle – of a body that either escapes or is reduced to representation. If we approach the body in terms of representation, the syntactical excision of gender from language destabilizes semantic meaning, and it fragments the body it seeks to describe. Similarly, race overdetermines the body, turning it into a crude representation of difference. But prosopopoeia and catachresis – as opposed to metaphor and metonymy – are not tropes of replacement; they do not belong to the realm of the referential. Instead, they are united in their purpose of literally producing figures and figuratively rendering of the literal. By approaching prosopopoeia and catachresis in terms of their original rhetorical functions, it becomes evident how prosopopoeia projects rather than imitates embodiment, where it would be absent on a representational level, while catachresis severs the referential link between the body and language that sustains race. In doing so, these tropes also provide an alternative to representational models of political visibility or presence, in which one thing stands in for another. This model of replacement or supplement has often been used to deny individuals closely aligned with the body – women, people of color, and others marked as different – from political representation. If the body is unrepresentable, then those defined by their bodies do not signify politically.

At the same time, the system of representation assumes that language indexes an actual, authentic subject. De Man reminds us language replaces phenomenal experience with signs that cannot carry the sensorial dimension to which they refer. Yet both repetition and aesthetic mystification anthropomorphize these signs, transforming the arbitrary connection between signifier and sign into a natural figure, and thus implying "the constitution of specific entities prior to their confusion."[47]

---

[47] Paul de Man, *The Rhetoric of Romanticism* (New York: Columbia University Press, 1984), 241.

This process "seems to be the illusory resuscitation of the natural breath of language," and aesthetic mystification that transforms language into an organic process.[48] De Man sought to deconstruct this pretense to presence, to demonstrate the irresolvable tension between "the semantic and the non-signifying, material properties of language."[49] Figures like catachresis and prosopopoeia themselves figure language's appropriative force – its attempt to collapse the difference between materiality and sign (they are "the figure, the trope, metaphor as a violent [. . .] deadly Apollo"[50]). De Man characterizes this in violent terms as "a device of language that never ceases to partake of the very violence against which it is directed."[51] This acknowledges, *pace* the New Critics, the materiality, even the embodied foundation, of poetic language. But he associates this materiality with a transcendental form of presence (an "ideology"), which ultimately conflates "linguistic with natural reality."[52] By dispatching embodiment to the non-figural, the non-signifying, he turns violence against the material body into a form of rhetorical or semantic misappropriation, or a misnaming, in catachrestic terms. Yet precisely in seeking to demonstrate how we "confuse the materiality of the signifier with the materiality of what it signifies,"[53] he transforms violence – a physical force that acts upon a material entity – into a semantic operation. Indeed, he characterizes deconstructive reading as engaging in this (textual) violence by repeatedly reenacting "the necessary recurrence of the initial violence."[54] Figuring the body in language resists the violent 'essentialism' of the natural body.

There is a way, I argue, of accounting for embodiment in language without making it appear a 'natural' figure or doing violence to it. This works by returning poetic and rhetorical figures and literary form to their embodied foundation, as I will do throughout this book. Prosopopoeia and catachresis – as well as other formal figures – make visible the conceit of representation, which naturalizes the act of standing in for something else. In giving voice to an absent person or inanimate object, prosopopoeia is the literal figure of the act of speaking for another. It reveals the *rhetorical* structure this political act. In turn, the catachrestic act of applying a figurative sense of language as if it was literal *denatu-*

---

48 De Man, *The Rhetoric of Romanticism*, 247.
49 De Man, *The Rhetoric of Romanticism*, 114.
50 De Man, *The Rhetoric of Romanticism*, 117–118.
51 De Man, *The Rhetoric of Romanticism*, 119.
52 Paul de Man, *The Resistance to Theory* (Minneapolis: University of Minnesota Press, 1986), 11.
53 De Man, *The Resistance to Theory*, 11.
54 De Man, *The Rhetoric of Romanticism*, 119.

ralizes the referential link between language and the body that sustains the exclusion from the political realm of those reduced to their bodies. At the same time, however, these figures allow us to grasp the presence of the body, because they are figures of and for embodiment – for the way embodiment gives rise to the very structures, figures, acts, and gestures of communication.

Rather than standing in for something absent or approximating an authentic self – both a key part of debates about who has the right to authentically speak on behalf of others – prosopopoeia and catachresis demonstrate the process whereby we create such figures and endow them with a presence and authenticity that representation appears to naturalize. The bodies that prosopopoeia and catachresis produce are *figurative* – they are not representations of actual bodies, whether gendered or racialized. These rhetorical figures demonstrate both the embodied foundation of poetic language and the formal construction of bodies. Embodied experience is composed, distributed, organized, and arranged. Far from undermining the political force of form, they throw into relief the processes of representation, both literary and political.

Chapter 3

"All life is figure and ground": Samuel Beckett and the Politics of Embodied Form

Samuel Beckett's bodies limp, crawl, grope, fall, collapse, and scream. They are broken, fragmented, disabled, prosthetic, imprisoned, and paralyzed. Like the disintegrating state of his bodies, his language stutters, falters, pauses, stammers, retreats, repeats, and ultimately fails to fully *mean*. More than any other writer in this book, and quite possibly in twentieth-century literary history, Beckett's works exemplify the failure of language to express the meaning it seeks to capture, and the failure of the body to mean in the absence of a language that can adequately represent it. Evidence for what has often been termed Beckett's 'aesthetics of failure' abound in comments he made on both his own work and on art in general. In *Three Dialogues* (1949), the Beckett persona speaks of a type of expression in which "there is nothing to express, nothing with which to express, no power to express, no desire to express, together with the obligation to express." The only way out of this impasse is to make "an expressive act [. . .] of its impossibility."[1] Elsewhere, Beckett

---

1 Samuel Beckett, *Disjecta: Miscellaneous Writings and a Dramatic Fragment*, ed. Ruby Cohn (New York: Grove Press, 1984), 139, 145. *Three Dialogues*, originally published in 1949, has often been taken as a statement of artistic intent. Leo Bersani argues that *Three Dialogues* is "the nearest thing we have to an explicit statement of [Beckett's] esthetic tastes or program," in Bersani, *Balzac to Beckett: Center and Circumference in French Fiction* (Oxford: Oxford University Press, 1970), 301. Thomas Trezise calls it the closest thing to "a statement of an artistic credo," in Trezise, *Into the Breach: Samuel Beckett and the Ends of Literature* (Princeton, NJ: Princeton University Press, 1990), 7. Ruby Cohn notes how *Three Dialogues* provides a well-worn "springboard for Beckett interpretation," yet she also identifies it as a key part of his "radical esthetic of failure," in Cohn, "Foreword," in *Disjecta: Miscellaneous Writings and a Dramatic Fragment*, by Samuel Beckett, ed. Ruby Cohn (New York: Grove Press, 1984), 15. Murphy et al. detail how Martin Esslin's inclusion of *Three Dialogues* in the collected volume *Samuel Beckett: A Collection of Critical Essays* (1965), alongside a number of now-canonical essays by Beckett critics, presents *Three Dialogues* as "a type of 'key' to Beckett's mature thinking on art" but "is made at the expense and exclusion of other aspects of Beckett's complex critical practice," in Peter John Murphy et al., *Critique of Beckett Criticism: A Guide to Research in English, French, and German* (Columbia, SC: Camden House, 1994), 17. Audrey Wasser is one of the few critics

emphasizes the need to break down the "terrifyingly arbitrary materiality of the word surface," characterizing language as "a veil which one has to tear apart in order to get to those things (or the nothingness) lying behind it."[2] He is similarly suspicious of formal wholeness. He assigns the artist the task of finding a form that accommodates "mess," which is "the very opposite of form."[3] He equally takes to task a monograph on Proust for imposing "a beautiful unity of tone and treatment" that "embalmed the whole."[4] Aesthetic unity equals a creative death.

These are powerful statements about aesthetics that cleave (to) the materiality of language, both splitting and adhering matter and form. They all gesture towards the power of aesthetics to represent the material body. Scholarship on Beckett likewise reproduces this ambivalence, frequently connecting Beckett's supposed aesthetics of failure to language's inability to render the body's materiality.[5] Leslie Hill refers to "the unrepresentable rhythmic pulse of the body" that supplements the failure of the corporealized subject to speak.[6] Christopher Ricks writes that the moments where words fail "speak of the body's failing."[7] Andrew Gibson argues that the "presentation of the body" is "caught up in and affected by the aporetic nature of Beckett's narrative discourse."[8] Reflecting the

---

to take seriously *Three Dialogues*' dramatic element and to argue that framing this text as evidence for an "aesthetics of failure" produces an abyssal argument in which, eventually, Beckett succeeds at failing to express, in Wasser, *The Work of Difference: Modernism, Romanticism, and the Production of Literary Form* (New York: Fordham University Press, 2016), 104. Her turn to the rhetorical function of language and form in Beckett is one of the most productive critical studies of him in recent years.

2 This is from the oft-quoted "German Letter of 1937" in Samuel Beckett, *The Letters of Samuel Beckett, Vol. 1: 1929–1940*, ed. Martha Fehsenfeld et al. (Cambridge: Cambridge University Press, 2009), 518–20.
3 Tom Driver, "Interview with Samuel Beckett," in *Samuel Beckett: The Critical Heritage*, ed. Lawrence Graver and Raymond Federman (London: Routledge and Kegan Paul, 1979), 219. Originally published in *Columbia University Forum*, Summer 1961.
4 Beckett, *Disjecta*, 64.
5 Ulrika Maude's *Beckett, Technology, and the Body* (Cambridge: Cambridge University Press, 2009) provides an important counterpoint to this tendency. This nuanced materialist study of the senses in Beckett challenges the prevailing consensus that Beckett's work "tends towards disembodiment, silence and stasis," in Maude, *Beckett, Technology, and the Body*, 4. I build on her careful attention to sensory experience and the body and her focus on the material body's agency. However, my formalist method departs from Maude's materialist approach, which reads Beckett's textual strategies in relation to historical and cultural changes, such as the technological advancements of the phonograph, tape recorder, and television.
6 Leslie Hill, *Beckett's Fiction: In Different Words* (Cambridge: Cambridge University Press, 1990), 147.
7 Christopher Ricks, *Beckett's Dying Words: The Clarendon Lectures 1990* (Oxford: Oxford University Press, 1995), 147.
8 Gibson, *Towards a Postmodern Theory of Narrative*, 263. Gibson is referring specifically to *Molloy* here, but similar critiques have been made about many of Beckett's narratives.

poststructuralist suspicion of transparent communication, Steven Connor has argued that Beckett's works "resist the notion of the innocent self-evidence of the body and its language, demonstrating instead that the body is knowable only in repetitions and representations."[9] Yoshiki Tajiri echoes Beckett's suspicion of imposing formal unity in Proust, arguing that his work exemplifies modernism's "formless body"[10] – an entity that can no longer contain a cohesive, autonomous subject.[11]

---

9 Steven Connor, *Samuel Beckett: Repetition, Theory, and Text* (Oxford: Basil Blackwell, 1988), 168. Connor's early analysis of the body in Beckett as a somewhat abstract entity has nevertheless given way to a sustained engagement with the materiality of language and embodiment in Beckett's writing. These include Steven Connor, *Beckett, Modernism and the Material Imagination* (New York; Cambridge: Cambridge University Press, 2014) and, for a very recent example, Steven Connor, "The Matter of Beckett's Facts," *Journal of Beckett Studies* 28, no. 1 (April 2019): 5–18.

10 Yoshiki Tajiri, *Samuel Beckett and the Prosthetic Body: The Organs and Senses in Modernism* (Basingstoke: Palgrave Macmillan, 2007), 75–76.

11 The body and the senses have, of course, always played a central role in Beckett studies. Early scholarship on Beckett tended to treat the body in terms of a Cartesian split between the mind and the body, in which the body is an impediment to be overcome or an imperfect machine. For examples of this see Edouard Morot-Sir, "Samuel Beckett and Cartesian Emblems," in *Samuel Beckett: The Art of Rhetoric*, ed. Edouard Morot-Sir, Howard Harper and Douglas McMillan III (Chapel Hill, NC: University of North Carolina Press, 1976) and Hugh Kenner, *Samuel Beckett: A Critical Study* (New York: Grove Press, 1961). Pierre Chabert's early paper on the body in Beckett's theatre was one of the first to call attention to Beckett's use of the actor's body as a dramatical material to be shaped and exploited like other stage apparatus. He insisted that Beckettian "dramatic tension" derives not only from "psychological conflict" but also a "genuinely physical conflict," in Chabert, "The Body in Beckett's Theatre," *Journal of Beckett Studies*, no. 8 (1982): 23–28, 23, 25. Later scholarship influenced by poststructuralism and deconstruction emphasized the discursive construction of the subject, relying on notions of "bodily inscriptions" that, as we have seen in the "Introduction," ultimately reduce materiality to textuality. The term "bodily inscriptions" comes from Hill, *Beckett's Fiction*, 111. The 'corporeal turn' saw Beckett criticism explore the body as a dynamic process rather than an obstruction to the mind, stressing the phenomenological experience of the body. Scholars in particular situated embodied experience within social, cultural, and technological changes, such as Beckett's engagement with sound technologies like the phonograph and the tape recorder. Such scholarship argued for the importance of materialism – as both material context and material substance – in Beckett's work. Representative examples of this scholarship include Connor's previously cited works; Tajiri, *Samuel Beckett and the Prosthetic Body*, which posits the figure of the prosthesis – an organic material that enfolds inorganic, alien matter – as paradigmatic of the disintegrating, disjointed Beckettian body; Maude, *Beckett, Technology and the Body*; and Anna McMullan, *Performing Embodiment in Samuel Beckett* (Abingdon: Routledge, 2010). McMullan picks up from Chabert and Maude with her investigation of embodied performance in Beckett's dramaturgy, exploring the tension between the physical presence of actors' bodies and the symbolism of absence. Despite the body's liminal position on the Beckettian stage, McMullan nevertheless asserts this body's contingency to the concrete experiences of historical, linguistic, and geographical dislocation Beckett underwent during WWII. Yet another advancement in Beckett studies has concerned how his work explores cognition, or the processes of the mind. See Marco Bernini, *Beckett and the Cognitive Method: Mind, Models, and Exploratory Narratives* (Oxford: Oxford University Press, 2021). Yet even the scholarship that has remained attentive to embodiment and embodied

The emphasis on both the body and language's formlessness, fragmentation, and failure recalls my discussion of counterviolence in the "Introduction" and in my recent discussion of *Sphinx*. Against the violence of representation, postmodernism has valorized undoing language, subjects, and bodies in order to escape normative strictures and institutions. If, as some scholars have noted, Beckett's narratives – and the narrative function in Beckett – seem to enact the Foucauldian order of discourse as power,[12] then the counter-violent breakdown of the embodied subject undermines exclusive metaphysical categories. Yet the celebration of counterviolence has also conflated power and violence, as well as reducing violence to rhetoric. As I noted in the "Introduction," Hanssen wonders whether the notion of violence as a kind of physical force has been "stretched beyond its former clearly demarcated boundaries" to include "such phenomenological elusive categories as psychological, symbolic, structural, epistemic, hermeneutical, and aesthetic violence."[13] The reduction of language to pure force has the potential to destroy the only site of a subject's potential agency: the body. Such are the dangers of 'stretching,' to use Hanssen's term, the representation of violence to the violence of representation and detaching violence from its relationship to concrete physical force.

In order to interrogate the 'stretching' of violence to representation and its consequences for embodiment, I turn to the rhetorical figure for extending and distorting: metalepsis. As I explored in "The Corporeal Urn," in classical literary criticism and rhetoric, metalepsis is the trope of the "far-fetched" – it "pulls things together which seem in principle to be far apart."[14] The phrase 'a lead foot' to describe someone who drives too fast is a prosaic example of metalepsis. A series of implied relationships connect 'lead' to 'heavy' and then to 'foot,' producing the figure of excessive speed through terms that are not directly related to either each other or the original abstract idea. Metalepsis also figures heavily in postmodernist narratology, in which it relates to the breakdown or intrusion of diegetic levels. This can occur when an actor breaks the fourth wall in theatre, directly addressing the audience, or when a narrator comments upon their narration, collapsing the distinction between

experience tends to insist upon the body's fragmentation and ultimately unrepresentable nature.

12 For examples of these approaches see David Watson, *Paradox and Desire in Samuel Beckett's Fiction* (Basingstoke: Palgrave Macmillan, 1991), in particular Chapter 1: "Narrative and Knowledge"; Gibson, *Towards a Postmodern Theory of Narrative*, 262–63; and Debra Malina, *Breaking the Frame: Metalepsis and the Construction of the Subject* (Columbus, OH: Ohio State University Press, 2002).
13 Hanssen, *Critique of Violence*, 9.
14 Cummings, "Metalepsis," 221.

the embedded tale and the frame narrative. Both uses of metalepsis are related to the question of *belonging*. The classical trope emphasizes the construction of attachments between seemingly disconnected things, whereas the postmodernist device focuses on how metalepsis can transgress repressive boundaries and calls attention to the way characters and narrative voices fit within different frames. But both uses of metalepsis can also entail failure, either when failing to fill in the classical trope's missing term, or when metalepsis leads to narrative breakdown in postmodernist fiction. Belonging – a state that Beckett's bodies seem incapable of achieving – is, fundamentally, a question of how bodies fit into political forms, as well as how bodily forms shape politics. Can metalepsis illuminate how bodies can be brought into forms even if representation fails? And is this operation ever possible without violence?

My focus on metalepsis works on several levels: first, in exploring the rhetorical operations of success and failure, it provides a corrective to the prevailing view of Beckett as a writer of limits and fragments. In other words, metalepsis – the trope for potential failure – interrogates the rhetorical structure of Beckett's 'aesthetics of failure.' It does this by accounting for both embodiment's elision and its excess, and it traces the outline of a body in form where representation offers it only in fragments. Whereas the breakdown of form forecloses belonging, metalepsis folds together bodily figments and figures into the ground of form. Second, I use metalepsis to reframe Hanssen's critique of the conflation of power and violence. I argue that in postmodernist criticism, violence itself has become metaleptic, stretched and reconfigured in a range of other disciplines and modes. This distortion is evident, for instance, in psychoanalytic theories of trauma that characterize the child's entrance into the symbolic realm of language as a form of violence.[15] This equation transforms physical violence into a universal experience at the center of all formations of the self, thus potentially minimizing specific forms of gendered, racial, or historical violence.[16]

---

15 Jacques Lacan, for instance, argues that "the symbolic order has to be conceived as something superimposed" in Lacan, *Seminar III: The Psychoses, 1955–1956*, ed. Jacques-Alain Miller, trans. Russell Grigg (New York; London: W. W. Norton & Company, 1997). Language, from which it is impossible to escape, is thus a system of control. This is a form of symbolic rather than physical violence. For a discussion of the role of violence in Lacan's conception of subject formation see Gavin Rae, "Forming the Individual: Castoriadis and Lacan on the Socio-Symbolic Function of Violence," in *Violence and Meaning*, ed. Lode Lauwaert, Laura Katherine Smith, and Christian Sternad (Cham: Palgrave Macmillan, 2019).

16 The 'stretching' of trauma from the historical specificity of certain contexts, such as the Holocaust, into ahistorical conditions of the psyche and subject formation is prominent

Reading metaleptically therefore traces where these physical, symbolic, structural, and rhetorical forms of violence cohere or differ, and where violence belongs – or should be omitted – in both language and form.

Beckett's work may seem like an odd place from which to begin an enquiry about how bodies can better fit into political forms. His texts are largely inhabited by male narrators and implicitly white subjects dislocated from time and space.[17] But the apparent autonomy of Beckett's formal worlds provides a space through which to explore the rhetoric of violence as 'pure' rhetoric, disconnected from a "material political geography."[18] I depart from referential or historicist readings of political violence in Beckett, focusing instead on the formal operations of speech and representations as they are enacted on and through bodies at the most literal level of physical force.[19] At the same time, I demonstrate how bodies can harness formal tropes and modes to resist the rhetoric of violence and even produce new forms, however nightmarish and undesirable.

In turn, this approach to metalepsis situates embodied form as an alternative to counterviolence – a 'counter-form,' if you will – that is not invested in the destituency of forms or bodies.[20] Beckett's works

in trauma studies. Cathy Caruth, for instance, draws on Lacan's notion of the past as a form of repetition, with historical trauma occurring belatedly, meaning that history cannot be conceived of in referential terms. See Caruth, *Unclaimed Experience*. This universal model of trauma has been critiqued by scholars who argue that it collapses the distinction between perpetrators and victims. For examples of this type of critique see Ruth Leys, *Trauma: A Genealogy* (Chicago: University of Chicago Press, 2000) and Dominick LaCapra, *Representing the Holocaust: History, Theory, Trauma* (Ithaca, NY: Cornell University Press, 1996).

17 I will focus most of my analysis on Beckett's prose, in which his narrators are almost exclusively men. Female characters appear much more in his dramatic pieces.
18 Peter Boxall, "Samuel Beckett: Towards a Political Reading," *Irish Studies Review* 10, no. 2 (August 2002): 159–70, 162.
19 For examples of historicist and materialist approaches to politics in Beckett see, amongst others, Mariko Hori Tanaka, Yoshiki Tajiri, and Michiko Tsushima, eds., *Samuel Beckett and Trauma* (Manchester: Manchester University Press, 2018); James McNaughton, *Samuel Beckett and the Politics of Aftermath* (Oxford: Oxford University Press, 2018); and McMullan, *Performing Embodiment in Samuel Beckett*.
20 There is little explicitly formalist or New Critical scholarship on Beckett, but the most influential Beckett scholars of the 1960s, including Ruby Cohn, Hugh Kenner, and Martin Esslin, approached Beckett through a combination of formalist and existentialist frameworks. Later works that focus on form also include Susan D. Brienza, *Samuel Beckett's New Worlds: Style in Metafiction* (Norman, OK: University of Oklahoma Press, 1987). These approaches largely eschew political or ideological readings of Beckett. For an overview of different critical trends in Beckett see Murphy et al., *Critique of Beckett Criticism*. Poststructuralist and postmodernist scholars explicitly positioned themselves against any claim that a humanist subject could be excavated from Beckett's work, equally turning away from implicitly formalist methods towards deconstructive

demonstrate that even if form is inescapable, it need not be unified. Turning to the politics of embodied form in Beckett thus helps critique the rhetorical violence of the violence of rhetoric. It reveals the consequences of celebrating the dissolution of political forms and transforming violence into a linguistic effect disconnected from the lived experience of embodied subjects. Rather than emphasizing metalepsis' destituent capacity to undo constraining forms, in this chapter I explore how metalepsis can account for bodies that are not fully present, whose speech has been muffled, whose mobility has been constrained, whose appearance has been eclipsed, and whose singularity has been subsumed into a generalized mass. Metalepsis reveals that there can be no forms without constraint. It also exposes the structure of such constraints – and thus enables the possibility of reorganizing them into attachments. At the same time, as the figure for (potential) failed figurality, metalepsis points to the consequences of overlooking or missing out elements of embodiment that need to be filled in. Failure to grasp how an embodied subject has been omitted, passed over, or excluded in political rhetoric can have concrete consequences for that person's ability to appear within the political regime of representation. The rhetoric of violence – of violence as rhetoric – has fractured and alienated bodies. Metalepsis provides a rhetorical structure through which we can perceive embodiment's occluded parts and thus reframes the body's relationship to language and political representation. As a formal or rhetorical device that is closely tied to embodiment, metalepsis lays bare the way political representation works upon the body, where the body can belong, and how it constitutes the elemental unit of political forms. If the rhetoric of violence has fractured and alienated bodies, metalepsis furnishes a figure for understanding the body's occluded parts, thus becoming a site of re-memberment and transforming detachment into attachment. Metalepsis offers a potential politics of belonging, but one that retains the speculative dimension of the figurative.

Figure

It is hard to read for a unified body in Beckett. His works are littered with body parts, dismembered limbs, and floating organs. His characters are often reduced to a single body part that distills their narrative func-

and symptomatic modes of reading. Trezise is representative of this critique, arguing that formalist and existentialist approaches "rely on an unexamined notion of the human subject," in Trezise, *Into the Breach*, ix.

tion. Thus, speech becomes Mouth in *Not I* (1973). In *Company* (1979), sight is embodied in a monstrous blinking eye, a "globe. All pupil" that fills "the whole field" of vision.[21] And a monstrous ear grows a head in *The Unnamable* (1958). The fragmentation of the body's form becomes an integral part of both Beckett's thematic landscapes and narrative devices. These organs and limbs, often described as "figments," become caught up in Beckett's repetitive syntactical forms, as if they are trying to reunite with a lost but generic body.[22]

The fragmentation – or perhaps 'figmentation' – of the body becomes more evident as Beckett's writing moves into the recursive territory of the trilogy novels *Molloy* (1951), *Malone Dies* (1951), and *The Unnamable*, which begin to dispense with traditional generic conventions like plot, story, setting, and character. Although Beckett had already forayed into the first-person narrative voice with such novellas and short stories as *First Love* (written 1946, published in 1970 in French and 1973 in English translation) and *The Calmative* (1946), the trilogy novels epitomize the Beckettian 'I' who will forever struggle to constitute itself. At the same time, bodies become increasingly illegible. They disintegrate but multiply. They are confined but spill out messily from their containers. They are dislocated in time and space. The breakdown of the body's recognizable form accompanies an increasingly indistinct gallery of characters who frequently bleed into each other, claim to be one another, and display freakishly similar characteristics. *Molloy* is narrated by the eponymous character in the first half who writes alone, confined to a room; his double, Moran, then takes over in the second part to narrate his search for Molloy, even as his physical deterioration mirrors Molloy's. In *Malone Dies*, Malone implies that he has created Molloy and Moran (and possibly other characters). Anticipating the 'closed space' stories like *Company*, place is reduced to a single room, with alternative settings existing only in the characters' memories. Bodily form is not attached to a cohesive identity or character.

The trilogy triangulates the three elements that seem to dominate Beckett's work thereafter: the breakdown of the self or the speaking 'I,' the deterioration of the body, and the composition of a writing marked

---

21 Samuel Beckett, *Nohow On: Company, Ill Seen Ill Said, Worstword Ho* (New York: Grove Press, 1996), 14. I cite here from *Company*, which will appear parenthetically with the abbreviation C.

22 The term "figment" often appears in Beckett's work to describe an incomplete or liminal condition, a "figment" of the imagination, like the "figment light never was but grey air timeless no sound" in Beckett, "Lessness," in *The Complete Short Prose, 1929–1989*, ed. S. E. Gontarski (New York: Grove Press, 2000), 199, or the woman who appears to the narrator as "pure figment" in Beckett, *Ill Seen Ill Said* in *Nohow On: Company, Ill Seen Ill Said, Worstword Ho* (New York: Grove Press, 1996), 58.

by its own limits, often signified by literal ellipses.[23] This culminates in the final novel, *The Unnamable*, in which the variously named Mahood, Basil, Worm, and "I" claims to be responsible for "all these Murphys, Molloys and Malones."[24] Human scraps confined to a jar that hangs outside a restaurant in what appears to be Paris, the shifting identity narrates the increasing breakdown of his body: "Having lost one leg, what indeed more likely than that I should mislay the other? And similarly for the arms. A natural transition in sum" (*U*, 43). Sight is reduced to a "great wild black and white eye" (*U*, 74), or a "paraphimotically globose" erotic orb that "seems to listen" (*U*, 87).[25] The narrator's compulsive need to speak is in turn embodied in the grotesque "image of a vast cretinous mouth, red, blubber, and slobbering" (*U*, 108). The variously shifting identities of the narrator mirror the body's form as a collection of bodily impulses (to speak and to move, in particular) and bodily figments.

The simultaneous breakdown of the body, identity, and language produces one of Beckett's most abject bodily figments in the short dramatic piece *Not I*. In the original stage version, there are two figures: Mouth, who is illuminated from below leaving the rest of the face in shadow, and Auditor, enveloped in a black, hooded cloak who appears to hover on an invisible podium above the stage.[26] While the two figures simultaneously occupy the stage and implicitly belong to a single body split in two, Mouth is at a distance from both the Auditor and the audience, appearing to some audience members like "a flickering candle-flame."[27] The separation between both figures and the audience proffers a form of suture that the play ultimately withholds: Mouth narrates an inexpressible life story, literally separated from the gesturing figure whose accompanying body language provides no narrative supplement. In the 1975 film version, in which Billy Whitelaw plays Mouth, the two figures have been combined into one monstrous figment that fills the screen, "as if the mouth had eaten the body."[28] The disturbing nature of Mouth's presence in the film version derives from the way it takes up the entire

---

23 See Wasser, *The Work of Difference*, 97–99.
24 Samuel Beckett, *The Unnamable* (London: Faber and Faber, 2010), 14. Hereafter referred to parenthetically using *U*.
25 Paraphimosis is a condition where the foreskin cannot be retracted, leading to potential infection.
26 Samuel Beckett, "Not I" in *The Complete Dramatic Works* (London: Faber and Faber, 1990), 376. Hereafter referred to parenthetically using *CDW* and the name of the play where necessary.
27 Connor, *Samuel Beckett*, 150.
28 Chabert, "The Body in Beckett's Theatre," 27.

space that a face would normally inhabit.²⁹ Yet even when the body prevails over the division of time and space, it does not offer either narrative resolution or bodily restoration. In its torrent of logorrhea, Mouth threatens to swallow the very source of its silence, "whole body like gone" (*CDW*, 380). The compulsive torrent of speech that issues from Mouth breaks down language into a series of figments: "just the mouth ... lips ... cheeks ... jaws ... never– ... what? ... tongue? ... yes ... lips ... cheeks ... jaws ... tongue" (*CDW*, 380). Mouth's language traces a recursive attempt to "crawl back in" to the "godforsaken hole" whence she came. This image recalls the womb and the anus – recurrent bodily passages and containers in Beckett's work – turning language and the body inside out, leaving her "speechless all her days ... practically speechless" (*CDW*, 381–82). Thus, even when actors' bodies are present in Beckett's dramaturgy – a physical presence that cannot be recreated in his prose narratives – embodiment can be figured as a lack. As Anna McMullan has noted, the body's absence or abjectness functions as a particular staging strategy in which a spectral presence (a voice, mouth, or even breath) undermines the body's external coherence.³⁰ Even physical presence is no guarantee of embodiment.

Moving into the later stages of his writing, Beckett's bodies become increasingly abstract and attenuated. The opening image of an unidentifiable figure in the dark in *Company*, for instance, revisits the sensory deprivation in *Murphy*. Yet this sensory deprivation also produces odd bodily excesses, such as an eye with "the hood slowly down. Or up if down to begin. The globe. All pupil" that cannibalizes "the whole field" of vision (C, 14). A roaming ear picks up the text's rustlings, murmurs, and stirrings, which is then echoed in the image of a "clenching and unclenching" hand (C, 20). This isolated clutching hand reappears in a series of jerking movements – "knee hand knee hand two. One foot" (C, 36) – that crystallize the limping, dysfunctional movement of the text, its constant "crawl" and "fall" within the narrative's confined, dark space (C, 37). Whereas the trilogy is narrated in the first person, *Company* shifts between second and third person, often commenting upon the relation between point of view and narrative function: "Use of the second person marks the voice. That of the third that cantankerous other" (C, 4). The occasional punctuation of the "I" seems to take *The Unnamable*'s breakdown of the self to the extreme: "The unthinkable last of all. Unnamable. Last person. I" (C, 17). The second-person

---

29 The looming presence of Mouth anticipates 'the eye. Filling the whole field. [...] The globe. All pupil. Staring up. Hooded. Bared. Hooded again. Bared again' (C, 14).
30 See McMullan, *Performing Embodiment in Samuel Beckett*, 118–119.

narration produces the uncanny sense of a figure that observes its own body at a remove: "You separate the segments and lay them side by side" (C, 30).[31] Like the ambiguity of "sole sound in the silence your footfalls," a single "foot falls unbidden in midstep," pacing out the body's impaired path through language. Echoing the clutching hand, the fragmented foot reappears as "a single leg" that allows "you [to] separate these segments and lay them side by side" (C, 30) in a parodic organization of bodily order. The foot is further subdivided into "half foot to half foot" in an infinite splitting until nothing remains but "bootless crawl and figments comfortless" (C, 39–40). Yet even when these disparate parts are reconstituted, they do not form a unified or recognizable body:

> Simultaneously the various parts set out. The arms unclasp the knees. The head lifts. The legs start to straighten. The trunk tilts backward. And together these and countless others continue on their respective ways till they can go no further and together come to rest. (C, 45–46)

This typically malfunctioning body, rusty with misuse, recalls the narrator's body in *The Unnamable*, which passes through different phases of deterioration from "the one-armed, one-legged wayfarer of a moment ago and the wedge-headed trunk in which I am now marooned," which are then revealed as "simply two phases of the same carnal envelope" (U, 43). Here, the body parts and organs strain in irreconcilable directions until they collapse exhaustedly into each other. The parody of human relations ends in a single word that exemplifies the Beckettian self: "Alone" (C, 46).

These figments often seem like a collection of defective parts knocking around inside the grotesque container of a disunited form – the "carnal envelope" cited above – struggling towards silence or isolation. Any reader of Beckett will recognize the felicitous feeling that accompanies the identification of a character, figure, or image from one work in another. Yet they are also frustratingly isolated from each other; their fragmented form overwhelms generic categorization. Ultimately, they refuse not only the 'personification' of character but also of the possibility of subjectivity. Thus, the figmentation of the body seems to accompany a breakdown of both the limits of the subject and expression. Both processes spur and reinforce each other in what critics have argued is a relentless interrogation of a modern, autonomous subject. These bodily figments undermine not only any recognizable identity

---

31 Maude connects the shift from first- to second-person narration in Beckett to the deconstructive gesture of eschewing an inner self in favor of an exterior surface or being, in Maude, *Beckett, Technology, and the Body*, 71.

for Beckett's characters, but indeed the conceptual basis for cohesive identity *tout court*.

Yet this type of reading relies upon the assumption that the subject is constituted in language. Beckett's fragmented language produces a fragmented body, and this fragmented body, in turn, acts as an index of the breakdown of the autonomous subject whose identity and embodiment cannot be integrated into a cohesive form. We are brought back, once again, to the dissatisfying circular insistence on aesthetic failure. But Beckett's bodies are rarely whole. Rather than seeing these figments as evidence of the body's fragmentation, or the impossibility of fully representing embodiment or subjectivity in language, I argue these figments are *figures*. They both stand in for characters, and they act as rhetorical or literary figures for embodiment. Indeed, these figments are characters whose outward forms coincide with their narrative function: Mouth speaks, the giant ear that grows a body in *The Unnamable* is the mediating "transformer in which sound is turned [...] to the rage and terror" of thought (*U*, 71). Their embodied shape is the literal figure for their formal function.

Beckett's literal figures – mouths, eyes, feet – are, to expand on Paul de Man's term, "metafigural."[32] They are ways of writing figuratively about bodily figures. Beckett's 'metafigures' comment not only upon how to write, but also how to write about the body in ways that are conscious of representation's fragmentary force. These metafigures demonstrate the bodily experience at the basis of poetic language by producing figures for their own bodily figuration. When Mouth speaks or *The Unnamable*'s giant ear hears, they bridge the gap between representation's alienating, objectifying function and the body's unsignifiable

---

32 Paul de Man, *Allegories of Reading: Figural Language in Rousseau, Nietzsche, Rilke, and Proust* (New Haven, CT: Yale University Press, 1979), 14. In his reading of Proust's metafigural language, de Man argues that the coincidence of "figural praxis and metafigural language" ultimately fails. Metafigural language demonstrates how literature always already deconstructs its own rhetorical mode, in de Man, *Allegories of Reading*, 15–17. The confrontation between literal and figurative language not only produces two (or more) different meanings, but inevitably leads to a process of constant undoing and contradiction. The counterpoint to de Man's insistence on an irresolvable contradiction in literary language would be the way the New Critics sought to suture aesthetic tension through figures like paradox and irony. My intention here is to neither resort to a naïve suspension of aesthetic or structural tension nor to insist that Beckett's work is constantly engaged in a process of its own undoing that constitutes an aesthetics of failure. It is also these tendencies in the New Critical and the deconstructive approach, as I demonstrated in the "Introduction," that lead them to elide embodiment from literature. Rather, I want to turn to a 'metafigment' to demonstrate how embodiment's movement between the subjective and the objective structures the very antinomies, inconsistencies, and irresolvable meanings in the text. These differences cannot ever be fully resolved by reading for form. But that is not the point.

excess, folding these two poles into a formal figure for this very process. Understanding these figments as literary figures helps us move beyond an unrepresentable or fragmented body, but it does not yet explain the relationship between embodiment and Beckett's fragmented form. To advance our understanding of this process, let us now explore figures for "carnal envelopes," bodily containers that function as figures of form. In doing so, they point to the embodied ground of figurality, and the importance of the ground – as both literal earth and dirt and the metaphysical stage of the self – to the figuration of embodiment.

Ground

In the previous section, I explored how Beckett's metafigures embody their formal functions. At the same time, their formal functions figure embodiment. This progresses beyond the aesthetics of failure, in which scholars have been too quick to alight upon figures of desuetude and deficiency. In this section, I will parallel these bodily figures with formalist tropes for containment and form, including jars, urns, tombs, and the ground.

The ground, in particular, is both the literal material of dirt and earth and the embodied foundation of figurality. Just as bodily figments condense the senses to individual body parts, these figures for form distill formal concepts like autonomy, suspension, integrity, and (re)production into material objects. Caressing the heteroclite objects in his possession, Malone ruminates on how their eidetic nature halts the unchanging mutations of matter: "the forms are many in which the unchanging seeks relief from its formlessness."[33] In *Proust*, the subject is the container combining these competing impulses for stasis and mutability, acting as "the seat of a constant process of decantation, decantation from the vessel containing the fluid of future time, sluggish, pale and monochrome, to the vessel containing the fluid of past time, agitated and multicoloured by the phenomena of its hours."[34] Murphy's instructor, Neary, bids him farewell with the didactic reminder that "all life is figure and ground."[35] Figure and ground are also realized in Molloy's yearning for "the earth

---

33 Samuel Beckett, *Malone Dies* (Harmondsworth: Penguin Books, 1975), 29. Hereafter referred to parenthetically using the abbreviation *MD*.
34 Samuel Beckett, *Proust* (New York: Grove Press, 1978), 4–5. Hereafter referred to parenthetically using the abbreviation *P*.
35 Samuel Beckett, *Murphy* (London: Calder Publications, 2003), 6. Hereafter referred to parenthetically using the abbreviation *M*.

to swallow" him up.³⁶ These organic, grounded images suggest recuperative life processes, as when Molloy hopes that the cyclical "labour of the planet rolling eager into winter" will rid his body "of these contemptible scabs" (*M*, 48). The notion of regeneration is echoed in the "word sacks" in *How It Is* (first published in French 1961 as *Comment c'est*, subsequently published in Beckett's own English translation in 1964), the embryonic form in which words coalesce into an organic "acervation."³⁷ In *The Unnamable*, bounded containers provide the increasingly fractured 'I' a cohesive form, however abject. The narrator's disintegrating body is "stuck like a sheaf of flowers in a deep jar" (*U*, 39) outside of a restaurant in Paris; recalling the variegated container of past experience in *Proust*, it is festooned "with its garland of many-coloured lanterns, and me inside it" (*U*, 47). To prevent his bodily scraps from sinking down, the proprietress fills the jar with sawdust (*U*, 44), in an ironic nod to Keats' urn embodying the absent remains of dust. The jar – or we might call it an urn – constrains the narrator, but it also holds him together.

At times these bounded containers of the body become the body as bounded container,³⁸ as in Beckett's repeated evocation of the womb or even, to extend the metaphor of body as bounded container to its most extreme form, the urn-like figure of the "wombtomb." In *Dream of Fair to Middling Women*, Belacqua describes "thought moving alive in the darkened mind gone wombtomb."³⁹ In a seeming riposte to Cleanth Brooks' conception of form as suspending or integrating irony and paradox, the "wombtomb" embodies its own unassimilable irony, for what "real living, living thought" could quicken in a tomb?⁴⁰ The womb's ambivalent conceptual space appears in a number of other works as a material place, including the play *Footfalls* (1975), in which May paces the stage, dimly perceiving a mother-like voice that emanates from an undisclosed space. Or again in *Company*, with its fetus-like figure curled up in the dark.

The evocation of earth, dust, urns, sacks, and "carnal envelopes"

---

36 Samuel Beckett, *Molloy* (London: Faber and Faber, 2009), 82. Hereafter referred to parenthetically using the abbreviation *MO*.
37 Brienza notes the organic dimension of this metaphor in *Samuel Beckett's New Worlds*, 104.
38 Hunter Dukes explores the function of bodily containers in Beckett's work, asking what makes these vessels "at once so contently bound to their materiality and so keen to serve as emergent sites of subjectivity, at once so mundane and so almost human?" in Dukes, "Beckett's Vessels and the Animation of Containers," *Journal of Modern Literature* 40, no. 4 (2017): 75–89, 77. Dukes is also interested in understanding the interchange between the body as container and contained, though within the context of psychoanalytic understandings of the self.
39 Samuel Beckett, *Dream of Fair to Middling Women*, ed. Eoin O'Brien and Edith Fournier (London: Calder Publications, 1993), 45.
40 Beckett, *Dream of Fair to Middling Women*, 45.

recalls formalist notions of organic and living form. Yet Beckett's bounded containers rarely contain for long. Even as Molloy lies in Lousse's dark garden wishing to become one with the ground, the "smell of damp earth" overwhelms him and he "forgot not only who I was, but that I was, forgot to be. Then I was no longer that sealed jar to which I owed my being so well preserved [. . .] a wall gave way and I filled with roots and tame stems" (*MO*, 48). The flowering, rhizomatic ground invades the bounded container of the self. Just as Molloy spills out of his sealed jar, *The Unnamable*'s narrator – a literal 'brain in a jar' – outgrows his confinement, metastasizing into a giant ear. Malone describes the contents of his head "streaming and emptying away as through a sluice [. . .] until finally nothing remained" (*MD*, 62). His bodily container is penetrated by a hand, "plunged in me up to the elbow" that delves "feebly into my particles" and lets "them trickle between its fingers" (*MD*, 63). This extended metaphor for a leaky bodily container culminates in the image of a fully dissolved body "when I go liquid and become like mud" (*MD*, 63). The organic here is precisely formless (or "informe").[41] The body's autonomous bounds are liquified, as if Beckett is suspicious of according living matter any kind of unity or autonomy. Even his frequent evocation of the womb or womb-like forms cannot be qualified as particularly organicist. Actual wombs rarely, if ever, feature. Rather, they are transformed into the living-dead space of the "wombtomb" or the dark space filled with "mush" and "stench" in *Company* (*C*, 22). These are forms that point to their own undoing, as in Beckett's description of the way characteristics pass between individuals in Proust in terms of "the disintegrating effect of loss that breaks the chrysalis and hastens the metamorphosis of an atavistic embryo" (*P*, 25). Or again, in the "godforsaken hole" in *Not I* that signifies the complete breakdown of speech. At its most extreme, the "word sacks" in *How It Is* turn into implements of torture, inscribed onto on the body as an instrument of pain.

This is not a release from form, however. Bodily figments are drawn down to the ground, demonstrating how forms constrain even as they distort (or distort through constraint). Beckett's bodily containers frequently spill their contents into the textual groundwater, while the ground becomes a prison for the body. Formal autonomy here becomes captivity. As Winnie is increasingly buried in *Happy Days* (1961), it becomes harder for her to distinguish between the ground and her body: "The earth is very tight today, can it be I have put on flesh. I trust not.

---

41 The term 'informe' comes originally from Georges Bataille. Yve-Alain Bois and Rosalind Krauss adopt the term to describe Marcel Duchamp's artistic experimentations. Tajiri brings both of these senses of the word to bear on his analysis of the "formless" body in Beckett in Tajiri, *Beckett and the Prosthetic Body*, 78, 107.

[. . .] The great heat possibly. [. . .] All things expanding, some more than others" (*CDW*, 149). Nag and Nell are confined to dustbins in *Endgame* (1957), which extend their bodies into the ground and the ground into their bodies. Yet rather than expanding their bodies' limits, they are stuck to the spot. Characters are drawn down to the ground with different degrees of violence. Some stumble, like Molloy, who "lapsed down to the bottom of the ditch" (*MO*, 93). Others, like the narrator's wife in *How It Is*, fall from a great height.[42] In *Company*, the ground's "pressure on his hind parts" provides the only indication of material space. Bodies fully merge with earth to form an indistinct ontological ground, like the "flatness endless little body only upright same grey all sides earth sky body ruins" in the short story "Lessness" (1970).[43] The gravity exerted by the ground can be characterized, as Connor has described it, as hypostasis, an accumulation or thickening of elements into an underlying substance, so that "the ground continues to organise the work, even in its absence."[44] In contrast to the fragmented figments of the body dispersed across Beckett's texts, these figures of form suggest accretion and concentration – a centripetal movement towards center and ground.

In a 1956 *New York Times* interview, Beckett stated that "at the end of my work there's nothing but dust – the namable. In the last book – *The Unnamable* – there's complete disintegration. No 'I,' no 'have,' no 'being.' No nominative, no accusative, no verb. There's no way to go on."[45] Echoing the final words of *The Unnamable* ("I can't go on, I'll go on" (*U*, 134)), this statement encapsulates the simultaneous breakdown of the subject and fragmentation of language that begins with the trilogy. It is tempting to follow Beckett's comments about *The Unnamable* and turn the solidity of the ground into the "complete disintegration" of dust, dispersed into the wind without an urn to contain them, to ensure that it cannot act as the ultimate end and origin. Certainly, postmodern approaches to Beckett have sought to recast organic processes like decomposition as language breaking apart under the weight of its own expression, or as the disintegration of the autonomous subject. Dust is the material trace of an irrecuperable body; it is the remains of an emancipatory failure to represent the body. But it is also possible to

---

42 Samuel Beckett, *How It Is* (London: Faber and Faber, 2009), 66. All further references to this text are cited parenthetically using the abbreviation *HII*.
43 Beckett, "Lessness," in *The Complete Short Prose*, 199.
44 Steven Connor, "Shifting Ground," http://stevenconnor.com/beckettnauman.html.
45 Israel Shenker, "An Interview with Samuel Beckett," in *Samuel Beckett: The Critical Heritage*, ed. Lawrence Graver and Raymond Federman (London; Boston: Routledge & Kegan Paul, 1979), 146–49. Originally published in the *New York Times*, 5 May 1956.

understand the ground as a function of form without reinstating it as the metaphysical ground of the self. An urn is a hole filled with matter. In contrast to the 'tears' and 'rents' that seem to dominate Beckett's commentary about his work, the jar, the urn, and the sack are a bounded forms, however abject. Thus, where identity, representation, and the self become most attenuated so too do logical forms for the body become increasingly important.

Is there a way of bringing together these bodily figments without falsely unifying them? Can we account for these instances of form without endowing them with an autonomy and integrity they do not possess? A potential answer to this conundrum lies in investigating what Neary in *Murphy* calls "figure and ground." On the one hand, bodily figments are figures for dispersal, diminishment, and etiolation. On the other hand, ground suggests concentration and accumulation. Rather than being caught up in a dialectical process of "creation and uncreation," or groping "toward the unword through a density of words,"[46] which many critics have read as evidence of an 'aesthetics of failure,' I argue that this simultaneous dispersal and concentration are functions of the same rhetorical figure: metalepsis. Metalepsis does not provide a final synthesis, unifying the body and representation into a single entity. It is, to appropriate Jean-Michel Rabaté's characterization of the relationship between silence and speaking (or writing) in *The Unnamable*, "a nondialectical fusion of the contraries."[47] Metalepsis points to the way embodiment and literary language mutually shape each other's form. Like the rhetorical and poetic tropes I have explored in other chapters, this both originates in embodied experience and condenses embodiment in literary form.

Form

Connor identifies hypostasis in Beckett's work, an accumulation that draws words, bodies, and objects down to the ground. At the same time, body parts, organs, and figments are strewn across his corpus. Concentration and dispersal compete with each other as organizing principles. Up until now, I have traced figments, forms, and fragments across a number of Beckett's texts. I now want to turn inward to closely explore the figurative process whereby inconsistency and antinomy are

---

46 Cohn, "Foreword," 12.
47 Jean-Michel Rabaté, *Think, Pig! Beckett at the Limit of the Human* (New York: Fordham University Press, 2016), 46.

given an embodied form. To do so, let us turn to a passage in *The Unnamable*, a novel, as I mentioned before, where Beckett dispenses of virtually any pretense to plot, story, and character as well as to any recognizable identity or cohesive body. Here we encounter the monstrous Worm, a head grown from an ear. While *The Unnamable* is marked by the extreme limits of both the subject and the body, it is also a remarkably recursive text, circling back again and again to the same figures, sensations, and forms. It is "littered with the discarded corpses of previous embodiments."[48] As the novel approaches its (anti)denouement, language seems to settle and accrete. This sedimentation occurs through a process whereby the body and figurative language coalesce into a shared form:

> Moreover, that's right, link, link, you never know, moreover their attitude towards me has not changed, I am deceived, they are deceived, they have tried to deceive me, saying their attitude towards me had changed, but they haven't deceived me, I didn't understand what they were trying to do to me, I say what I'm told to say, that's all there is to it, and yet I wonder, I don't know, I don't feel a mouth on me, I don't feel the jostle of words in my mouth, and when you saw a poem you like, if you happen to like poetry, in the underground, or in bed, for yourself, the words are there, somewhere, without the least sound. I don't feel that either, words falling, you don't know where, you don't know whence, drops of silence, through the silence, I don't feel it, I don't feel a mouth on me, nor a head, I do feel an ear, frankly now, do I feel an ear, well frankly now I don't, so much the worse, I don't feel an ear either, this is awful, make an effort, I must feel something, yes, I feel something, they say I feel something, I don't know what it is, I don't know what I feel, tell me what I feel and I'll tell you who I am, they'll tell me who I am, I won't understand, but the thing will be said, they'll have said who I am, and I'll have heard, without an ear I'll have heard, and I'll have said it, without a mouth I'll have said it, I'll have said it inside me, then in the same breath outside me, perhaps that's what I am, the thing that divides the world in two, on the one side the outside, on the other the inside, that can be as thin as foil, I'm neither one side nor the other, I'm in the middle, I'm the partition, I've two surfaces and no thickness, perhaps that's what I feel, myself vibrating, I'm the tympanum, on the one hand the mind, on the other the world, I don't belong to either [. . .]. (*U*, 99–100)

This passage circles back to earlier images of "a hairless wedge-head" that is "broad at the base, its slopes denuded, culminating in ridge or crowning glory strewn with long waving hairs like those that grow on naevi" (*U*, 27–28). It revisits a description of Worm for whom "a head has grown out of his ear" (*U*, 70). This recalls the narrator "dashing

---

48 Anna McMullan, "Versions of Embodiment/Visions of the Body in Beckett's '. . . but the clouds . . .,'" *Samuel Beckett Today / Aujourd'hui* 6 (1997): 353–64, 357.

my head angrily against the neck of the jar" (*U*, 42), in which he is confined, or contemplating a time when "I was freer to turn my head than now [...] And sometimes I don't confuse myself with my jar, and sometimes I do" (*U*, 53–54). The confusion between figure and form extends to other bodily combinations: "I say what I am told to say, in the hope that some day they will weary of talking at me. The trouble is I say it wrong, have no ear, no head, no memory" (*U*, 59). These are only a small selection of instances where heads and ears, as well as other bodily parts, morph into or are confused with each other, or where the boundary between the body and the container becomes indistinct. The passage combines, builds upon, and slightly alters a series of previous figures in the novel. This centrifugal movement outwards through the narrative is accompanied by a centripetal one in which the repetition of words, clauses, body parts, and syntactical constructions gradually accumulate into a rather monstrous bodily figment: a giant ear. The body is at once dispersed, fragmented, and expelled across the text. But it is also concentrated and distilled into specific forms.

Is there a way to make sense of the simultaneous transference and disconnection, which gradually coheres into the monstrous form of an ear – or, to be more precise, a tympanum, itself a distillation of the ear's function to its most important component? This dual process of dispersal and thickening can also be understood in terms of metalepsis. Metalepsis is a trope that at once pulls in and pushes away, concentrates and disperses, omits the central term and stretches it to the outer possibilities of signification. Might metalepsis be the trope of Beckett's aesthetics of failure – something that incorporates even as it pushes away? Like the other tropes and figures discussed thus far, its figural function as something that mediates coincides with the body's form. Quintilian translated the term in Latin as *transumptio*, designating translation, transfer, and transmutation. Transumption shares the same root words as 'transubstantiation,' or the transformation of Christ's body into objects that literally become his body. It thus signals the way objects or images both stand in for and elide the body's materiality.

Indeed, metalepsis could be the figure for the unrepresentable body – a body that can only be grasped through second or third order aspects of language (like representation) in a process that also simultaneously reveals the body's presence as a form of discursive or rhetorical mediation. Embodiment provides the ground of poetic language and aesthetic form, and poetic figures are themselves figures of and for embodiment. Metalepsis is thus the figure for the failure of figurality – the failure to 'figure,' to shape, to form, all concepts that are themselves extensions of embodiment. Indeed, metalepsis is less figure than *figment*. It is a fragment that points to its own inability to fully figure, even as this figure for failed figurality gives form to the body beyond the failure of representation. My rather dizzying elaboration of the relation between metalepsis and embodiment here can be summed up as follows: if we read for metalepsis we can fill in the body's fragmented form, or at least identify the (missing) middle term. The failure to represent the body, then, is not an aesthetic failure but a failure of *reading*. As the figure for failed figurality, it helps us grasp where literary representation appears to elide embodiment.

Let us return to the passage to more fully understand this process. The tympanum is one of the bodily organs that mediates between inside and outside. This figment is the figure for the embodiment of metalepsis – distilling metalepsis' mediating function to a bodily form – and the metalepsis of embodiment, which extends, distorts, and stretches the body beyond a recognizable form. The passage layers a number of rhetorical tropes, including aporia, chiasmus, catachresis, and other metalepses, which are themselves condensed to an embodied state. Aporia, or the expression of doubt, is expressed through the image of an absent mouth, the organ of speech that declares uncertainty about its own existence ("I don't feel a mouth on me, I don't feel the jostle of words in my mouth"). It repeats the novel's opening pages, which are themselves an expression of aporia.[49] In an image that resonates closely with Merleau-Ponty's notion of chiasmus as the enfolding of the body and the world, the ear surmises that "I'm neither one side nor the other, I'm the middle." At the end of the image, chiasmus seems to metaleptically replace aporia; it pushes past aporia's physical impediment through repetition. But these tropes are also folded into each other (like the flesh of an ear), as well as repeated.[50] This enfolding is reproduced through the metaleptical return to the metalepsis of "drops of silence." Moreover, the passage – like the book or even Beckett's corpus as a whole – acts as a reflection on catachresis, or the (im)possibility of naming. *The Unnamable*'s title is already a catachresis; it seeks to name a concept that has no proper referent through a word that refers to its own inability to fully name. The passage questions what it means to be without any proper referent ("I'll tell you who I am, they'll tell me who I am, I won't understand, but the thing will be said, they'll have said who I am, and I'll have heard").

---

49 See Amanda Dennis, "Radical Indecision: Aporia as Metamorphosis in *The Unnamable*," *Journal of Beckett Studies* 24, no. 2 (2015): 180–97, 183.

50 We will remember from the chapter on *Sphinx* that an aporia is a rhetorical expression of doubt that also implies the impossibility of physical passage (from the Greek *a-poros*, or 'without passage'). In Garréta's text, the aporia of the racialized body is made concrete in the sphinx's material figure, which blocks the reader's (interpretive) passage.

This is part of a longer reflection in the text on how to name concepts, substances, or states that have no proper referent. "It's time I gave this solitary a name," the narrator decides, "nothing doing without proper names. I therefore baptize him Worm" (51); or later, "I remember Worm (that is to say, I have retained the name). And the other (what is his name? what was his name?) in his jar" (*U*, 114). Like a catachresis, this baptism produces a new form ("Worm is first of his kind" [*U*, 51]), but one that does not capture the ontological status of the subject: "Someone says 'you'? It's the fault of the pronouns. There is no name for me, no pronoun for me" (*U*, 123).

Metalepsis deforms aporia, chiasmus, and catachresis beyond their established formal functions. It transforms catachresis into an impossible figure of speech: an ear that talks. It stretches aporia beyond the point of obstruction, resulting in an expression of ontological certainty ("I'm the tympanum"). It multiplies chiasmus to the point where it no longer provides emphasis but rather ubiquity. It enfolds metalepsis, turning itself over and over as a parody of itself. These tropes act as middle terms, in other words, a key feature of metalepsis, which passes over and through them. This ongoing process of figuration both interrupts and extends embodiment. At times, for instance, the passage comments upon its metaleptical processes ("perhaps that's what I am"). At other moments, embodiment *is* metalepsis; it is the "middle" and "the thing that divides the world in two." The tympanum, a mediating membrane, is the bodily organ that enables transference, and which stops communication when it is impaired.

The metalepsis makes itself into a figure – the ear – for the very thing it professes to represent, namely the failure to hear or to communicate. Through this thickening and layering of tropes, metalepsis turns the figure into the ground – the medium of communication. This ear is a metafigure that self-consciously reflects upon the body's figuration. Its gigantic dimensions might even qualify it as a *mega*-figure, whose mediation of inside and outside literally embodies the act of metalepsis. The umbrella trope of metalepsis further illuminates this process by demonstrating how the ear itself becomes the master figure of embodiment in the novel, a formal container. Embodiment does not necessarily fully 'figure' in the figure here. Rather it does something even more difficult to grasp: it provides the medium of transition or transference; it is, in other words, the mediating ground between word and thing – the material basis of metaphor.[51] Embodiment is the metaphorical 'hinge' that structures the text's formal and representational logic. It structures

---

51 See Cummings, "Metalepsis," 227.

metalepsis and metalepsis structures Beckett's form – the transition between the bodily and the rhetorical itself is a form of metalepsis.

Metalepsis reframes the oscillation between fragmentation and concentration in Beckett's writing, and his writing of the body in particular. It helps bring into view previously elided embodied forms, especially monstrous or invisible bodies. Metalepsis, in this sense, is the poetic trope that helps discern the absence and presence of bodies that do not register within normative forms of representation. Indeed, the metalepsis of the tympanum embodies the act of reading; the trope's twisting and turning requires an active reading stance that follows its different figurative projections and inversions. Its bodily form figures the act of turning a deaf ear to particular bodies, of seeing or tuning them out.

Discipline and Punish

In the previous section, I proposed that metalepsis accounts for the constant movement between silence and speech, stasis and movement, repetition and originality in Beckett's texts. Metalepsis exposes the rhetorical structure of Beckett's supposed aesthetics of failure – why it is so persuasive in convincing us of its validity. The logic of metalepsis underpins the repetition, replacement, and substitution of other figures in Beckett's text, from the endless parade of slightly altered names and the recycling of specific images to the constant return of specific spaces. At the same time, metalepsis does not resolve or suspend these internal contradictions, folding them into a falsely unified form. It demonstrates how form need not be unified to have a shape. Metalepsis is the trope for constant formal movement, which never alights upon a definitive term or resolution. These different metaleptical dimensions pertain in particular to the Beckettian body, whether etiolated and inaccessible or grotesquely, exorbitantly present, like the giant ear.[52] Reading metaleptically allows us to understand how embodiment is stretched, expanded, contorted, distributed, and fetched from afar by constellating a range of other tropes and figures, while at the same time it is concentrated, condensed, isolated, and distilled in bodily figments. This constant process of projecting and introjecting embodiment gives it a form beyond the fragmentation of representation.

---

52 The abject, grotesque, and monstrous body in Beckett has received a great deal of scholarly attention. See Gibson, *Towards a Postmodern Theory of Narrative*, 258–273 and Maude, *Beckett, Technology, and the Body*, 99–103, 106–110. Rather than seeing the grotesque body as exceeding or signifying the limits of representation, however, I focus on how it is distributed in literary form.

My analysis of metalepsis thus far has drawn on the classical tradition, in which a (successful) metalepsis can demonstrate how "language pulls things together which seem in principle to be far apart."[53] This differs from the way postmodernist literary criticism approaches metalepsis as a metafictional narratological device that disrupts the boundaries between narrative levels.[54] This sense of intrusion implies a degree of violence, which is largely absent from its use as a rhetorical trope. The postmodernist approach to metalepsis critiques the notion of whole or teleological forms, which construct boundaries and assimilate difference into a single entity – a drive that postmodern narratology itself conceives of as a violent flattening or exclusion of difference. In postmodernism, the deconstruction of the essential self goes hand in hand with the construction of a discursive body. Postmodernist criticism on metalepsis thus often emphasizes how language violently undoes and fragments the body as a container for the authentic self. Language itself does violence to the body, either through excess or breakdown.

As I explored in the "Introduction," this violent undoing of the body and the subject is a form of counterviolence – a discursive force that seeks to undo hegemonic categories and forms of logic. Postmodernist approaches to metalepsis often have a much more explicit political function; they emphasize the figure of the boundary as something that regulates belonging. Unsurprisingly, approaches to both politics and metalepsis in Beckett have tended to insist upon its destituent potential as a form of counterviolence. Peter Boxall has argued that in its constant movement between antinomies, Beckett's work both constructs a boundary and violently contests it – a confrontation that is fundamentally political. (And also, though he does not explicitly label it as such, metaleptical.)[55] He describes a process similar to metalepsis in which "the writhings and contortions endured by Beckett's narrators and characters are orchestrated around a relentless confrontation between a poetic demand for a right to silence, and a political demand for speech."[56] The reverberations of the violent clash between antinomies are felt most keenly on the body – its "writhings and contortions" – as the locus of speech and the object that is silenced. In this sense, Beckett's works seem to incarnate the postmodernist emphasis on discursive violence, or the structural violence of discourse and rhetoric. The counterviolence in

---

53 Cummings, "Metalepsis," 221.
54 Metalepsis' metafictional dimension is not confined to postmodernist fiction by any means, however. *Don Quixote*, arguably the earliest novel, uses metalepsis in this way.
55 Cummings describes metalepsis as a "borderline figure" that "interrogates the boundaries of figurative language," in Cummings, "Metalepsis," 223.
56 Boxall, "Samuel Beckett: Towards a Political Reading," 160.

Beckett's work, according to Boxall, lies in its allegorical undoing of these oppressive forms.

Debra Malina, too, takes up the figure of the boundary in Beckett, arguing that the "*erection* of the boundaries" is inherently violent.[57] She explicitly invokes the figure of metalepsis to argue that "narrative constitutes the subject in part by *breaking down* the very structures that apparently define subjects and lend them their air of stability."[58] This breakdown resists the discursive production of boundaries and categories that submit the subject to forms of power. The destituent – rather than constitutive – understanding of metalepsis aligns with the postmodern "collapse of master narratives, the dismantling of the category of the real, and the deconstruction of binary and hierarchical systems of understanding."[59] Metalepsis frequently involves acts that question "the ontological status of fictional subjects or selves," such as when omniscient narrators suddenly reveal themselves as characters in the novel, or when a character from an extradiegetic or hypodiegetic frame bursts into the diegetic narrative. For this reason, metalepsis is a prism through which to explore "the dynamics of subject construction in an age that has witnessed [. . .] the deconstruction of the essential self in favor of a subject constituted in and by narrative."[60] Like Beckett's supposed violations of narrative conventions, which end in violent consequences, metalepsis transgresses narrative structures and reading conventions, which are often framed as violent intrusions.[61] Metalepsis acts as a form of counterviolence that resists the restrictive "policing" of representation by producing formless entities of non-expression, including the connection between character and identity, chronology, plot, and setting, amongst others.[62]

The violence of metaleptical transgression – the intrusion of different voices and narrators not only within embedded frames of specific texts but also across Beckett's entire corpus – is closely tied up with the fragmentation of bodies. The deconstruction of the self is necessarily enacted in and through the narrative fragmentation of the body, a process that is often violent and painful.[63] In this sense, Beckett's works seem to incarnate the postmodernist emphasis on the structural

---

57 Malina, *Breaking the Frame*, 1–2, italics in original.
58 Malina, *Breaking the Frame*, 10.
59 Malina, *Breaking the Frame*, 1–2.
60 Malina, *Breaking the Frame*, 2.
61 See Malina, *Breaking the Frame*, 4.
62 See Watson, *Paradox and Desire in Samuel Beckett's Fiction*, 17, for an example of this type of reading.
63 Violence is often identified as one of the techniques that Beckett uses to stage his 'aesthetics of failure.' See Llewellyn Brown, ed., *La violence dans l'oeuvre de Samuel Beckett: Entre*

violence of discourse and rhetoric. And indeed, Beckett's bodies are subjected to forms of power that are as repressive as they are absurd. His bodies are constantly surveilled, interpellated, controlled, and pursued by shadowy authority figures: the absent but omnipresent Godot, the detective Moran, the oppressive Lousse.[64] They are deprived of speech; they frequently end up institutionalized; they are confined to spaces that bring together the authoritarian control of the prison and the prison-like structures of the mind. At the most extreme end, discourse is literally inscribed on the body as a form of violence, as when the narrator of *How It Is* tortures Pim by carving his name into his buttocks with an old can opener. Yet silence and fragmentation can also help Beckett's characters and narratives to elude control.

I thus propose using the rhetorical figure for mediation, translation, and carrying over to explore the boundary between rhetorical, formal, and poetic violence and material, physical violence. As I will demonstrate in this section, counterdiscourse in Beckett's work is not associated with a kind of unrepresentable embodied experience that slips through the overdetermination of political power. Rather, form itself becomes a counterprinciple through embodiment. Embodied form exposes the structural violence of rhetoric and the rhetoric of structural violence by creating rather than undoing forms. The forms and tropes enact a counterviolence not by fragmenting the body or placing it beyond signification, but by making embodiment a constitutive element of form. My analysis of metalepsis in this section argues that approaching violence through metalepsis as a rhetorical or formal trope, rather than a narratological device, momentarily puts violence back in its place. It makes sense of the consequences of treating language as violence by turning violence into a purely formal principle. The consequences of this, as Beckett's texts demonstrate, require us to revisit the counter-discursive celebration of formlessness. Formlessness does not lead to emancipation from oppressive political forms. It leads to forms entirely devoted to the subjugation of bodies to rhetoric, discourse, and representation – forms where the enactment of violence upon bodies becomes the only organizing principle.

To think about the relationship between form, violence, and the body, I want to turn to one of Beckett's most difficult, most violent, and also most formally ordered texts, *How It Is*, in which a narrator describes his torture of a figure he names Pim whom he encounters in

---

langage et corps (Paris: Lettres Modernes Minard, 2017). Many of the essays in the collection focus on *How It Is* as the exemplary text of narrative torture and violence.
64 See Watson, *Paradox and Desire*, 2.

an expanse of mud.⁶⁵ The book is divided into three sections: before Pim, during Pim, and after Pim. It is constructed through a series of ordering units that gradually build on each other: single words coalesce into approximately twenty repeated phrases that then merge into bodily figments (hands, nails, sacks),⁶⁶ circulate as motifs of form (the skin as writing surface, the sack as an embryonic shape, matter as "primeval mud" [*HII*, 7]), and cohere into "word blocks" or "collocative sets" that use no punctuation and do not follow standard rules of syntax.⁶⁷ It is only by reading the text out loud that normal speech patterns emerge – a kind of "midget grammar" (*HII*, 66), as the narrator calls it. These word sets, largely of a comparable size until they begin to fracture at the book's end, organize the limited semantic, syntactical, and phrasal units into an unmistakable, if seemingly arbitrary, pattern. *How It Is* is obsessed, too, with algebra, geometry, and the laws of physics; it contains a number of schematics and formulas, including calculations of movement and speed, and the narrator strives to categorize different species.

Beyond its strikingly formalist structure, *How It Is* is also, fundamentally, a book about the production of forms. The narrator sets out to use specific devices and techniques for each section, although this largely fails.⁶⁸ He begins the first part ("before Pim") with the imperative that "we follow I quote the natural order more or less my life last state last version what remains bits and scraps" (*HII*, 3). The narrator suggests that he shapes Pim from the ground of form, "primeval mud": "Pim never be but for me anything but a dumb limp lump flat for ever in the mud but I'll quicken him you wait and see how I can efface myself behind my creature" (*HII*, 44). And the narrator's tortures are all oriented towards creating attachments and constraints, sometimes literal, as when he pins Pim to the ground. The basic unit of the couple produced in section two becomes the foundation for a monstrous body politic in the third section, a *polis* literally composed of bodies, organized around a mathematical formula. The expanse of mud draws the text's language back to itself, producing a closed textual ecology. This is a highly formalized, autonomous space in which formal principles

---

65 It is also one of Beckett's funniest books.
66 Ruby Cohn has identified around twenty repeated phrases in the text in Cohn, *Back to Beckett* (Princeton, NJ: Princeton University Press, 1974), 233.
67 This is, in fact, the only work Beckett composed that uses no punctuation. Édouard Magessa O'Reilly describes them as "word-groups" in Magessa O'Reilly, "Preface," in *How It Is*, by Samuel Beckett, ed. Edouard Magessa O'Reilly (London: Faber and Faber, 2009), x. Brienza describes them as "collocative sets," a term from linguistics that describes a set of words arranged semantically, in Brienza, *Samuel Beckett's New Worlds*, 90.
68 Brienza, *Samuel Beckett's New Worlds*, 102.

replace conventional political relations of community, negotiation, organization, and belonging.

The production of these forms – both bodily and political – is inseparable from violence. Indeed, the violent imposition of language on the body produces form. The text's enclosed, autonomous form offers a site for pushing ('stretching') the effects of political rhetoric on embodiment to its most extreme limits. This offers a pure distillation of the way power shapes and fragments bodily form, while also demonstrating political form's embodied foundations. Both the violent training or *dressage* of bodies and the substitution of figures in this enclosed formal space recalls Sade's *120 Days of Sodom* ("Sadism pure and simple" [*HII*, 54], the narrator admits of his torture of Pim),[69] another text in which an autonomous formal space becomes the site of indiscriminate experiments on bodies, a power that does not respect individuality. However, the shape of these forms is contingent; there is nothing essential about the linguistic patterns that emerge, just as the violence against bodies seems gratuitous. Indeed, the violence of representation, discourse, and rhetoric is the only thing innate in *How It Is*.

Rather than offering formlessness as a way of counteracting the violence of form and language, Beckett demonstrates there is no way of out of forms. The forms that emerge from this experiment are nightmarish exercises in pure violence, which demonstrates why it is necessary to distinguish between different types of violence. If the language that is organized into patterns, arrangements, and structures contains within it an implicit force of violence, then any emerging forms – even progressive ones – will not be able to overcome this structural violence. Beckett thus seems to reverse poststructuralism's emphasis on language as violence, suggesting that violence is a system of language – a language that expresses itself through embodiment.

This understanding of violence as a type of language is captured by the figure of metalepsis, which both breaks down and creates attachments. Let us now trace a metaleptical movement across the enclosed violence of *How It Is* in order to understand the relationship between discursive and actual violence. There are a number of different metalepses in the text; however, I want to focus on one that emerges with particular prominence in the second section, which is also the most violent (and absurd) part. Here the narrator recounts his relationship with Pim, moving between the past and the present. This diegetic move-

---

[69] On similarities between *120 Days of Sodom* and *How It Is* see Elsa Baroghel, "Samuel Beckett, lecteur de Sade: *Comment c'est* et *Les Cent vingt journées de Sodome*," Samuel Beckett, *La Revue des lettres modernes*, no. 4 (Paris: Classiques Garnier, 2017).

ment is framed by a self-reflexive commentary on the novel's structure: "here then at last part two where I will have to say how it was as I hear it in me that was without quaqua on all sides bits and scraps of how it was with Pim vast stretch of time," which itself anticipates the "vast tracts of time part three and last in the dark the mud my life murmur it bits and scraps." As if to confirm that the narrator still exists in living, breathing form in the present tense of diegesis, he moves his hand over his body, which "hangs a moment it's vague mid air then slowly sinks again and settles firm and even with a touch of ownership already on the miraculous flesh perpendicular to the crack the stump of the thump and thenar and hypo balls on the left cheek the four fingers on the other the right hand" (*HII*, 43). His hands eventually reach his buttocks "when contact with the right cheek less pads than nails" elicits a "second cry of fright" (*HII*, 44). The pain of his nails – later described as "some always long others presentable" (*HII*, 45) – on the sensitive flesh of his buttocks provides another narrative frame for his torture of Pim. Before the metaleptical movement between diegetic levels can take place, the narrator seems to remember that "quick my nails a word on them they will have their part to play" (*HII*, 44). This self-reflexive commentary on the book's diegetic layers suggests that the narrative constitution of the subject is enacted through violence – bringing us back to the narratological conception of metalepsis and its connection to the violence of rhetoric.

Yet this narrative metalepsis exists in tension with the formal trope of metalepsis, which provides a counter-form. As the narrator has promised, his nails do play an important, indeed fundamental role in the section's representation of violence and the body and the violence of representing the body.[70] As the narrator moves his hands over his body, he not only moves between past and present diegesis, his body and Pim's, but also into another metaleptical mode that is based on the metalepsis of "quick my nails" (*HII*, 44). "Quick my nails" is a metalepsis of 'to cut to the quick,' meaning to injure someone, often through words. The meaning of "quick" on which this metalepsis depends is not the adverb describing motion (an adverb that would rarely be used to describe the halting movement of Beckett's characters), but rather the Biblical figure for living, as in 'the quick and the dead.'[71] This meaning of quick is also evident in the archaic notion of 'quickening,' the moment when the fetus

---

70 My characterization of the chiasmatic relationship between violence and representation draws on a subheading in Sanyal, *The Violence of Modernity*, 28.
71 *How It Is* is replete with Biblical imagery and language, not least the irony of creating ('animating' or 'quickening') Pim from mud. For a discussion of Biblical imagery in the text see Brienza, *Samuel Beckett's New Worlds*, 98–99.

shows the first stirrings of life. "Quick" thus means alive and is associated with the living flesh of the body, hence the 'quick of the nails,' or the sensitive flesh under the 'dead' material of the nail. Etymologically, 'quick' is a cognate for the Latin *vīvus* and, by extension, the Greek *bios*, both meaning life, whence the French *vivant* and *vif*, and the English 'vivid' and 'vital.'

The metalepsis of "quick my nails" thus projects and performs the rhetorical violence that the idiomatic figure of speech 'to cut to the quick' describes. In omitting the central action, it literally excises from language its own act of 'cutting,' while also separating the violence of the figure of speech from the 'quick' of the body's living flesh. It supplements the extended meaning of 'quick' metonymically associated with "my nails," filling in the formal excision through a bodily figure. This initial metalepsis sets off a series of different formal operations that both extend and 'cut out' the body, often in relation to a metaleptical reflection upon the narrative construction of the subject: "my part but for me he would never Pim we're talking of Pim never be but for me anything but a dumb limp flat for ever in the mud but I'll quicken him you wait and see and how I can efface myself behind my creature when the fit takes me now my nails." This then jumps to the next word block, which begins with "quick a supposition" and, after five lines wondering about the reality of the mudscape in which the narrator, along with "billions of us crawling and shitting," lives, ends with "more now my nails" (*HII*, 44). The metalepsis is reprised in the repetition of "my nails" at the beginning of the next block of words, which then ends with a reflection upon death, the opposite, in other words, of the 'quick.' This is immediately extended into the following block of words, which provides metalepsis as repetition: "til his hour of death it is not said at what age having done this / the hour of his death at what age it is not said."[72] This 'quick' metaleptical movement turns back again to the paradox of "his nails his death," which is reinforced by a bathetic image that opposes 'quickening': "all his life thus lived died at last saying to himself latest breath that they'd [his nails] grow on" (*HII*, 45). "They'd" thus performs another metalepsis, ambiguously standing in for the bodily figure. The metaleptical process that begins with the omission of "quick my nails" (*HII*, 44) structures the "life" (the 'quick') of their relationship: thus, with this seemingly gratuitous act of violence, "our life in common we begin" (*HII*, 47).

The French text provides us with a different configuration of the linguistic relationship between violence and the body. The movement

---

72 The forward dash here indicates a line break between block paragraphs.

of the narrator's nails over his body recalls the colloquialism *jusqu'au bout des ongles*, meaning completely or entirely. It suggests that his body's form is fully apprehensible but only to himself. The next mention of nails, in the passage where we encounter the metalepsis in English, does not explicitly contain a metaleptical figure of speech: "mais vite un mot sur mes ongles ils vont avoir leur rôle à jouer" [but quickly a word on my nails they will have their role to play].[73] Yet the implied association of *jusqu'au bout des ongles* connects with other figures of speech, namely phrases including *à vif*. This includes *couper à vif/couper la chair* [the flesh] *à vif*, which also means completely and derives from the same etymological root of *vīvus*, setting off a similar chain of associations, in which the sense of living flesh is also very strong. The insistence that "je vais [...] animer" Pim's "carcasse inerte et muette"[I'll quicken (his) dumb limp lump] (CC, 82) also recalls the notion of 'quickening' (*animer* in French), this time transforming a lifeless form into a sentient thing. The omitted term of *vif* is nevertheless reinstated under another guise through the adverb "vite," which is then stretched through other words and figures, including "plus vivant" [more lively] (CC, 81), "vite une supposition" [quick a supposition] (CC, 82), and "toute sa vie vécu mourut enfin" [all his life thus lived died at last] (CC, 83), amongst others. Thus, as in the English rewriting, the narrator's nails are caught up in an extended trope of both creating forms and cutting flesh.

If I have taken you through these rather dizzying metaleptical movements – and this only covers the second section's first pages – it is to demonstrate how the body is imbricated in these different forms of metalepsis in ways that cannot simply be defined according to fragmentation or violence. The body is the surface on which language is literally inscribed, providing the stark figure for the subject constructed by discourse. But it is also the embodied foundation of rhetorical form. The 'quick' of living flesh structures the distribution of the figure for both rhetorical and actual violence: the nails. Thus, just as language undoes itself and by extension the discursive subject through a rhetorical operation of injury, it also redistributes, extends, and stretches embodiment beyond the effects of rhetorical injury. The body is the central figure connecting these two kinds of metalepsis. As the narrator moves his hands over his body, he not only moves between past and present, his body and Pim's, but also into another metaleptical mode that is based on the metalepsis of "quick my nails" (*HII*, 44). The body mediates between

---

73 Samuel Beckett, *Comment c'est* (Paris: Les Editions de Minuit, 1961), 81. All further references will be given parenthetically with the abbreviation CC. The translations of the passages I cite from *Comment c'est* are my own.

metalepsis as a violent breakdown of the subject and its form-giving, extending, and locating dimensions.

This understanding of metalepsis thus helps account for the violence of representation – and the representation of violence – while also providing a counter-form that is not exclusively enacted through the breakdown of the body or the subject. This extended metalepsis gives form to the relationship between the body, violence, and representation. It figures violence as a structural element of representation; it is a laceration (a 'cut') into language and the body ("quick my nails a word"). Yet it does not come to rest upon this state. It moves on, and it enfolds other elements. While not falsely restoring the body, it provides a way of tracing embodiment within the text's structure and form, even when the experience of pain shatters both language and subjectivity. In accounting for embodiment beyond representation, it also provides an alternative relationship between the body and rhetorical violence – one that is, however, far from ideal, as we shall see.

In *Sphinx*, prosopopoeia projects embodiment beyond the constraints of representation, and catachresis disrupts the referential connection between language and the body. However, in *How It Is* metalepsis does not have the same emancipatory function. It stretches violence beyond physical force, and it reduces rhetoric to pure violence. But it is thus also useful for allowing us to trace the rhetorical operations of the postmodernist conflation of representation and violence and the valorization of formlessness as a type of counterviolence. Metalepsis demonstrates the consequences of conflating speech, discourse, and representation with physical violence. The narrator designs a series of lessons to ascertain whether Pim "can speak" (*HII*, 48), which are organized around various tortures: "first lesson theme song I dig my nails into his armpit right hand right pit he cries I withdraw them thump with fist on skull his face sinks in the mud his cries cease end of first lesson" (*HII*, 54). Although Pim vocalizes a range of noises, they never quite reach the level of speech; either "the mud muffles or perhaps a foreign tongue" (*HII*, 48), "he sings a little tune" (*HII*, 47), or he simply cries out in pain. If for Elaine Scarry, pain "actively destroys" language,[74] here pain becomes the only medium of communication. Physical violence both controls this form of pure corporeal noise and replaces language: "the thump on the skull signifying stop at all times and that come to think of it almost mechanically at least where words involved" (*HII*, 55). The coincidence of Pim's tortured body and shattered speech demonstrates the consequences of turning discourse into violence. Pim's fragmented body gives

---

74 Scarry, *The Body in Pain*, 4.

form to his lack of agency; he can offer no resistance to violence. His body cannot figure itself in language or speech:

> I draw his arm towards me behind his back it jams [...] released at last the arm recoils sharp a little way then comes to rest it's I again must put it back where I found it way off on the right in the mud Pim is like that he will be like that he stays whatever way he's put but it doesn't amount to much on the whole a rock. (*HII*, 50)

Perhaps in a different situation, the narrator muses, "I would have been a different man more universal" (*HII*, 57), but within the *huis clos* of the text's 'total' form, language is reduced to pure force on the body.

How It Is provides an autonomous formal space where the consequences of reducing political representation to bare violence can be stretched to their most extreme limits. Beckett strips violence, representation, and politics of their referential or identity function. Excised – 'cut out' – from concrete political contexts or cause and effect, Pim and the narrator's relationship reveals the violent mechanics of power reduced to its most basic volition: "why mechanically why simply because it has the effect the thump on skull we're talking of the thump on skull the effect of plunging the face in the mud the mouth the nose and even the eyes and what but words could be involved in the case of Pim a few words what he can now and then." This is not an ethical violation ("I am not a monster," he declares [*HII*, 55]), because constituting one's subjectivity by literally cutting one's initials into another's body makes perfect sense within the text's formal ecology of violence. The instrument of violence is once again the metaleptical figure of nails, which carves the very form of *How It Is* into Pim's body: "unbroken no paragraphs no commas no a second for reflection with the nail of the index until it falls and the worn back bleeding passim it was near the end like yesterday vast stretch of time" (*HII*, 61). In other words, the novel presents violence as a formal principle, or something that organizes figurative language into an embodied form.[75]

The narrator wields power in order to enact fundamental political acts: he brands Pim with his initials and thus announces himself as a subject while erasing the subjecthood of the other; he enslaves Pim in order to experience his own freedom; he exercises agency as a pure will to subjugate; he takes up speech in order to silence another; he sticks his finger up Pim's arse to remind himself that his body remains intact. Literal relations of power are enacted on the figurative body. In other

---

75 I build on Sanyal's astute analysis of violence as a formal principle that can be deployed across a range of fields, including politics and aesthetics, in the work of Charles Baudelaire and Albert Camus, in Sanyal, *The Violence of Modernity*, 177.

words, violence constitutes bodies purely in form, whether constructed in language or molded from mud. Yet, constrained to the relationship between the narrator and Pim, these power relations have not taken on the shape of a political community. Thus, while the production of embodied form in the novel's second section has political valences, the way in which violence is wielded as a formal principle – and the political consequences of this act for embodiment – is most apparent in the book's third section. Here, the relationship between discursive violence and the body stretches outwards yet again, beyond the foundational unit of the couple. It creates a body politic – a political space literally made up of bodies: "a hundred thousand prone glued two by two together vast stretch of time." The narrator and Pim pull apart and reform couples with an endless cycle of Bems, Boms, Krims, and Krams: "at the instant Pim reaches the other to form again with him the only couple he forms apart from the one with me Bem reaches me to form with the only couple he forms from the other one" (*HII*, 98). Yet the formation of these bodies into a single political unit is animated ('quickened') by only one motivating objective. Violence is the primary formal principle of this body politic: "all these same couples that eternally form and form again [...] always two strangers uniting in the interests of torment" (*HII*, 105). This violence is inscribed into the materiality of bodies, as well as taking on the linguistic structure of a chain of significations ("all along the chain in both directions" [*HII*, 123]), in which "tormentors those whose turn it is on and off" enact violence against the next in line in a choreography of torture: "right arm claw the armpit for the song carve the scriptions plunge the opener pestle the kidney" (*HII*, 98). The narrator eventually provides a schematic for this violent ordering of embodied form, tracing out how "victim of number 4 at A en route along AB tormentor of number 2 at B abandoned again" (*HII*, 103), *ad infinitum*.

If this body politic is made up of bodies "agglutinated two by two in the interests of torment" (*HII*, 100), it also comes to breathe, act, and move as one, "glued together like a single body in the dark the mud" (*HII*, 106). In other words, this body politic brings together figure and ground, body and form, into one political entity. These "millions and millions there are millions of us" (*HII*, 99) set off together with the Beckettian body's spasmodic movements, "a procession advancing in jerks or spasms like shit in the guts" (*HII*, 108). The collective exertions of this great sensing body leave it breathless, "panting wilder more and more animal in want of air." Recalling the monstrous tympanum in *The Unnamable*, this body politic listens with "an ear like ours" and speaks of "this life in the dark and mud its joys and sorrows journeys intimacies and abandons as with a single voice" (*HII*, 121). The suggestion that this voice, which seems to both emanate from and speak to this collective body, might represent agency is quickly dispatched. In a parody of elective government, "every twenty or forty years according to certain of our figures" this body politic exposes the pretense of political representation as an expression of individuality, "recall[ing] to our abandoned the essential features" (*HII*, 121). This embodied form, composed entirely through the violence of rhetoric, can offer no guarantee of political representation, which relies upon individual differences: "in reality we are all one and all from the unthinkable first to the no less unthinkable last glued together in a vast imbrication of flesh without breach or fissure" (*HII*, 122).

The embodied form of *How It Is* eventually presents a terrifying expanse of pure physical force and suffering. However, rather than taking this as evidence for the dangers of understanding embodiment through form, and vice versa, I argue that Beckett's forms are instructive in providing the negative image of embodied form's possibilities. *How It Is* throws into relief what happens when form is abandoned to totality and formlessness is celebrated as resistance. Much postmodernist criticism has also been concerned with exposing structural violence – the violence of exclusion and of conforming that inheres in all normative structures. Yet in renouncing form as hegemonic and celebrating formlessness as a type of counterviolence, such approaches have abandoned the affordances of form, including attachment, organization, persuasion, and agency, leaving form in the service of oppression. *How It Is* exposes both structural violence and the consequences of surrendering form to a kind of totalitarianism. The brief glimpse of the possibility "to conceive of another world as just as ours but less exquisitely organized" (*HII*, 125) is not an emancipatory gesture. It acknowledges that there can be no political organization without form. The task must be to create different forms. Rather than formlessness, "formulation to be adjusted assuredly in light of our limits and possibilities but which will always present this advantage that by eliminating all journeys all abandons it eliminates at the same stroke all occasion of sacks and voices quaqua then in us when the panting stops" (*HII*, 123).

Through its 'strict' formalism, *How It Is* demonstrates the consequences of conflating rhetoric and violence. It distills language to pure physical force wielded against bodies, metaleptically stretching to the extreme of postmodernism's ambivalent disavowal of and investment in the violence of rhetoric. Indeed, this relationship is more easily grasped as a purely formal configuration. It is stripped of social conventions, political contexts, and specific identities; linguistic forms and textual spaces exist as highly autonomous formal realms. Paradoxically, in transforming violence into a formal principle, and transporting it into a purely textual realm, *How It Is* demonstrates the concrete consequences of severing violence from the lived reality of embodied subjects – that is, of omitting bodies as the mediating term between politics and representation.

Rather than eliding embodiment and the body from the system of political representation, in other words, *How It Is* metaleptically strips the relationship between representation, the body, and violence down to the 'quick.' Violence is purely rhetorical, and yet it literally cuts to the quick, such as when the narrator claws his fingernails in Pim's armpit or carves his name in his buttocks. The novel reveals the fundamentally embodied foundation of both politics and form, as well as the nightmarish consequences of reducing discourse, representation, and language to pure violence. Metalepsis, then, demonstrates the embodied consequences of stretching violence across a vast range of categories beyond physical force, while also concentrating the effects of this distribution in the body's form itself. Beckett uncovers the violence of discursive violence, that is, the material excision that the insistence on discourse as violence enacts. *How It Is* exposes the consequences of creating a political form that rests upon the fragmentation of the body, but it also throws into relief the consequences of a counterviolence of destituency. Crucially, the novel demonstrates the *formal* dimension of these things; they exist as rhetorical, poetic, and discursive structures that cannot be simply transposed onto political realities, while at the same time they provide the form for exploring and imagining the 'unimaginable,' Hopefully to avoid it ever taking form.

Totality's Violence

In this chapter, I have sought to demonstrate how metalepsis brings together bodily figments and grounded figures in the form of the body politic – a form, as *How It Is* reminds us, that is literally made up of bodies – while also demonstrating the consequences of reducing rhetoric to violence. The monstrosity of this political form, which is orientated purely towards the torture of bodies, demonstrates what happens when violence is metaleptically stretched out of shape. Indeed, some readers may argue that I myself have stretched metalepsis beyond its capacities and exaggerated the consequences of postmodernist counterviolence in order to vaunt the potential of embodied form. Exaggeration is an important element of metalepsis, enabling it to cut to the quick of language's living flesh. In deciding what is included and what is cut out, what is whipped into shape and what is left in the margins, the act of critique can also be a form of rhetorical violence – a *policing* of the borders of knowledge. Indeed, as Hanssen reminds us, the term critique derives from the Greek word *krinein*, meaning to cut, separate, distinguish, as well as to decide and to judge.[76] Sometimes, the 'cut' of critique can render representation or form violent in ways that collapse rhetoric and materiality, language and embodiment. This metalepsis of cut and critique is of course another exaggeration, which I use to demonstrate the importance of separating and distinguishing between different forms of violence.

My reading of Beckett through the figure of metalepsis and its relationship to embodiment, form, and violence has thus sought to understand how rhetorical violence both coincides with and differs from material forms of power, and how literary form can distribute embodiment in ways that elude political forms of representation. While political representation or power is frequently wielded as a form of violence against bodies, this material violence needs to be carefully weighed and evaluated in terms of its similarity to rhetorical violence. Rhetoric can produce physical violence, whether through hate speech's incitement to violence or the embodied experience of pain and terror that comes from encountering racist and sexist speech and symbols.[77] Indeed, perpetrators of hate speech often fall back on the excuse that 'mere words' cannot be equated with physical violence. The violence of literary form illuminates and may even give shape to our conceptions of how violence breaks apart bodies, but in treating all discourse as structurally violent literary criticism can also obscure the material consequences of political violence, conflating the fragmented, unrepresentable body of postmodernist counterdiscourse with bodies broken by political power and killed by structural violence.

This all-pervasive power can lead to a sense of impotence. If we think that all violence is discursive violence, we may be less likely to act when physical and affective violence occurs or feel that there is no way of resisting it, since it is part of the very foundation of the self.[78] As

---

76 Hanssen, *Critique of Violence*, 3–4.
77 See Judith Butler, *Excitable Speech: A Politics of the Performative* (New York: Routledge, 1997), 99–100. Many African Americans have spoken about the terror they feel when faced with a confederate flag, for instance. This visual symbol has the potential to cause actual physical pain.
78 The counterpart to this is the widespread notion that reading literature makes us more empathetic, and that empathy can spur us to act. In other words, identifying with experiences that are different from ourselves in texts inherently makes us more open to respecting and protecting such differences in the public sphere.

Debarati Sanyal has argued in relation to her critique of modernity as a form of trauma, while "recent theory has led to sophisticated accounts of the decentralized and ungraspable quality of power, its dissemination in academic circles and in general public culture has tended to foster melancholy resignation or even cynicism rather than a sense of possibility, resistance, or agency."[79] By fragmenting and dislocating the very site on which power makes itself felt most strongly, criticism has undermined political agency. Understanding where rhetorical and concrete violence, whether historical or contemporary, intersect and differ helps identify what type of violence is affecting bodies at a particular time. It thus helps formulate appropriate forms of resistance, contestation, and organization, which originate in embodied, lived experience itself.

Indeed, we can partly trace one of these boundaries for differentiating violence in relation to the two ways I have explored metalepsis in this chapter. As a rhetorical or poetic trope, it draws attention to the boundaries between lived experience and literary form, whereas its use as a figure for the undoing of forms enables the textualization of violence, turning all experience into discourse. It is much easier to torture, maim, or kill a body in the text than to recognize violence as an actual force acted upon bodies and experienced by subjects. The textualization of violence – turning all representation into a form of violence, and all violence into a process of representation – actually takes a formalist turn. It divorces violence from its real-world contexts and the material force it exerts on bodies and subjects. Beckett's works demonstrate the consequences of metaleptically extending and stretching material violence into aesthetic, discursive, and symbolic configurations, by transforming such formal figures into pure vehicles of violence.

Beckett's formalist distillation of discursive violence to *actual* violence reveals how the valorization of counterviolence elides the material violence (which need not be purely physical) of the fragmented, unrepresentable body. It is important to emphasize that Beckett's formalist violence is not emancipatory. Beckett's characters and bodies rarely belong in the spaces where they are confined. They are deprived of speech even as they cannot stop screaming. They are interpellated by the law and imprisoned, but also excluded and 'cut out.' Terror, pain, and surveillance are part of the texts' formal logic. Formalist violence demonstrates the consequences of celebrating the dissolution of shaping structures. Yet in revealing the rhetorical structure of structural violence, it also exposes the interconnected systems of representation that enable

---

79 Sanyal, *The Violence of Modernity*, 2.

some bodies and their pain to be visible and expressible and others to be invisible and inexpressible. As I argued in the "Introduction," postmodernism's crisis of representation has placed the embodied experience of those most vulnerable to political violence outside of our perceptual sphere. This subjects embodied experience to *ellipsis*. It does not emancipate the body from representation. It makes it more susceptible to violent forces emanating from and sanctioned by those who enjoy full political representation and whose experience implicitly shapes our governing forms. Beckett's works help us understand how the language of counterviolence too often omits the material violence experienced by those refused political representation.

We can bring this discussion back to a more concrete political context in relationship to the simultaneous elision of gender and the overdetermination of race in *Sphinx*. In that chapter, I focused on the way prosopopoeia projects embodied presence in the absence of a gendered discursive subject, and I argued that catachresis can disrupt the representation of race by reordering the body's formal composition beyond seemingly self-evident racial codes. Catachresis, in this sense, acts metaleptically; it stretches the body beyond its recognizable boundaries and invites us to fill in the missing forms left by race's excision. Yet metalepsis also draws attention to the dangers of overlooking missing terms, such as the narrator's whiteness, which structures the text's scopic regime and which persists in the text's form – and my analysis of it – even when I thoroughly deconstructed blackness. By failing to fully read whiteness, I left it intact. I reinforced whiteness as the assumed structure of embodied form, itself a type of boundary 'policing.' Whiteness remained as the default form into which black bodies must assimilate. In this case, the mediating term that structures metalepsis, which must be filled in by the reader (and the critic!), became simply an ellipsis; it is a permanent omission symbolically represented by an indexical sign pointing to absence (three successive dots, a dash, or brackets, mirroring the inscription of A***'s name in *Sphinx*). To read race through metalepsis, then, may help fill in the missing terms rather than wielding metalepsis as a form of exclusion. However incongruous the comparison with *Sphinx*, *How It Is* demonstrates the dangers of using metalepsis as a form of 'policing' that violently regulates the presence of bodies in political forms and the forms of political rhetoric enacted upon bodies. This understanding of metalepsis demonstrates what happens when we fail to read formally – when we read only for political representation.

By coming back to my analytical omission of whiteness in *Sphinx*, I have demonstrated that deconstruction is not enough. We must try to produce new political forms or risk leaving intact the residues of previous incarnations. Postmodernist approaches to metalepsis have celebrated its potential to break forms apart – to disrupt the kinds of confinement, containment, and enclosure of which postmodernism is (rightly) suspicious. By contrast, I have approached metalepsis in order to understand the material effects of wielding language as violence on the body. Beckett's works are crucial in this regard because they transform violence into a purely formal principle. As I noted above, there is no emancipatory gesture to an 'outside' or 'elsewhere' in Beckett. Bodies remain mired in mud, broken down, stuck in place. What Beckett's texts demonstrate is that there is no way *out* of form. Formlessness does not lead to the dissolution of oppressive political forms, but rather to forms entirely devoted to subjugating bodies to rhetoric, discourse, and representation – forms where the enactment of violence upon bodies itself becomes the only organizing principle. His bodies and embodied forms do not offer a liberation from such nightmarish forms. Instead they provide a glimpse at the nightmare of a political order that metaleptically omits the bodies that compose it.

The Beckettian body politic provides the stark negative image of a utopian politics of belonging, but one that reveals the close imbrication of embodiment and form – both poetic and political. Beckett's body politic exposes the embodied foundation of the most essential political form. At the same time, it reveals the consequences of treating representation or discourse as violence, for it fragments the only site of political agency: the body. Form is unavoidable, but it does not mean that we must accept current political organizations. What haunts this body politic is the possibility of a political form that is explicitly ordered, arranged, distributed, and organized around different embodiments. The form of texts like *How It Is* demonstrates the necessity of creating new ones, which recognize and valorize their embodied foundations, while the formal properties of *The Unnamable* point towards new ways of reading for, and thus conceiving of, these embodied forms. When fully engaged, metalepsis helps guard against monolithic or totalitarian forms. Rather than 'policing' belonging or breaking down the subject, metalepsis can connect seemingly disconnected things, like the fragmented body, or put other things, like violence, back into place so that they do not infect the entire structure of language. Metalepsis pops into view, disguises itself, turns on its heels, goes on the lam, and hides in plain sight in ways that evade the vigilant surveillance of political representation and power. Metalepsis enables the body to appear in defamiliarized forms, to inhabit unorthodox places, and to require new modes of description and recognition. When we halt at de-forming the body or deconstructing narrative, then violence ensues. But metalepsis helps produce new forms to take its place. Instead of celebrating formlessness, Beckett's enclosed spaces and subjected bodies demonstrates what happens when we give form over to order as violence.

Chapter 4

The Unbearable Lightness of Being: Chiasmus, Embodiment, and Interpretation in Maurice Blanchot

This chapter on Maurice Blanchot turns *Formal Matters* into a chiasmus. It is the point at which two very different concepts of writing and the body cross over. On one side is the abstract formalism of Garréta and Beckett, in which embodiment takes shape beyond representation, theme, and identity by providing the ground for poetic language. On the other side, as the reader will come to see, is Primo Levi's testimonial literature, whose self-conscious objective of providing an account of the Holocaust is inseparable from the demands of representation, particularly the representation of the body. Blanchot provides the fulcrum on which this calibrated system rests. The slight structural imbalance that emerges is an essential facet of chiasmus, a rhetorical figure in which the two inverted clauses rarely perfectly mirror each other, providing an asymmetrical rhetorical formulation.[1] The formalist autonomy of Garréta and Beckett combines to provide an uneven counterpoint to the historical specificity of Levi. Looked at from another perspective, however, the concrete materiality of Levi's work, anchored in the weight of representation – of representation *as* a weight – grounds Garréta and Beckett's allusiveness. This chapter thus demonstrates how embodiment shapes the boundaries of thought and interpretation, as well as literary form.

Like all the other tropes *Formal Matters* has thus far explored, chiasmus is important in both ancient and classical rhetoric and postmodernist thought. It is also, however, the trope that has the most phenomenological dimension, as explored in Merleau-Ponty's analysis of chiasmus, which represents the perceptual interweaving of the body and the world beyond the realm of vision, a haptic form of sensibility that interrupts the primacy of vision. I bring chiasmus' phenomenological and rhetorical dimensions together with its use in postmodernist

1 Antimetabole is the figure for mirroring per se.

deconstruction to explore the work of Maurice Blanchot. Or rather, I use his final short *récit*, *The Instant of My Death* (1994, *L'Instant de ma mort*), to illuminate the relationship between embodiment, form, and interpretation beyond absence.

Blanchot has often been considered a writer of extreme negativity and fragmentation, for whom writing figures an un-figurable presence, "a radical passivity of the self" that is excluded "from the domain of that which can appear, exile[d] from the realm of experience." Early on, he argued that "language must renounce being at once the expression of obvious certainty and the expression of the universal; there is no continuity between sensation and words."[2] Here, Blanchot seems to argue that language cannot make embodied experience comprehensible, breaking the link between "bodily sensation and the language used to describe or otherwise designate such perception."[3] However, I read the discontinuity between language and the body in terms of chiasmus. These concepts are part of a crisscrossing movement that also implicates their opposites, namely sensory experience and embodiment. The figure of chiasmus in *The Instant of My Death* demonstrates how embodiment emerges through interpretation. By throwing into relief the work of analytical labor, chiasmus reveals how embodiment is neither an *a priori* essence nor a purely discursive product of representation. The movement of reading – like a trope's twisting and turning – gives shape to an otherwise indistinct or amorphous phenomenal experience.

Chiasmus

Of all the poetic and rhetorical figures *Formal Matters* explores, chiasmus has the closest relationship to the body, in both a literal and a figurative sense. The figure resembles the interwoven double helix of DNA (itself a visual representation of a bodily structure imperceptible to the naked eye),[4] and it is used to describe the X-shaped structure of optic nerves, connecting its visual function to concepts of sight and transparency. The 'X' of chiasmus derives from the Greek letter χ, *chi*. In *Timaeus*, Plato links it to the rhythms of breath – "inhaling" and "exhaling" – as well as

---

2 Maurice Blanchot, *Faux pas*, trans. Charlotte Mandell (Stanford, CA: Stanford University Press, 2001), 89.
3 Crispin T. Lee, *Haptic Experience in the Writings of Georges Bataille, Maurice Blanchot and Michel Serres* (Oxford; New York: Peter Lang, 2014), 111. Lee recognizes this seeming separation but goes on to provide a compelling analysis of the way haptic experience operates in *The Instant of My Death*.
4 On the similarity between the DNA double helix and chiasmus see Thomas, "Chiasmus in Art and Text," 50.

the metaphor of weaving into an X shape.⁵ This could refer to fabric, as in the notion of the woven veil of the soul (*diaplakeisa*), which is made of the same stuff as breath. Breath and air share the same constitution as the soul, as well as similar forms of movement.⁶ The body's literal material and figurative movements are thus braided together, like the cruciform figure of chiasmus.

As a poetic or rhetorical figure, chiasmus is deceptively simple. In its most basic form, it entails the rhetorical inversion of two clauses in an AB:BA pattern. The neatness of this crisscrossing effect led a number of rhetoricians to treat it as contrived or ornamental.⁷ However, chiasmus can also act as structuring principle of thought, shaping it into a cohesive form. This is evident in the principle of *hysteron proteron*, or 'the latter first,'⁸ which helped the narrator (or *rhapsode*) of Homeric epic to "hold the attention of his listener with a minimum of effort on the part of the latter."⁹ Rather than mere ornament, then, chiasmus "may give structure to the thought pattern and development of entire literary units, as well as to shorter sections whose composition is more dependent on immediate tones and rhythms."¹⁰ Yet, as Rodolphe Gasché makes clear, the importance of chiasmus is not found in either its grammatical/rhetorical or mnemonic/psychological uses, but rather in the way it constitutes "an original form of thought" that "allows oppositions to be found into unity." In this way, it helps identify the forms of difference that a totality yokes together. Chiasmus "allows the drawing apart and bringing together of opposite functions or terms and entwines them within an identity of movements," linking together pairs of opposites in a process that secures "by the very movement of the inversion of the link that exists between opposite poles [...] the agreement of a thing at variance with itself."¹¹ Chiasmus provides the figure for intellectual or analytic unity.

Postmodernist thinkers sought to deconstruct chiasmus' unity or totality. For de Man chiasmus emerges from a void, "a lack that allows

---

5 On "inhaling" and "exhaling" and the braiding of fabric see Plato, *Plato's Timaeus*, trans. Peter Kalkavage (Newburyport, MA: Focus Publishing, 2001), 78D and 36B–D.
6 For a discussion of how these metaphors have been used in Plato see Nicoletta Isar, "Undoing Forgetfulness: Chiasmus of Poetical Mind – a Cultural Paradigm of Archetypal Imagination," *Europe's Journal of Psychology* 1, no. 3 (August 28, 2005), https://doi.org/10.5964/ejop.v1i3.370.
7 See Henri Morier in the *Dictionnaire de poétique et de rhétorique*: "the chiasm would only be a sort of silly affectation were it not motivated by a superior reason, the desire for variation, the need for euphony and expressive harmony," quoted in Gasché, "Reading Chiasms," xvi.
8 Welch, *Chiasmus in Antiquity*, 251.
9 Quoted in Gasché, "Reading Chiasms," xvii.
10 Gasché, "Reading Chiasms," xvi.
11 Gasché, "Reading Chiasms," xvii.

for the rotating motion of the polarities."[12] Derrida builds upon this notion of chiasmus in a series of readings of Blanchot's *récits* in which he associates Blanchot's writing with a "double invagination," in which it is impossible to differentiate the interior from the exterior, the limit from the center.[13] Andrzej Warminski, drawing on de Man and Derrida, uses chiasmus to interrogate the appearance of totality in rhetorical form "as a simulacrum of the transcendental."[14] Merleau-Ponty, too, notes the similarity between chiasmus and invagination, using the figure of "flesh" to argue that chiasmus does not lead to a final synthesis, but to a perpetual enfolding of the embodied matter of perception. In this sense, the rhetorical clarity of chiasmus' reversible structure can produce forms of obscurity, opacity, or thickness. Merleau-Ponty also uses chiasmus as a figure for interpretation, a way of getting at inchoate experience before it has been 'worked over' by processes of thought.

Clarity and lightness, on the one hand, and opacity and weight, on the other, are the two inseparable elements of chiasmus. This dialectical movement never leads to a synthesis. It thus helps account for the body's simultaneous solidification and dematerialization in language and form. Chiasmus brings together the two opposite terms that make up its own meaning: the physical, material body and the figurative form of language and thought. It embodies the inseparability of the body's literal and figural dimensions, without fully unifying these dimensions. Chiasmus illuminates how the body overlaps with itself as both subject and object, and traces the boundary between the body and language, representation, and form as a self-conscious process of interpretation.

Absence Embodied

Let us now turn to *The Instant of My Death*.[15] The text appeared in 1994, and it is Blanchot's final *récit*, a short form of fictional narrative.

12 De Man, *Allegories of Reading*, 49.
13 Jacques Derrida, "Living On," in *Deconstruction and Criticism*, by Harold Bloom et al. (London: Seabury Press, 1979), 100–101.
14 Andrzej Warminski, *Readings in Interpretation: Hölderlin, Hegel, Heidegger* (Minneapolis, MN: University of Minnesota Press, 1987), 8
15 The critical reception of Blanchot's final *récit* has been dominated by Jacques Derrida's essay, *Demeure: Fiction and Testimony*, which is published in English along with in a dual-language edition of *The Instant of My Death*. See Maurice Blanchot and Jacques Derrida, *The Instant of My Death/Demeure: Fiction and Testimony*, trans. Elizabeth Rottenberg (Stanford, CA: Stanford University Press, 2000). I will henceforth cite Blanchot's text parenthetically from this edition. Derrida's essay explores the boundary between testimony, philosophy, and literature. Subsequent analyses have tended to eschew the *récit*'s literary dimension, emphasizing its philosophical, juridical, or political aspects. See, for instance,

It appears to depict Blanchot's near execution at the hands of a Russian–German firing squad during WWII.[16] It thus provides a form of testimony for his early political activities, which had long been shrouded in secrecy.[17] It also draws on Blanchot's philosophical interest in the limit between life and death, the neuter, the exhaustion and withdrawal of language, and *désœuvrement* or 'worklessness,' a kind of constitutive undoing of literature and philosophy.[18] Such concepts would seem to preclude an analysis of embodiment, and indeed little work has been done on the body and the senses in Blanchot's thinking.[19] Yet Blanchot's engagement with withdrawal, neutrality, and passivity provides a site through which to explore how embodiment takes form in figures for its own attenuation. If Blanchot has rarely, if ever, been studied via his engagement with the body it is because embodiment remains incipient in his work. It is never fully realized, expressed, or represented. For

Thomas S. Davis, "Neutral War: *L'Instant de ma mort*," in *Clandestine Encounters: Philosophy in the Narratives of Maurice Blanchot*, ed. Kevin Hart (Baltimore, MD: Johns Hopkins University Press, 2004) and Hent de Vries, "'Lapsus Absolu': Notes on Maurice Blanchot's The Instant of My Death," *Yale French Studies*, 93 (1998), 30–59. Philippe Lacoue-Labarthe explores the *récit*'s literary value, but also hints at the difficulty of writing on the *récit* after Derrida in Lacoue-Labarthe, "Fidelities," *The Oxford Literary Review*, 22 (2000), 132–51: 133.

16 On 20 July 1994, the same year that Blanchot published *The Instant of My Death* and the fiftieth anniversary of his near execution by a Russian-German firing squad, he declared in a letter to his friend Jacques Derrida that "fifty years ago, I knew the happiness of nearly being shot to death," in Derrida, *Demeure*, 52.

17 See Leslie Hill, *Maurice Blanchot: Extreme Contemporary* (London: Routledge, 1997), 17 for a brief discussion of this. Jacques Derrida describes it as a text that "gives the condition under which autobiographical testimony presents itself 'in the manner of a work of art,'" a term that Derrida takes from Blanchot's *The Writing of the Disaster*, which suggests that "to write one's autobiography, in order either to confess or to engage in self-analysis in order to expose oneself to the gaze of all, *in the manner of a work of art*, is perhaps to seek to survive, but through a perpetual suicide – *total insofar as fragmentary death*," in Derrida, *Demeure*, 44. The quotation from Blanchot is found in Maurice Blanchot, *The Writing of the Disaster*, trans. Ann Smock (Lincoln, NE: University of Nebraska Press, 1995), 64. Derrida has added the emphasis.

18 Blanchot returns to the notion of *désœuvrement* throughout his lifetime, but he first introduces it as "an impression of being ever so strangely out of work" [*l'impression d'un désœuvrement des plus étranges*], in Blanchot, *The Space of Literature*, trans. Ann Smock (Lincoln, NE: University of Nebraska Press, 1989), 23.

19 A notable exception to this is Lee, *Haptic Experience*. Similarly, Blanchot's association with deconstruction, underpinned by Derrida's sustained commentary on Blanchot's work, has led scholarship to largely overlook the role of the body, embodiment, and the senses in his oeuvre. There has been some work on Blanchot's engagement with phenomenology, but this is generally focused on tracing phenomenological influences in his thinking. See Arthur Cools, "Intentionnalité et singularité: Maurice Blanchot et la phénoménologie," in *Blanchot et la philosophie*, ed. Eric Hoppenot and Alain Milon (Paris: Presses Universitaires de Paris 10, 2010) and Marlène Zarader, *L'Être et le neutre: à partir de Maurice Blanchot* (Paris: Verdier, 2001).

this reason, his work demonstrates how embodiment forms through interpretation, as it requires an active reading mode.

At the level of the story (one can hardly call it a plot), the *récit* describes how a young *maquisard* is seized by Nazi commandos who transpire to be a unit from the collaborationist Russian army led by Andrey Vlasov. He is led out of the chateau where he has been hiding with his family and faces a firing squad. Suddenly, fellow Resistance fighters create a diversion. As the Nazi lieutenant leading the unit leaves to investigate, the Russian soldiers allow the young man to escape. Retaliation for the young man's evasion is dispensed unevenly: his aristocratic family faces only having the chateau searched and a manuscript stolen, while three young farmers, entirely innocent, are executed. Afterward, the young man is forever tormented by a sense of injustice. After the war, he returns to Paris where he tells the novelist André Malraux about the missing manuscript, a collection of reflections on art, which despite Malraux and Jean Paulhan's searches never reappears.

The *récit*'s testimonial dimension, easy to reconstitute at the level of representation, is counterposed with an overwhelmingly sensorial register, in particular the "feeling of extraordinary lightness" [*le sentiment de légèreté extraordinaire*] (5) that the protagonist experiences on the threshold of his death – a sensation of permanent abeyance. The *récit* both directly presents this sensation through the repeated evocation of lightness and related sublime experiences of "elation" [*l'allégresse*], "beatitude," and "ecstasy" (5) and gives shape to these sensations at the level of syntax through chiasmus. The *récit* brings the ephemeral, ineffable sensation of lightness – a feeling characterized by *absence* – into literary form. In this way, the *récit* enables critics and readers to trace how seemingly inexpressible embodied experiences can take form in literary language.

Lightness structures a series of chiastic figures, including life and death, past and future temporalities, opacity and clarity ('lightness' in English or *lumière* in French), and narrator and protagonist. It also underpins the narrative movement between suspended moments and clear historical markers, including the Allied landing in Europe (3); reference to "that year 1944," and the date 1807 inscribed on the façade of the chateau where the protagonist dwells (7), which refers to the postwar period and Napoleon's campaign; and the protagonist's meeting with Malraux, who attempts to find the missing manuscript (11). In turn, chiasmus drives the text to vacillate between direct testimony and mediated sensation. Thus, lightness acts as the pivot on which a series of formal, thematic, and conceptual pairings rotate. The thematic and conceptual pairs are given form at the level of syntax, while the syntactical units are absorbed into abstract concepts or thematic identities. They are so intertwined that it is impossible to separate these different elements. The constant vacillation between the syntactical and the thematic, the formal and the conceptual, the ineffable and the directly stated produces the sensation of lightness, itself the embodied experience of absence.

Mirroring Beckett's *The Unnamable*, which begins with an aporia that structures the text's "impasse,"[20] *The Instant of My Death* begins with an unbalanced chiasmus: "I remember a young man – a man still young – prevented from dying by death itself" (3). This is followed by others, including "I know – do I know it," "the encounter of death with death," "dead – immortal" (5), and "as if the death outside of him could only henceforth collide with the death in him" (9). The fine but slightly uneven balancing between two inverse clauses and two inverse concepts produces a sense of counterpoise, a kind of weightless suspension. These sensations are, in turn, produced through the *absence* of weight. But these sensations are nevertheless embodied. They are the embodied experience of the absence of representation, made present in the *récit*'s formal structure. Lightness is both an embodied state and a formal literary property.

Take for instance the moment death is put into abeyance. The protagonist and his family have been dragged out of the house. He asks that his family be spared having to witness his death. They form "a long, slow procession, silent, as if everything had already been done" (5). At that moment, the narrative voice asserts its mediating presence:

> I know – do I know it – that the one at whom the Germans were already aiming, awaiting but the final order, experienced then a feeling of extraordinary lightness, a sort of beatitude (nothing happy, however) – sovereign elation [*allégresse*]? The encounter of death with death?
>
> In his place, I will not try to analyze [*à sa place, je ne chercherai pas à analyser ce sentiment de légèreté*]. He was perhaps suddenly invincible. Dead – immortal. Perhaps ecstasy. Rather the feelings of compassion for suffering humanity, the happiness of not being immortal or eternal. Henceforth, he was bound to death by a surreptitious friendship [*une amitié subreptice*]. (5)

Within this brief passage we have all the elements of chiasmus, including its syntactical, rhetorical, conceptual, thematic, and embodied dimensions. The friction produced by the narrative's vacillation between life and death, past and present, self and other (the narrator made other to

---

20 See Dennis, "Radical Indecision," 183.

himself) is given form by the inverted, but slightly unbalanced syntactical clauses. The vacillation produces friction, emitting the embodied sensation of lightness, an affect that ties together two radically different poles in a relation of intimacy (*une amitié*).

Throughout the short text, the chiasmus' rotational movement is counterpoised with moments of suspension or immobility: the interruption of the protagonist's death by firing squad, the Germans' "immobility that arrested time," the narrator's tentative description of the protagonist who seems to float off into the "dense forest" [*le bois épais*] before rediscovering "a sense of the real" (5), and the "feeling of lightness that I would not know how to translate" (7), a lightness that "remains" [*demeure*], just as death is "in abeyance" [*toujours en instance*] (11). Thus, the narrative's crisscrossed diegetic temporalities pause at moments to produce the formal suspension of oppositions; these brief moments embody both the sense of temporal suspension and physical weight.

The association between lightness and the "dense forest" where the protagonist finds himself links the physical sensation of levity to philosophical notions of light or *la lumière*,[21] an unobscured realm of human activity and reason similar to the notion of *une clairière*, or a 'clearing' in the woods.[22] The relationship between *légèreté* and *lumière* emerges in the text's interplay between the revelation of the senses – the sense of entering the 'real' – and the obscurity of intentions. For instance, he owes his life to the fact that he belongs to a "noble class" even "in the eyes of the Russians" (16), yet this reason, presented with such clarity, remains highly opaque – it is an "unanalyzable feeling" (17), a sensation "I would not know how to translate" (16).

Lightness also signifies something that can be easily moved or displaced. Embodiment's linking of the opposed conceptual terms helps disperse and distribute embodied experience, before then reversing this movement and anchoring it in an inescapable materiality, such as death, the facticity of historical context, or even the physicality of sight and vision (being 'fascinated').[23] Materiality also undoes itself. The trope's twisting and turning is accomplished with an elegant *légèreté* or elan that is made manifest through textual balance, as in the conceptual

---

21 *La légèreté* has a different etymological root from *la lumière*, but they share conceptual relations in terms of materiality and perception, for instance in Descartes' theory of air being a body, which is linked to transparency and metaphors of vision. See Stefanos Geroulanos, *Transparency in Postwar France: A Critical History of the Present* (Stanford, CA: Stanford University Press, 2017), 32–35.
22 See Alfred Ernout, Antoine Meillet, and Jacques André, *Dictionnaire étymologique de la langue latine: histoire des mots*, 4th ed. (Paris: Klincksieck, 2001), 368.
23 Lee, *Haptic Experience*, 177.

inversion "I am alive. No, you are dead," or the stylistic suspension that forms the *récit*'s open-ended conclusion: "All that remains is the feeling of lightness that is death itself, or, to put it more precisely, the instant of my death henceforth always in abeyance" (20).

Over and over again, chiasmus *produces* the embodied sensation of lightness, a weightlessness found at the level of textual structure: the *récit*'s slight form, the clarity and transparency of its style, the economy of its repetition of reversible terms, and even the appearance of words spaced evenly on the page in the slim, almost insubstantial original Fata Morgana edition, printed on ivory vellum, a transparent, semi-opaque paper often used to communicate the gravity (that is, *weight*) of an event.[24] The embodied weight of chiasmus is thus what produces the text's crystalline style, its almost transparent form. However, the text's chiastic movement is slightly asymmetrical; it does not lead to a false unity. The chiasmus brings together the fragmentary form of Blanchot's writing with the integrity of embodiment, but it does not unify them in a relation of identity. Chiasmus produces the sensation of lightness in Blanchot's *récit*, which is, precisely, the embodied sensation of *absence*.

The Interpretation of Embodiment

In *The Infinite Conversation*, Blanchot suggests that the narrative voice exists only within the text; it is never prior to it. At the same time, however, it cannot exist in the text. It has only a sort of neutralizing function.[25] Blanchot describes this narrative voice in terms of an absent embodiment:

> The narrative voice that is inside only inasmuch as it is outside, at a distance without there being any distance, cannot be embodied [*ne peut s'incarner*] [...] it is always different from what utters it: it is the indifferent-difference that alters the personal voice. Let us (on a whim) call it spectral, ghostlike.

---

24 The text was originally published by Fata Morgana, the same *maison d'édition* that printed Blanchot's *The Madness of the Day* (1973, *La Folie du jour*): Maurice Blanchot, *L'Instant de ma mort* (Montpellier: Fata Morgana, 1994). This edition is itself extremely lightweight. It is about half the size of a normal book, and it is printed on semi-transparent paper vellum. It was then reprinted in a dual-language version alongside Derrida's commentary, cited above, which also loses the original edition's materiality. Perhaps the publishing house's slightly provincial and marginal status chimed with Blanchot's attraction to the *récit*'s 'minor' status, which Leslie Hill characterizes as its "relation to another time, a time outside of time and at a distance from time, a time that is the time of the *récit* itself," in Hill, *Maurice Blanchot*, 143.

25 See Hill, *Maurice Blanchot and Fragmentary Writing*, 12.

Not that it comes from beyond the grave, or even because it would once and for all represent some essential absence, but because it always tends to absent itself in its bearer and also efface him as the center.[26]

The narrative voice cannot give itself a form; it is associated with those disembodied figures of the specter and the ghost. And yet, as I have shown in my reading of *The Instant of My Death*, its own abstention or withdrawal is a form of embodiment. By way of conclusion, then, I want to explore the interpretive processes whereby this narrative voice gains a body. Chiasmus will be instructive because it is a rhetorical figure closely tied to the act of interpretation.

Merleau-Ponty gestures to a chiastic mode of interpretation in "The Chiasmus – The Intertwining," in which he begins by critiquing philosophical methods that are set up as "reflections" – methods that implicitly install a distance between experience and theoretical outcome. In order that philosophy does not prejudge its findings, it must "install itself in a locus where" reflection and intuition "have not yet been 'worked over.'" This locus offers "us all at once, pell-mell, both 'subject' and 'object,' both existence and essence, and hence give philosophy resources to redefine them." This aesthetic experience, which includes "seeing, speaking, even thinking" is "irrecusable and enigmatic." Though they are given names, these names only convey "significations in tufts [*en touffe*], thickets [*des buissons*] of proper meanings and figurative meanings" whose repetition is "the insistent reminder of a mystery as familiar as it is unexplained, of a light [*lumière*] which, illuminating [*éclairant*] the rest, remains [*demeure*] at its source in obscurity." Blanchot will later strongly evoke this language in the young man's return to the real within the wood's obscurity. For Merleau-Ponty, the task is to try to "rediscover within the exercise of seeing and speaking some of the living reference that assign them such a destiny in a language," teaching individuals "how to form our new instruments, and first of all to understand our research, our interrogation, themselves."[27]

Blanchot's *récit* acts as a space in which inchoate "pell-mell" experiences exist before reflection. This takes place in the vacillation between narrator and young man, between a narrative voice made present and one that effaces itself, in the abrupt jumps between past and present, and in the contrast between the concrete realm of historical events and the euphoric indeterminacy of temporal suspension. At the same time, a mode of interpretation is needed that makes *sense* of the indeterminate

---

26 Maurice Blanchot, *The Infinite Conversation*, trans. Susan Hanson (Minneapolis, MN: University of Minnesota Press, 1993), 386.
27 Merleau-Ponty, *The Visible and the Invisible*, 130.

events at the narrative's center. By reading chiasmus as the *récit*'s central figure – its structuring principle – I have sought to actively bring embodiment into form, to give shape to the narrative voice's spectrality in the text's embodied structure. In a similar manner to prosopopoeia, this projects the voice of the critic into the text, using the narrator as a kind of ventriloquist. The chiasmus between these voices endows embodiment with an opacity – a form of weight produced through weightlessness. At the same time, chiasmus' lightness produces a sense of effortlessness that belies the work done by the text and the interpreter to pull together the elements of embodiment into a cohesive form. Against the absence of representations of the body and the representation of lightness, I have demonstrated how absence can itself be embodied. Echoing the phenomenological principle that existence precedes essence – that presence, in other words, is brought about by action – I argue that embodiment is the *product* of literary criticism. There is no bodily essence that exists before or beyond representation, but equally the body is not merely a discursive construct. My reading of Blanchot has demonstrated how literary criticism can produce the object of its study – in this case, embodiment – beyond limit or boundary.

The Form of the Disaster

Blanchot reprises a ghostlike figure in *The Writing of the Disaster*, a work whose form brings together extreme fragmentation and negation as an ethical gesture that acknowledges the past's absent presence, a kind of passivity of being (a 'lightness'):

> passivity is measureless: for it exceeds being; it is being when being is worn down past the nub – the passivity of a past which has never been, come back again. It is the disaster defined – hinted at – not as an event of the past, but as the immemorial past (*Le Très-Haut*) which returns, dispersing by its return the present, where, ghostly, it would be experienced as a return [*revenant*].[28]

The revenant embodies the past, and this disaster, without ever being directly named, is the Holocaust, which forms the horizon of ineffability that Blanchot seeks to write from and towards.[29] The ghost is the figure of

---

28 Blanchot, *The Writing of the Disaster*, 17.
29 Blanchot uses the term "holocaust" several times but never as a proper noun, emphasizing its ancient definition as an all-consuming or sacrificial fire that heightens the event's alienness to thought: "*the holocaust, the* absolute *event of history – which is a date in history – the utter-burn where all history took fire, where the movement of Meaning was swallowed up*," in Blanchot, *The Writing of the Disaster*, 47. Emphasis in original.

disembodiment, while the disaster points to the limits of writing through its negative expression of the Holocaust. They are both reflected in what Blanchot calls "a passive that is thought," a form that approaches representation and presence but "cannot make itself present, or enter into presence, and is still less able to be represented or to constitute itself as a basis for representation." Echoing the movement of chiasmus, he characterizes this double movement as an "oscillation" that risks constituting itself as a cohesive form of thought that does not recognize its own limits: it "does not know it must be sovereignly patient – in other words, passive outside of all sovereignty."[30] Against the oscillation that figures itself as a figure in language, Blanchot gestures towards a writing of ruins that creates traces through effacement: "writing which distinguishes itself by deleting from itself all distinguishing marks, which is to say perhaps, ultimately, by effacing itself [. . .] for it seems to leave indelible or indiscernible traces."[31] This is a kind of formlessness: "to write, 'to form,' where no form holds sway, an absent meaning."[32]

Dematerialization or disembodiment permeates *The Writing of the Disaster*. Ghosts and revenants haunt the ruins of representation; writing de-faces itself, scraping off its own distinguishing features. The absence of form points to the impossibility of figuring the presence of the past. "*The danger,*" Blanchot writes, is "*that the disaster acquire [sic] meaning instead of a body.*"[33] In Blanchot's thinking, the ineffability of embodiment signals the limits of representing the Holocaust, while the limit the Holocaust places on language situates the body outside of signification. This is an emancipatory gesture to the extent that it is a form of passivity that avoids the violence of representation, the opposite pole to passivity. A writing "where no forms hold sway" – entailing a 'lightness' of touch – helps elude the kinds of power and violence that emerge through representation.

Yet, as I argued in the "Introduction" and in my analysis of Beckett, relegating the body to the realm of the inexpressible makes it more vulnerable to violence, not less. Rather, as I have tried to show with my reading of chiasmus in *The Instant of My Death*, it is possible to give form to the body without reifying it in representation. The sensation of lightness is the experience of death suspended. It is a kind of *resistance* and not simply a passivity. If Blanchot's works often partake in a radical gesture of withdrawal as a form of ethics, then understanding the chiastic form of embodiment – a body absent at the level of representation,

---

30 Blanchot, *The Writing of the Disaster*, 33.
31 Blanchot, *The Writing of the Disaster*, 34.
32 Blanchot, *The Writing of the Disaster*, 41.
33 Blanchot, *The Writing of the Disaster*, 41. Emphasis in original.

theme, or identity, but present at the level of lexis, syntax, figure, and form – helps account for the demands of the body in an ethical project that tries to make sense of the disaster. Even when the body may seem most attenuated, it can be found at the level of form. Chiasmus writes the ineffability of embodiment into the disaster without giving it over to representation. Indeed, it is embodiment that gives this 'writing of the disaster' its form.

In this sense, my reading of Blanchot here also helps pivot between Samuel Beckett and Primo Levi. In the chapter on Beckett, I explored how his autonomous literary worlds wield force as a formal principle that allows us to explore the consequences of treating language as rhetorical violence enacted upon the body. This is a world divorced from the ethical demands of representation. Primo Levi's works, on the other hand, take up the ethical demands of writing and representation posed by Blanchot. His works anchor the kind of formal violence that operates in *How It Is* in the material world of the concentration camp. If *How It Is* cautions against giving form over to violence, Levi's testimonies provide the material evidence for this principle when it is metaleptically stretched into the real world. In Levi's writing, embodiment provides the foundation of testimony; the body cannot be separated from the process of transforming itself into language. The consequences for understanding testimony's embodied foundation are important. It changes the relationship between representation and the body into one of adequacy and necessity. Here, too, the unbalanced dimension of the chiasmus proves fruitful for *Formal Matters*. It tilts the scales towards a theory of the relationship between embodiment and writing that demonstrates that embodiment takes shape in form and that it can also be *represented* directly in language.

Chapter 5

The Hunger Artist: Testimony, Representation, and Embodiment in Primo Levi

The Holocaust stands as the ultimate limit experience in postmodernist thought. It is an event so traumatic, terrifying, and even sublime that it defies all attempts to figure it in language. From Theodor Adorno's famous (and misunderstood) dictum about the barbarity of writing poetry after Auschwitz to Claude Lanzmann's insistence on the "obscenity in the very project of understanding,"[1] the event's extreme violence seems to defy aesthetic figuration and requires strict ethical norms for artistic representation, often leading to abstraction and minimalism.[2] The historian Saul Friedlander highlights a similar tension in relationship to historical evidence, arguing that the "monstrous manifestation of human 'potentialities'" should "not be forgotten or repressed," but equally "this record should not be distorted or banalized by grossly inadequate representations [. . .] there are limits to representation *which should not but can easily be transgressed*."[3] Jean-François Lyotard, one of the most prominent thinkers of what some have called the "Holocaust sublime,"[4] argues that representing "Auschwitz" is a form of forgetting:

1 The statement is "to write poetry after Auschwitz is barbaric," in Theodor W. Adorno, "Cultural Criticism and Society," in *Prisms* (Cambridge, MA: MIT Press, 1983), 34. Claude Lanzmann, Cathy Caruth, and David Rodowick, "The Obscenity of Understanding: An Evening with Claude Lanzmann," *American Imago* 48, no. 4 (1991): 473–95, 478.
2 While minimalism and abstraction, on the one hand, or an emphasis on individual stories, on the other, have come to dominate the representational conventions of the Holocaust, Kathryn L. Brackney demonstrates how these aesthetic norms have a history and excavates an alternative model of uncanny, surrealistic Holocaust representations in the post-war period, in Brackney, "Remembering 'Planet Auschwitz' During the Cold War," *Representations* 144, no. 1 (November 1, 2018): 124–53.
3 Saul Friedlander, "Introduction," in *Probing the Limits of Representation: Nazism and the "Final Solution,"* ed. Saul Friedlander (Cambridge, MA: Harvard University Press, 1992), 3. Emphasis in original.
4 On the "Holocaust sublime" see Zachary Braiterman, "Against Holocaust-Sublime: Naive Reference and the Generation of Memory," *History and Memory* 12, no. 2 (2000): 7–28.

"it cannot be represented without being missed, being forgotten anew, since it defies images and words."[5] Art should only bear witness to the *differend*, "the unstable state and instant of language wherein something which must be able to be put into phrases cannot yet be."[6] Drawing on the *differend* as that which exceeds language, Michael Bernard-Donals and Richard Glejzer argue that "what is redemptive in representations of the Shoah – what one sees – is precisely the production of this sublime excess, which troubles testimony and narrative and forces the reader to confront the horror of the limit."[7]

This excess or absence also haunts the language of testimony by Holocaust survivors. Elie Wiesel suggests that "the word has deserted the meaning it was intended to convey – one can longer make them coincide."[8] Jean Améry writes about how difficult it was to learn "the ordinary language of freedom" after his liberation, a type of language that he continues to speak "with discomfort and without real trust in its validity."[9] Aharon Appelfeld categorizes the Holocaust as "the type of enormous experience which reduces one to silence."[10] Writing in *The Drowned and the Saved* (1986, *I sommersi e i salvati*), Primo Levi insists that "we, the survivors are not the true witnesses [. . .] we are those who by their prevarications or abilities or good luck did not touch bottom. Those who did so, those who saw the Gorgon, have not returned to tell about it or have returned mute."[11] Even while rejecting the Holocaust's

---

5 Jean-François Lyotard, *Heidegger and "the Jews,"* trans. Andreas Michel and Mark S. Roberts (Minneapolis, MN: University of Minnesota Press, 1990), 26. In using 'Auschwitz' to stand in for the Holocaust, Lyotard effectuates a common metonymy in Holocaust studies that tends to posit the event as the universal model for trauma or history. As Jan Kott writes: "at the limit of that experience, Auschwitz is no exception but the rule. History is a sequence of Auschwitzes, one following the other," in Kott, "Introduction," in *This Way for the Gas, Ladies and Gentlemen*, by Tadeusz Borowski, (New York: Penguin Books, 1976), 25.
6 Lyotard, *The Differend*, 13.
7 Michael F. Bernard-Donals and Richard R. Glejzer, *Between Witness and Testimony: The Holocaust and the Limits of Representation* (Albany, NY: SUNY Press, 2001), 5.
8 Elie Wiesel, *From the Kingdom of Memory: Reminiscences* (New York: Summit Books, 1990), 14.
9 Jean Améry, *At the Mind's Limits: Contemplations by a Survivor on Auschwitz and Its Realities*, trans. Sidney Rosenfeld and Stella P. Rosenfeld (Bloomington, IN: Indiana University Press, 1980), 20.
10 Aharon Appelfeld, *Beyond Despair: Three Lectures and a Conversation with Philip Roth* (New York: Fromm International, 1994), 79.
11 Primo Levi, *The Drowned and the Saved*, trans. Raymond Rosenthal (London: Abacus, 2002), 64. Hereafter cited parenthetically as *DS*. The book was originally published in Italian with the title *I sommersi e i salvati* in 1986. *Sommersi* does not strictly signify 'drowned'; it can also mean 'submerged.' Lyotard, who was not a Holocaust survivor, puts it in less poetic terms: "To have 'really seen with his own eyes' a gas chamber would be the condition which gives one the authority to say that it exists and to persuade the unbeliever.

supposedly "unspeakable" condition as a form of religious mystification, the philosopher Giorgio Agamben has drawn on Levi's figure of the drowned to posit that "the aporia of Auschwitz" constitutes "a reality that necessarily exceeds its factual elements." At its core, testimony contains a "lacuna" that arises from the fact that "the survivors bore witness to something it is impossible to bear witness to."[12]

We are familiar with the language of excess, absence, silence, limit, and aporia. This register also dominates postmodernist approaches to the body. In this chapter, I explore the body's aporetic relationship to representation through the Holocaust testimony of Primo Levi, a writer who has had a strong influence on philosophical approaches to testimony as a form of aporia. Aporia, I argue, is closely related to both the embodied structure of testimony and the testimony of embodiment. As I noted earlier, the term derives from the Greek term *a-poros* or 'un-passable,' and it describes a condition of epistemological puzzlement. Platonic metaphors connected it to states of numb speechlessness or physical paralysis. This sense of immobility extends to the body's proprioceptive experience of its physical environment, as aporia describes a vertiginous state. In rhetorical terms, it expresses doubt, whether in the form of a question or a statement. Primo Levi himself offers an apt example of the interconnection of aporia's phenomenological, spatial, rhetorical, and epistemological dimensions in relationship to testimony when he interrupts his narration of a chemistry examination he underwent at Auschwitz in order to be chosen for a special Kommando, which almost certainly saved his life: "Today, at this very moment as I sit writing at a table," he says, "I myself am not convinced that these things really happened."[13] The rhetorical expression of doubt brings together the phenomenal experience of sitting at a table in the space of the present with uncertainty about his knowledge of the past. However, as we saw in my earlier discussion, postmodernist engagements with aporia have tended to elide the figure's embodied dimension, emphasizing its spatial relations in order to illustrate the limits of metaphysical concepts. This

---

Yet it is still necessary to prove that the gas chamber was used to kill at the time it was seen. The only acceptable proof that it was used to kill is that one died from it. But if one is dead, one cannot testify that it is on account of the gas chamber," in Lyotard, *The Differend*, 3–4.

12 Agamben, *Remnants of Auschwitz*, 32, 12–13. Note here that even while arguing against the mystification of the Holocaust, Agamben uses the metonymical term 'Auschwitz' to describe it.

13 Primo Levi, *If This Is a Man/The Truce*, trans. Stuart Woolf (London: Abacus, 1991), 109. This British edition brings together Levi's 1947 work, *Se questo è un uomo* (*If This Is a Man*), which details his experience in Auschwitz, and *La tregua* (*The Truce*), published in 1963, which depicts his journey home after his liberation. Hereafter I will cite these works as either *IM* and *T*, respectively.

disembodiment has, in turn, effaced the figure's rhetorical function as an expression of doubt, reifying it into an inexpressible absence at the heart of testimony.

The aporia of the Holocaust, the limit of representation, and the silence of the body converge in the figure of the eyewitness in Holocaust and trauma studies. Describing a Holocaust survivor's collapse on the stand at Eichmann's trial, Shoshana Felman writes that it "can be read as a parable of the collapse of language in the encounter between law and trauma"; it is "a dimension of speechless embodiment, which brings to the fore through the very failure of words the importance of the witness's body in the courtroom."[14] Yet even though the witness's body is the only guarantor of presence at the event, it nevertheless contains an aporia, because "the act of witness is only available in another place and another time,"[15] as a representation in speech or in narrative. Representation thus entails a process of dematerialization. James E. Young describes this in strikingly physical terms as the author leaving behind the linguistic trace of presence: "what was evidence for the writer at the moment he wrote is now, after it leaves his hand, only a detached and free-floating sign" that also divests the word of its "evidentiary authority, the only link it ever had to its object in the world."[16] This embodied absence is itself layered upon the absence of those Levi called the "true witnesses," who are not here to testify to the full extent of the Holocaust precisely because they experienced it. These *Muselmänner*, a problematic term to which I will return, have "lost the ability to observe, to remember, to compare and express themselves" (*DS*, 64). Their lack of speech is reflected in their "faceless presences" (*IM*, 109); their capacity for language hollowed out like their empty bodies. They are the physical form of testimony's aporia, while the lacuna of witnessing points to the inability to render the body in language.

Scholars have nevertheless questioned the notion that the Holocaust represents a limit event or an unassimilable excess in language. Dominick LaCapra has trenchantly critiqued both sublime models of the Holocaust and those that transform embodied, historical trauma into a universal experience, arguing they are a form of aestheticization that averts political action. He counters that "the discursive symptom" of theory's fetishization of limits "is the repeated, moth-to-flame movement towards paradox, aporia, or impasse that 'sublimely' brings language

---

14 Shoshana Felman, *The Juridical Unconscious: Trials and Traumas in the Twentieth Century* (Cambridge, MA: Harvard University Press, 2002), 9.
15 Bernard-Donals and Glejzer, *Between Witness and Testimony*, 58.
16 James E. Young, "Interpreting Literary Testimony: A Preface to Rereading Holocaust Diaries and Memoirs," *New Literary History* 18, no. 2 (1987): 403–23, 413.

to a halt and renders impossible (or situates as hopelessly naïve) any form of recovery or viable agency."[17] Jacques Rancière, too, is highly critical of the paradigm of the unrepresentable. In a similar manner to LaCapra's criticism of transhistorical appeals to the unrepresentable, Rancière questions the conditions under which something might be said to be "unrepresentable." He locates any such unspeakability not in the artwork's aesthetic features or in its subject matter, but in ethical and moral norms that are not proper to either one. Yet while LaCapra looks askance at aesthetics as a potential mystification of historical experience and fact, Rancière argues that aesthetic representation has a fundamentally political dimension. It helps determine the sensory field in which some segments of society – such as the witness – will be heard or seen and others will be silenced.[18]

Such approaches have demonstrated how the aporetic paradigm of the unrepresentable undermines agency. They have also noted how the unrepresentable is a normative gesture, rather than a property of art or literature. However, few scholars have connected the sublimation of the Holocaust and the aporia of testimony to the elision of the body in postmodernist thought. Indeed, as I argue in this chapter, these are inseparable. The repeated invocation of the Holocaust's unrepresentable nature, whose aporia turns on an irrecoverable embodied experience to which the figure of the witness can only gesture, forecloses both embodied and political action.

It is important to recover or strengthen the body's agency because Holocaust perpetrators were fundamentally oriented towards the goal of destroying the most important pieces of evidence: the eyewitnesses themselves. The Nazi project of biological racism was waged as a war upon Jewish and other racialized bodies in order to excise them from the German body politic, conceived of as a somatic terrain of blood and soil. By transforming Jewish victims into abject physicality, Nazis persuaded themselves they were killing "a form of slime, vomit, or excrement" rather than a human being.[19] As Hannah Arendt writes, fascism and totalitarianism sought "to manipulate the human body – with its infinite possibilities of suffering – in such a way as to make it destroy the

---

17 LaCapra, *Representing the Holocaust*, 192.
18 Rancière critiques the unrepresentable across a range of his writings, but most centrally in Jacques Rancière, "Are Some Things Unrepresentable?" in *The Future of the Image*, trans. Gregory Elliott (London: Verso, 2009); Jacques Rancière, "Why Emma Bovary Had to Be Killed," *Critical Inquiry* 34, no. 2 (January 1, 2008): 233–48; and Jacques Rancière, "L'irreprésentable en question. Entretien avec Jacques Rancière," *Europe*, no. 926–927 (2006): 425–54.
19 Christopher E. Forth, "The Body," in *Writing the Holocaust*, ed. Jean-Marc Dreyfus and Daniel Langton (London: Bloomsbury Academic, 2011), 161.

human person as inexorably as do certain diseases of organic origin."[20] Dehumanizing and objectifying the body dis-figures the locus of speech and the inviolable guarantor of presence. Since the body was the brute site of genocide, we must be careful not to reinforce its disintegration, fragmentation, or unspeakability, because this is also what makes it the primary site of agency and resistance. It is the embodied locus of speech and sensation. By insisting on both the unspeakability of the Holocaust and the unrepresentability of the body, postmodernist scholarship problematically echoes the body's devaluation.

The repeated invocation of the unrepresentable also fails to understand the rhetorical dimension of this gesture and risks silencing both historical event and embodied experience. In her critique of the "unspeakable," Naomi Mandel notes that "to say something is unspeakable is not only to conjure 'something' and describe it; it is, moreover, an act of speech, a discursive move that produces knowledge even as it gestures towards knowledge's limits."[21] In contrast to the mystification of the Holocaust, Mandel focuses on speech's embodied dimension, which "conjoins the act of physical articulation, the performative quality of language, the space (however virtual) of a public arena, and the presence of a community."[22] Speech originates in the body, is articulated in space – either physical or implied – and presumes the existence of others who respond with their own embodied act of listening. When we invoke the unspeakable – or other analogous terms like the unrepresentable – we efface the embodied subject who speaks.[23] Mandel continues: "by drawing attention to the semantic (language's limits), the unspeakable directs the critical gaze away from physical presence, effecting a certain dissociation from the body of the speaker and from her act of speech."[24] To invoke the unspeakable is a rhetorical act of *silencing*. But not only that: it elides the embodied presence that is both the origin and the guarantor of testimony, the form on which so many of the *facts* of the Holocaust have depended for their telling.[25]

20 Hannah Arendt, *The Origins of Totalitarianism* (New York: Harcourt Brace Jovanovich, 1973), 453.
21 Naomi Mandel, *Against the Unspeakable: Complicity, the Holocaust, and Slavery in America* (Charlottesville, VA; London: University of Virginia Press, 2006), 37–38.
22 Mandel, *Against the Unspeakable*, 38.
23 While not entirely commensurate, the unrepresentable has a similar function to the unspeakable in both Holocaust studies and postmodernist criticism. As I explored in the "Introduction," representation, too, has a close relationship to the body, not least through the Platonic valorization of speech. Throughout this chapter, I take the unrepresentable and the unspeakable as conjoined rhetorical gestures.
24 Mandel, *Against the Unspeakable*, 38.
25 The witness's body has received ample attention in Holocaust scholarship, but the vast majority of it insists upon the way trauma fragments embodiment. Apart from Mandel,

In this chapter, I restore the link between embodiment and speech in the Holocaust testimony. Or rather, I will seek to restore the link between embodiment and *representations of* Holocaust testimony, of testimony as an inherently representational form. Focusing on this work as not only historical, juridical testimony but also as a representation of speech shifts the terms of the debates around what is unrepresentable. As Mandel notes, there is "a distinction between the survivor's inability or unwillingness to speak, on the one hand, and the rhetorical work of the unspeakable, on the other. [. . .] *Representations* of survivor testimony are representations of such speech, not of the (presumably unrepresentable) Holocaust, nor of the (too often sacralized) survivor."[26] My focus on the relationship between embodiment and representation, as with my focus on embodiment and form in earlier chapters, demonstrates the *rhetorical* function of so many assumptions about what a body or language can or cannot do. Whereas previous chapters in *Formal Matters* have explored how form affords more opportunities for accounting for the presence of embodiment beyond representation, this chapter attends to the relationship between the body and representation. I argue that while witnessing might only be grasped through its absence – that is, by its *representation* – embodiment structures this relationship. Postmodernist thought remains beholden to an aesthetic model in which representation can only afford a crude form of mimesis, and thus turns to the sublime or the ineffable. By contrast, I engage with the work of Rancière to argue that literary language can represent embodied experience through an "immediate adequation of thought and sensible materiality."[27] The immanence of embodied experience, which can be rendered in language and representation at the very level of syntax, challenges the unrepresentability of the Holocaust and the body.

Literary testimony about the Holocaust – a genocide which annihilated the vast majority of its potential witnesses as pure bodily objects – poses significant challenges to representation. Virtually every scholar

---

Michael G. Levine is one of the few scholars to shift away from a focus on the unrepresentable by attending to the witness's body and how this body both seeks to express the trauma of the Holocaust and, when it cannot, where texts signify this silence. He puts forward the notion of the "body as witness," or bodies that are "transfused with and mutely driven by historical energies that have yet to be metabolized, how they are inhabited by memories painfully lodged in particular openings, organs, tissues, and cavities," in Levine, *The Belated Witness: Literature, Testimony, and the Question of Holocaust Survival* (Stanford, CA: Stanford University Press, 2006), 2.

26 Mandel, *Against the Unspeakable*, 100. Italics in the original.
27 Jacques Rancière, "The Aesthetic Revolution and Its Outcomes: Emplotments of Autonomy and Heteronomy," *New Left Review*, no. 14 (April 2002): 133–51, 135.

of the Holocaust has been at pains to point this out. Yet this does not mean we should turn away from representation or invoke its limits. Rather, it is *only* through representation that we can apprehend the witness's embodied speech. This does not, in turn, signal that the body somehow escapes representation or signification. On the contrary, the responsibility to represent the speaking witness – an action that is inextricably tied up with the witness's body – may lead to more modes of representation, not less. Embodiment confers weight, presence, and veracity upon representations of testimony. Holocaust testimony does not point to the limits of representation; nor does the body fundamentally escape signification. The inseparability of testimony and embodiment lead to the opposite: they disclose how such limits are themselves rhetorical rather than intrinsic qualities of either representation or experience.

I explore these questions through the testimonial literature of the Holocaust survivor, Primo Levi, in particular his literary memoirs, *If This Is a Man* (1947, *Se questo è un uomo*) and *The Truce* (1963, *La Tregua*), and *The Drowned and the Saved*, a collection of essays. *If This Is a Man* describes how Levi, a native of Turin, Italy, was arrested in December 1943 fighting with an Italian partisan group affiliated with the Resistance. After passing through a detention camp, he was deported to Auschwitz III or Auschwitz Monowitz, the labor camp affiliated with the chemical company IG Farben. A chemist by training, Levi was eventually selected to work in the Chemical Kommando, a squad of skilled prisoners tasked with chemical production. This turn of events, combined with his "good fortune" (*IM*, 15) to be deported to Auschwitz in January 1944, when labor scarcities meant that the Nazis had reduced indiscriminate killings, helped Levi survive the war. *The Truce* takes up Levi's liberation from the camp, detailing in often absurd vignettes his Odyssean journey home to Italy via the Soviet Union. Levi insisted upon the testimonial project of his writing; it is grounded in historical and phenomenological fact. But his works are also self-consciously literary, drawing attention to the means and processes of representation. They frequently reflect upon the nature of representation and its relationship to lived, historical realities.

Levi's work reminds us that *all* testimony and speech is a form of representation, even when it emerges extemporaneously from one's mouth immediately after one has seen something with one's eyes. Levi frequently describes brute physical sensations like pain, hunger, cold, and fatigue (sensations that often provide the impetus for him to tell his story), as well as the embodied affects of shame, disgust, and desire. Levi's work has also often been cited as evidence for the aporetic structure of testimony,[28] while scholars have also largely overlooked the importance of embodiment in his work.[29] Indeed, little scholarship has explored the connection between embodiment and testimony in his writing. In fact, the insistence on the aporetic structure of testimony and the disembodied dimension of his narratives goes hand in hand: if one foregrounds embodied experience in Levi's work then it becomes clear that testimony is not aporetic.[30] Embodiment is what gives testimony its representational weight.

The relationship between representation, testimony, and embodiment is far from straightforward, however. Levi identified a lacuna at the heart of testimony, as I cited earlier. Yet these rhetorical gestures towards incompleteness or absence are counterbalanced by a sensorium and sense of materiality that saturate all levels of language. For instance, he often notes that the Lager – his preferred term for the concentration

---

[28] This is largely as result of Giorgio Agamben's extensive engagement with Levi's *The Drowned and the Saved* in *Remnants of Auschwitz*, in which Agamben elaborates his notion of the lacuna or aporia of testimony.

[29] The early elision of the body in studies of Levi's work often reflects Levi's own ambivalence about the body as a fragile but inescapable carapace, or "container," as Charlotte Ross describes it. Ross has provided the most extensive study in English of embodiment in Levi's oeuvre. Considering the entirety of Levi's corpus, Ross argues that the body acts as a container of the self, an ambivalent figure of both containment and porosity that incarnates Levi's humanist anxieties about the body, in Ross, *Primo Levi's Narratives of Embodiment: Containing the Human* (Abingdon: Routledge, 2010). Marco Caracciolo has also explored Levi's work in the context of narrative theory, embodied consciousness, and cognitive science in Caracciolo, *Embodiment and the Cosmic Perspective in Twentieth-Century Fiction* (New York; Abingdon: Routledge, 2020). For Italian scholarship that addresses the body in Levi, see Giuseppina Santagostino, *Primo Levi: metamorfosi letterarie del corpo* (Moncalieri: Centro interuniversitario di ricerche sul viaggio in Italia, 2004) and Pierpaolo Antonello, *Il ménage a quattro: Scienza, filosofia, tecnica nella letteratura italiano del novecento* (Florence: Le Monnier, 2005).

[30] Indeed, much of the scholarship on Levi emphasizes the humanistic tradition that he was educated in and on which he often drew, including his valorization of science and reason and the influence of Homer, Dante, and the classical canon. See, for instance, Risa B. Sodi, *A Dante of Our Time: Primo Levi and Auschwitz* (New York: Peter Lang, 1990) and Lynn M. Gunzberg, "Down Among the Dead Men: Levi and Dante in Hell," *Modern Language Studies*, 16 (1986): 10–28. This humanistic strand of thought often devalues the body, positing it as the material extension of the mind. Postmodernist criticism later reexamined Levi's work in relation to 'posthumanist' thinkers like Foucault, Agamben, Adorno, and Lytoard, arguing that Levi in fact problematizes the Enlightenment figure of the universal man and thus also interrupts narratives of progress and reason that many postmodernist thinkers have associated with the Holocaust. In addition to Ross, *Primo Levi's Narratives of Embodiment*, see also Jonathan Druker, *Primo Levi and Humanism After Auschwitz: Posthumanist Reflections* (New York: Palgrave Macmillan, 2009). Apart from some notable exceptions, however, this postmodernist criticism still largely occludes the role embodiment plays in Levi's work, not least because it often emphasizes the aporetic nature of testimony, which pivots around the embodied absence of the 'true' witness, the one who by virtue of having experienced the full extent of the camps does not return to tell the tale.

camp – deformed language, and, as he expresses in his metaleptical breakdown of the narrative levels between writing and the camp, he sometimes has trouble believing such events took place. But his writing also registers the constant hum of embodied experience:

> At a distance of forty years we still remember, in a purely acoustic form, words and sentences pronounced around us in languages [*lingue*] we did not know and did not learn afterwards. [. . .] These foreign voices became engraved on our memories as on an empty, blank magnetic tape; in the same manner, a famished stomach rapidly assimilates even indigestible food. (*DS*, 73)

The term *lingue*, meaning both 'languages' and 'tongues' evokes the materiality of language. It is consumed and broken down by the body, like the act of digesting. This passage implicitly connects the deeply embodied nature of his memories to the act of representation, depicted in the metaphor of the magnetic tape that literally records speech and sound in a physical form, allowing it to endure.

I argue that Levi's work reveals testimony's embodied structure rather than an absence or lacuna. This chapter will focus largely on two figures that seem to point to the limits of testimony and the unrepresentability of the body: aporia and objects. As I noted above, aporia, or other related terms like lacuna and the unspeakable, feature heavily in both witness testimonies and critical theorizations of the Holocaust. I explore aporia as a material terrain of language through which the embodied subject moves in order to make language – representation – meaningful. The second aspect I focus on is the relationship between subjects and objects. The Holocaust violently objectified humans as a precursor to their murder, but objects also form the boundary between life and death in the Lager. In this sense, the aporia of witnessing is embodied in the primacy of objects: they are often more valuable than human life. Drawing on Rancière's critique of the unrepresentable, I explore the 'paratactic' relationship between bodies and objects in Levi's writing. This reframes the relationship between bodies and objects from one of metonymic replacement to mimetic correspondence, affording more opportunities for representation, not less.

The Substance of Testimony

Before I explore aporia and objects – putative figures of testimonial doubt and embodied absence – I will reflect upon the relationship between the representation of testimony and embodiment. Debates about the most appropriate way to represent the Holocaust – and whether one should even attempt to represent it in the first place – have often been heated. The role of fiction (or 'aestheticization') has been a particular flashpoint.[31] Responding to what he saw as inexcusable aesthetic transgressions in the American mini-series *Holocaust* (1978) and *Schindler's List* (1993), Claude Lanzmann asserts that "fiction is the worst transgression for the history of the Holocaust." What fiction betrays, however, is not so much historical accuracy, but rather an attempt to represent such facts at all. Instead of pointing to its own limits, fiction fails to fill the gaps, what Lanzmann calls its "nothingness" [*le néant*].[32] For similar reasons, literary and historical scholars of the Holocaust have often focused their attention on modernist representation, with its tendency towards abstraction, fragmentation, and self-referentiality – all aesthetic strategies that defamiliarize the representational process.[33] Such approaches, as I noted above, emphasize how language cannot fully assimilate traumatic experience and historical fact, breaking down under its own weight and revealing the limits of representation. However, while Holocaust survivors who wrote testimonial literature often express incomprehension of or disbelief in their experience, they also frequently suggest that language, specifically in its aesthetic or fictional form, is the only way to represent such memories. Levi insists upon language's necessity rather than its insufficiency. He does not so much voice an anxiety about language failing him but rather that no one will *listen*.

The shift away from the insufficiency of language to a concern about the refusal to listen changes the terms of the debate around the limits of representation. In the "Introduction," I discussed how aesthetic acts like speaking, listening, and acting are ways of making subjects visible within political spaces of representation. Depriving individuals of the right to speak or to be heard, in a courtroom for instance, renders their embodied experience invisible, that is, *unrepresented*. But this failure of representation is not proper to either the embodied subjects that seek to make their experiences heard, nor to the linguistic vehicle or medium of

---

31 See, for instance, the heated debates around *Schindler's List*. Essays addressing these debates are found in Yosefa Loshitzky, *Spielberg's Holocaust: Critical Perspectives on Schindler's List* (Bloomington, IN: Indiana University Press, 1997). These anxieties continue to resurface periodically, particularly with works that self-consciously play with the boundary between fiction and history, such as Jonathan Littell's controversial *The Kindly Ones* (2006, *Les Bienveillantes*), written from the viewpoint of a Nazi perpetrator.
32 Lanzmann states that "la fiction est la transgression la plus grave dans une histoire pareille." This is quoted in David Carroll, "The Limits of Representation and the Right to Fiction: Shame, Literature, and the Memory of the Shoah," *L'Esprit Créateur* 39, no. 4 (1999): 68–79, 71.
33 See, for instance, Hayden White, "Historical Emplotment and the Problem of Truth," in *Probing the Limits of Representation: Nazism and the "Final Solution,"* ed. Saul Friedländer (Cambridge, MA: Harvard University Press, 1992).

this experience. The failure of representation derives from a refusal on the part of others to recognize language's incontrovertible materiality: the eyewitness as the embodiment of language.

Over and over again, Levi comes back to the disjunction between the materiality of language and the refusal to listen. In a short commentary on the theatrical adaptation of *If This is a Man*, Primo Levi likens himself to "the ancient mariner in Coleridge's ballad," *The Rime of the Ancient Mariner*, compelled by an incontrollable need "to tell my story even before my physical hunger was satiated." Although he repeats his tales "dozens of times in just a few days, to friends, enemies and strangers," he is not assuaged; he has "not finished even now."[34] Narrative becomes a primary lifeforce: "we hope not to live *and* tell our story," Levi continues in the same commentary, "but to live *in order to* tell our story."[35] Levi returns to this compulsive, insatiable need to tell in his preface to *If This Is a Man*, noting that "the need to tell our story to 'the rest' [*gli altri*] to make 'the rest' participate in it, had taken on for us, before our liberation and after, the character of an immediate and violent impulse, to the point of competing with our other elementary needs." The "rest" here is not only those who were not imprisoned in the camps, but also the more abstract conception of the "others" (*gli altri*), as if an enormous experiential gap exists between the two groups. This embodied compulsion structures the book's "fragmentary character" (*IM*, 15), in which episodes are presented "not in logical succession, but in order of urgency" (*IM*, 16). But the book's "fragmentary" (or rather, episodic) form points to the body's drive to 'fill up' on words and stories, rather than testifying to its absence. Hunger is a structural imperative of Levi's testimony. At the most fundamental level, embodied experience is what organizes and determines the relation between words in Levi's testimony.

Throughout *If This is a Man* and *The Truce*, Levi yokes together the representation of testimony and the embodied experience of hunger. The prisoners all experience the same dreams, which meld into one another. In the first dream, Levi sits down at a bountiful table and begins to tell the tale of his "hunger and of the lice-control, and of the Kapo who hit me on the nose." The sensation of telling his story "is an intense pleasure, physical, inexpressible, to be at home, among friendly people and to have so many things to recount." Yet gradually he notices that no one is listening to him; the audience is "completely indifferent."

---

34 Primo Levi, "Note to the Theatre Version of *If This Is a Man*," in *The Black Hole of Auschwitz* (Cambridge: Polity Press, 2005), 24. This stanza from Coleridge's poem also forms the epigraph of *The Drowned and the Saved*.
35 Levi, "Note to the Theatre Version," 4.

The intense pleasure gives way to "a desolating grief," a "pain in its pure state, not tempered by a sense of reality and by the intrusion of extraneous circumstances" (*IM*, 66). At this point, the dream dissolves into another, in which "you not only see the food, you feel it in your hands, distinct and concrete, you are aware of its rich and striking smell; someone in the dream even holds it up to your lips, but every time a different circumstance intervenes to prevent the consummation of the act" (*IM*, 67). Every night "the dream of Tantalus and the dream of the story are woven into a texture of more indistinct images: the suffering of the day, composed of hunger, blows, cold, exhaustion, fear and promiscuity, turns at night-time into shapeless nightmares of unheard-of violence, which in free life would only occur during a fever" (*IM*, 68). The entire sensorium is present here, melding the substance of language and embodiment, creating the "distinct and concrete" image Levi provides. (He elsewhere describes a "hunger and desolation so concrete" [*IM*, 122].) The limit here is of reception rather than expression. Levi expresses anxiety that no one will listen to what happened, not that he is unable to represent it.[36] The act of telling is thus accompanied with a process of evacuation that leaves Levi "alone in the center of a grey and turbid nothing" (*T*, 379).

The physical act of telling is accompanied by a negative gesture of disembodiment that results from a failure to listen rather than a failure to speak. The gesture's ethical failures bring us back to the dangers of postmodernism's focus on the impossibility of representing or witnessing. The limit is not metaphysical, ahistorical, or abstract. Perpetrators, bystanders, spectators, readers, critics – *gli altri*, "the others" – impose this limit through their refusal to recognize the enormity of this embodied experience. Emptying out signifies a refusal to listen to and acknowledge the physical body's incontrovertible evidence, what Michael G. Levine calls the "body as witness."[37] These two actions converge in the figure of the *Muselmann*, the faceless, hollowed-out container of a human being, the 'true' witness who has lost the ability to speak.

---

36 The difficulty that Levi faced publishing *If This Is a Man* after writing it demonstrates that there was some basis to his anxieties. This is a common worry in Holocaust testimony, and it challenges the long-held 'myth of silence,' which holds that in the post-war period Jewish survivors of the camps did not want to tell their stories. As Hasia Diner has demonstrated in the American context, Holocaust survivors and Jewish communities widely commemorated and memorialized the Holocaust. It was subsequent generations who distanced themselves from this history, from which gradually emerged the truism of a culture of 'forgetting.' See Hasia R. Diner, *We Remember with Reverence and Love: American Jews and the Myth of Silence after the Holocaust, 1945–1962* (New York: New York University Press, 2009).

37 M. Levine, *The Belated Witness*, 2.

The *Muselmann* is the physical embodiment of the aporia of testimony – the "embodied product of the Lager."[38] The *Muselmänner* are "faceless presences," whose capacity for language is hollowed out like their bodies, "too empty to really suffer" (*IM*, 96). The *Muselmann* is "a staggering corpse, a bundle of physical functions in its last convulsions."[39] They are "nameless hulks" or *Figuren* – figures, dolls, or "puppets," as Levi often describes them.[40]

Levi's representation of the *Muselmann* – like the term itself – is highly problematic but also remarkably influential, not least in Agamben's characterization of the aporia of testimony in *Remnants of Auschwitz*.[41] I earlier noted that Levi describes the *Muselmänner* as "those who saw the Gorgon" (*DS*, 64). In Greek mythology, the Gorgon is the female creature with serpent hair whose gaze kills by turning the viewer into stone. Agamben explores the etymology of this metaphor, arguing that since in Greek the etymology of face (*prosopon*) designates "what stands before the eyes, what gives itself to be seen," the Gorgon does not, properly speaking, have a face. It is an "anti-face" – or *antiprosopon* – that "represents the impossibility of vision" or "what cannot *not* be seen."[42] The task of bearing witness on behalf of the *Muselmann* is a kind of *antiprosopopoeia*, or an 'unmaking' of faces and figures. The *Muselmann* is the figure stripped of its figurality, turned into pure *Figuren*. This 'living dead' figure – deprived of speech through the material conditions of the camp – embodies the aporia of testimony as an elision of embodiment from language. The *Muselmann*'s negative form, then, seems to point to the difficulty of representing embodiment.

On the one hand, Levi's representation of the *Muselmänner* presents them as faceless figures and walking corpses – abject forms of embodiment. The *Muselmann*, deprived of a face, is unable to speak. On the other hand, the embodied structure of representation in Levi's testimony – the compulsive urge to tell – enacts a kind of prosopopoeia. This is an aestheticization of the figure that helps fill up a hollow form, preventing those who listen from turning away. Thus, we might think of the

---

38 Sharon B. Oster, "The Female Muselmann in Nazi Concentration Camp Discourse," *The Journal of Holocaust Research* 34, no. 3 (July 2, 2020): 198–219, 199.
39 Améry, *At the Mind's Limits*, 3.
40 Agamben, *Remnants of Auschwitz*, 48.
41 See Sharon B. Oster, "Impossible Holocaust Metaphors: The *Muselmann*," *Prooftexts* 34, no. 3 (2014): 302–48, for an astute critique of the way Holocaust studies has uncritically adopted the term from Levi's work. Oster demonstrates how the *Muselmann* was not an absolute ontological category that destined one to death or silence; prisoners could move in and out of this state. The focus on the *Muselmann* as a fixed category forecloses communication and agency.
42 Agamben, *Remnants of Auschwitz*, 53.

Muselmann as coming into existence when we turn our faces away, an aporia of testimony that emerges not from a limit of representation but from an ethical failure to listen. The limit of representation is not intrinsic to either the experience or the work of art, but rather emerges from a refusal to engage with the aesthetic dimension of Holocaust testimony, which is the only way to render the embodied materiality of this experience in language. As I will demonstrate in the next section, the aesthetic figure of prosopopoeia helps trace an embodied path through this aporia, projecting a vital figure of language in the face of the living dead, the subject without speech.

The Embodied Terrain of Aporia

It has now become commonplace in Holocaust studies to assert that testimony is inherently aporetic. Aporia relates to both moral, ethical injunctions about the need for highly referential, accurate representations of the Holocaust (anchored in the figure of the eyewitness) and the Holocaust's supposedly unspeakable, unrepresentable, or irretrievable nature. These two opposed injunctions are actually tied to each other: when most of the eyewitnesses never survived, how can referential, accurate, and thorough representations exist? In the absence of the eyewitness, the event can only be represented obliquely, by calling attention to the gaps in testimony. This aporia, I argue, is not proper to either the Holocaust or our methods of representation. It emerges from an ethical imperative to ensure that representations of the Holocaust do justice to the suffering of those involved, even as the evocation of limits and ineffability obscures the normative operations of this gesture.

As I noted in "The Corporeal Urn," this employment of aporia, characterized by Agamben's work, effaces its own origins as a rhetorical figure for doubt, reifying it into an inexpressible absence at the heart of testimony. In turn, by eliding the rhetorical dimension of aporia, such approaches also efface its embodied origin. In this chapter, I recover aporia's embodied dimension as a state of paralytic speechlessness and bring it into dialogue with its spatial facets. While prosopopoeia and catachresis have a direct relationship to embodiment, either performing or projecting it, aporia provides the material realm of language in which the body moves. Aporia is the terrain of linguistic form that the subject struggles through in a physical quest to understand and bear witness to embodied experience. Levi's testimonial literature often depicts aporia both as an embodied form of speech – the "flickering" tongue of language in *If This is a Man* (an image to which I will return) – and a literal *topos*, or place; it is rhetorical doubt made concrete in the physical space of the Lager. If elsewhere I have explored how embodiment provides the grounds for poetic and rhetorical figures, here aporia provides the ground for the figuration of embodiment. Aporia is an untamed, savage material terrain, the vast space of the Lager that one must physically traverse (and survive) in order to try and understand it.

The work of the French philosopher and Holocaust survivor Sarah Kofman is particularly enlightening in terms of understanding aporia as a wild, physical terrain. For Kofman, philosophical knowledge or wisdom (*metis*, meaning wily intelligence or cunning) is a way of discovering *poroi*, passages through aporia. This form of cunning, exemplified by Odysseus, "progresses by twists and turns,"[43] in a similar manner to the contortions of the term 'trope.' It "allows us to blaze a trail, a *poros*, a way, to find a path through obstacles, to discover an expedient (*poros*), to find a way out (*poros*), of a situation from which there is no way out, which is aporetic." The aporia of witnessing or of the body in the Holocaust is often conceived as a limit. Yet Kofman argues that aporia is in fact found "wherever indeterminacy (*apeiras*) reigns, wherever there are no limits and no directions, whenever we are trapped, encircled or caught in inextricable bonds," at which point *metis* "discovers stratagems, expedients, tricks, ruses, machinations, [...] which allow us to move from the absence of limits to determinacy."[44] *Poros* "is a matter of blazing a trail where no trail exists, of crossing an impassable expanse of territory, an unknown, hostile and boundless world, an *apeiron* which it is impossible to cross from end to end." *Poros* is associated with the sea, hence the centrality of Odysseus, but it also describes "a passage opened up across a chaotic expanse which it transforms into an ordered, qualified space by introducing differentiated routes, making visible the various directions of space, by giving direction to an expanse which was initially devoid of all contours, of all landmarks." Rather than just a sea space, it is associated with "the image of chaos itself," Tartarus, or "a realm of wild swirling squalls where there are no directions, no left and no right, no up and no down, where there are no fixed directions, where one can find no landmarks, no bearings to travel by." *Poroi* are not just sea-routes through this chaos but are also related to "*peirata*, the landmarks, the points of light that mark a sailor's course," or equally *poros* "can take the form of a link that binds, just as the action of linking can sometimes take on the appearance of making a traverse, of making one's

---

43 Sarah Kofman, "Beyond Aporia?" in *Post-Structuralist Classics*, ed. Andrew E. Benjamin (London; New York: Routledge, 1988), 8.
44 Kofman, "Beyond Aporia?" 9.

way."⁴⁵ Thus while Tartarus is the "aporetic place *par excellence*," buffeted by "the irresistible violence of the winds that rage there," it is also a realm without exit: "it links forever. It is impossible to flee; Tartarus extends to form a gigantic mesh which has no end and no bounds," akin to "the hunting nets and fishing nets which the *metis* of men invents to defeat the *metis* of animals and to trap them."⁴⁶

Kofman's analysis of aporia is strikingly similar to Levi's description of the Lager throughout his work. The Lager is Tartarus – the wild realm of aporia battered by violent winds in which one cannot establish a firm footing. The Lager is aporia made concrete, a vast plane governed by senseless regulations and rituals: a slave camp that never produced any products, a place where "everything is forbidden" (*IM*, 35) but also "everything was free" (*IM*, 152). The Lager's inexplicable logic is encapsulated by an exchange between Levi and a camp guard upon his arrival. "'*Warum?*'" [Why?] Levi asks, to which a guard responds, "'*Hier ist kein warum*'" [There is no why here] (*IM*, 35). Another prisoner carves "*Ne pas chercher à comprendre*" [Do not seek to understand] (*IM*, 109) into the bottom of his bowl to continually remind himself of the camp's absence of meaning. Just as the Lager suspends the normal rules of logic and meaning, so too does it divest the conventional markers of human existence, including time, space, and language, of sense. The future is "an invincible barrier" (*IM*, 123); time is "sterile and stagnant," a "superfluous material" that collapses into an endless "world of mud" (*IM*, 122–23). This world of mud – the formalist universe of Beckett's *How It Is* manifested as a terrifying reality – reveals the hidden form of human agency, transforming new arrivals into "miserable and sordid puppets" (*IM*, 32) whose existence is subordinated to objects: shoes, bowls, and spoons. Although the Lager is "a perpetual Babel, in which everyone shouts orders and threats in languages never heard before" (*IM*, 44), its senselessness requires a new register:

> Just as our hunger is not that feeling of missing a meal, so our way of being cold has need of a new word [*un nome particolare*]. We say "hunger," we say "tiredness," "fear," "pain," we say "winter" and they are different things. They are free words, created and used by free men who lived in comfort and suffering in their homes. If the Lagers had lasted longer a new, harsh language would have been born; and only this language could express what it means to toil all day in the wind, with the temperature below freezing, wearing only a shirt, underpants, cloth jacket and trousers, and in one's body nothing but weakness, hunger and knowledge of the end drawing near. (*IM*, 129)

---

45 Kofman, "Beyond Aporia?" 10.
46 Kofman, "Beyond Aporia?" 11.

Throughout his testimonial literature, Levi often frames everyday terms with quotation marks, defamiliarizing their normative uses and highlighting their representational function. Yet this seemingly insufficient language, which belongs to "free men," nevertheless produces a language of embodiment, not least to describe "the prescribed hunger, that chronic hunger unknown to free men, which makes one dream at night, and settles in all the limbs of one's body" (*IM*, 43). Because the Lager is organized around the destruction of the body, the body also forms the primary site of resistance: "One has to fight against the current: to battle every day and every hour against exhaustion, hunger, cold, and the resulting inertia" (*IM*, 98). Embodiment is a form of *poros*. It carves a path through aporia. It lays down boundaries, markers, and points of light – however precarious and fragile such landmarks are – making the space visible and comprehensible. The body does not point to the limits of testimony, but rather shapes the physical terrain of witnessing into an embodied ground of understanding.

This notion of embodiment as *poros*, carving out a passage through the wild terrain of aporetic chaos, is evident in one of the central chapters of *If This Is a Man*, "The Canto of Ulysses," which takes its title from a passage in Canto XXVI of Dante's *Inferno*. This chapter brings together many aspects of Kofman's characterization of *poros* and aporia, the aporetic expanse of Tartarus, the figure of Odysseus (here Ulysses) navigating squalls, the cunning of *metis* and the search for knowledge, and the figure of speech as a body. While many scholars have posited this chapter as evidence for Levi's humanism and, by extension, the sovereign humanistic subject, it is noticeable that, as Jonathan Druker notes, it is "framed by an actual quest for food" and Levi's attempted recitation of the Canto is performed "with the urgency of a fundamental physical need."[47] As I noted earlier, Levi often yokes together telling and hunger. The compulsive need to tell mirrors the prisoners' once inescapable hunger, with the mouth serving as the organ of both speech and mastication. The prisoners often chew on language as if it was food in their sleep, dreaming of telling their story at dinner tables.

Here, it is not so much language that replaces foodstuffs, but rather a physical quest through the space of the camp that becomes a metaphorical attempt to carve a route through aporia – to give language a body. One spring day, Levi is permitted to accompany his Kommando's Pikolo, or messenger-clerk, to fetch the pot of soup for lunch. This Pikolo, Jean, represents the wily intelligence of *metis*: "he had chosen the path cleverly so that we could have to make a long detour" (*IM*, 117), thus

---

47 Druker, *Primo Levi and Humanism After Auschwitz*, 37.

prolonging their time away from manual labor. Jean confesses to Levi that he would love to learn Italian: "Why not immediately, one thing is as good as another, the important thing is not to lose time, not to waste this hour." Levi suddenly feels the urge to teach Jean Italian through the Canto. There is "no time to change"; Jean "*will* understand" (*IM*, 118). As Jean leads Levi through the Tartarus of the camp, the vast terrain governed by the law of incomprehension ('there is no why here'), speech surges like a bodily force. Levi recites:

> Then of that age-old fire the loftier horn
> Began to mutter and move, as a wavering flame
> Wrestles against the wind and is over-worn;
> And, like a speaking tongue vibrant to frame
> Language, the tip of it flickering to and fro
> Threw out a voice and answered: 'When I came . . . (*IM*, 118)

> [*Lo maggior corno della fiamma antica*
> *Cominciò a crollarsi mormorando,*
> *Pur come quella cui vento affatica.*
> *Indi, la cima in qua e in là menando*
> *Come fosse la lingua che parlasse*
> *Mise fuori la voce, e disse: Quando . . .*][48]

Aporia is spatialized. It is an exposed terrain that "wrestles against the wind," or, more literally in Italian as "that which the wind exhausts" [*Pur come quella cui vento affatica*]. Within this wild terrain, language begins to flicker precariously, as an "age-old" flame that wavers or sputters, picking up strength and vitality as it becomes increasingly embodied in the figure of "a speaking tongue" [*la lingua che parlasse*]. Playing on the double meaning of *la lingua*, which can mean both language and tongue (as opposed to the system of language, *il linguaggio*), speech is condensed to its bodily organ.[49] This flickering tongue of language rises out of the terrain of aporia, which organizes a series of discursive impasses: the wind that seeks to extinguish the flame of language, the "hole" (*IM*, 118) or "lacuna" (*IM*, 120) in Levi's memory that prevents him from reconstructing the Canto in its entirety, and the dangers of passing SS officers and spies. The flickering tongue of language lights the way through aporia, like the *peirata* that once illuminated a sailor's route.

---

48 Levi is translating the Canto from French to Italian for Pikolo, although it is in Italian in the original version. Levi alludes to the difficulties of translating: "Here I stop and try to translate" (*IM*, 118).
49 Indeed, a third meaning of *la lingua* as a flame's tongue complements the notion of language as a force that penetrates or marks the body. I thank Rosa Mucignat for drawing my attention to this meaning.

As Levi and the Pikolo move through the camp, then, they also move through the aporia of discourse, captured in the image of the sea's vast expanse, which represents aporia's limitless space: "... So on the open sea I set forth," Levi recites. Yet this action is bolstered by the figure of speech as a body, a flickering tongue. Levi sets forth [*misi me*] across this expanse, casting language down like "a chain which has been broken" as if "throwing oneself on the other side of a barrier." Embodied speech, in other words, creates boundaries and limits, as well as providing a *poros* across "the open sea." This open sea is made material in the aporetic image of "uncharted distances" that one sets off to explore in order to "follow after knowledge and excellence." Even though words, especially translation, continually fail Levi, he is sustained by the "impulse" to tell, an embodied urgency to move through the discursive aporia of the camp carried along on language's tongue. At this moment, Levi interjects to say that it was as if he "was hearing [the Canto] for the first time: like the blast of a trumpet, like the voice of God" (*IM*, 119). Evoking "the loftier horn" that "threw out a voice," with which he began, *poros* becomes prosopopoeia, the making of the face or the figure of figurality, so that momentarily, as Levi recites again from Dante, "my little speech made every one so keen ..." [*Li miei compagni fec'io sì acuti ...*] (*IM*, 120). *Acuti* in Italian has multiple valences. It can mean keen and acute, as well as suggesting a sharp physical sensation or a sense of shrewdness (embodied in Ulysses himself). The figure of prosopopoeia projects the physical sensation of movement – of 'throwing out' – into the body of language. It produces the flickering tongue of language, lighting the way, establishing a boundary that can be traversed, making a figure as a stratagem of moving through a dangerous limitlessness.[50]

Certainly, embodiment remains a fragile force, flickering under the constant threat of being extinguished by the great squalls of the Lager's aporetic space. This is captured in the Canto's final lines: "And over our heads the hollows seas closed up" (*IM*, 121). Evoking the watery image of the "submerged" – the *Muselmänner* "who followed the slope to the bottom, like streams that run down to the sea" (*IM*, 96) – the flickering tongue of language is extinguished of its figurative force, returned to the body's bare existence, to the banal but inescapable sensation of hunger and the quest for food. Yet there are techniques, strategies, and methods for shoring up embodiment against aporia's tides. Levi presents speech – representation – as a physical necessity. Indeed, he condenses speech to its embodied origins in "the speaking tongue," making a figure for

---

50 Kofman describes this action as a "move from the absence of limits to determinacy," in Kofman, "Beyond Aporia?" 9.

the 'figure' of speech. The aporia of witnessing is situated not in speech or representation, but in the material constraints – hunger, cold, fatigue, terror, imprisonment, disinterest – that are also what make this speech necessary.

Aporia and Mimesis

Levi's work turns the aporia of representation – the embodied lacuna at the center of testimony – inside out, transforming it into the Lager's representational field. It is a *topos* that requires a trope in order to twist and turn through it, like the serpentine hair of the Gorgon. This provides the body a linguistic form that helps carve a passage through aporia. By materializing the rhetorical figure of aporia in the space of the camp, Levi's work conceives of a relationship between embodiment and representation beyond absence or doubt.

The Hungarian Holocaust survivor and Nobel Laureate Imre Kertész also describes the concentration camp as a representational space. "I did have to invent Auschwitz and bring it to life [. . .] through the magic of language and composition," he professes in *Dossier K*, which is staged as an 'interrogation' between Kertész and his editor about Kertész's "autobiographical novel" *Fatelessness*. He continues: "From the very first lines you can already get a feeling that you have entered a strange sovereign realm in which everything" and "anything can happen. As the story progresses, the sense of being abandoned increasingly takes hold of the reader; there is a growing sense of losing one's footing."[51]

He frames the concentration camp as a space that suspends the normal landmarks of literary language and representation. This, in turn, leads the reader into the increasingly wild hinterlands of aporia, which are entirely disconnected from a mimetic relationship to reality. This is not a withdrawal from the ethical demands of representation; on the contrary, it is an acknowledgment that there is no 'direct' access to the concentration camp: "the concentration camp is imaginable only and exclusively as literature."[52] Rather than mystifying the Holocaust or situating it beyond language, Kertész aestheticizes it. This denaturalizes the different power relations and forms of violence that led to and circulated within the camp, framing them as forms and norms of representation.

---

51 Imre Kertész, *Dossier K*, trans. Tim Wilkinson (Brooklyn, NY: Melville House, 2013), 9.
52 Imre Kertész, "Who Owns Auschwitz?," trans. John MacKay, *The Yale Journal of Criticism* 14, no. 1 (2001): 267–72, 268. This quotation is originally from Imre Kertész, *Gályanapló* (Budapest: Holnap Kiadó, 1992).

Levi is not as sardonic as Kertész, but he also constructs the Lager as a space that interrupts normal mimetic conventions. This is particularly the case with his description of the "gray zone," a physical and a conceptual space that suspends the conventional moral and ethical frameworks of judgment for Jewish prisoners (though not for perpetrators). Like Levi's evocation of the *Muselmann*, the gray zone has been remarkably influential in Holocaust and trauma studies, as well as in sociology, philosophy, and history, enabling scholars to theorize different forms of complicity and trauma that arise under extreme situations of duress.[53] It is important to remember, however, that Levi theorizes the gray zone as a representational space. The gray zone cannot be understood as a reflection of the real world. It is more like a warped mirror that distorts the body into an unrecognizable form. Levi is at pains to demonstrate how this redrawing of ethical relations is done through a redistribution of the conventional rules and figures of mimesis. He emphasizes the material topography of the camp as a space that can only be entered through representation, thus distinguishing between the moral complicity of the camp and other social and political spheres. He poses the question of complicity in terms of mimesis and identification:

> power was sought by the many among the oppressed who had been contaminated by their oppressors and unconsciously strove to identify with them. This *mimesis*, this identification or *imitation*, or exchange of roles between oppressor and victim, has provoked much discussion. True and invented, disturbing and banal, acute and stupid things have been said: it is not virgin terrain; on the contrary it is a badly plowed field, trampled and torn up. (*DS*, 32, my emphasis)

This passage echoes Kertész's description of the Lager as knowable only through literary representations, but which nevertheless makes one lose "one's footing." Here, it is "a badly plowed field, trampled and torn up" that the reader stumbles on. I draw out the circulation of mimesis and identification in Levi's description to demonstrate how the gray zone exists as a rhetorical space that suspends the normal rules and conventions governing representation. It is graspable *only* as a form of representation, but one that also redraws the normative grounds of mimesis. As we shall see, this has a significant impact on the relationship between embodiment and representation.

---

53 For recent examples of Holocaust studies scholarship that productively builds on the gray zone see Debarati Sanyal, *Memory and Complicity: Migrations of Holocaust Remembrance* (New York: Fordham University Press, 2015) and Michael Rothberg, *The Implicated Subject: Beyond Victims and Perpetrators* (Stanford, CA: Stanford University Press, 2019).

Let us now explore some of the representational roles and relations that take place in the materialized space of aporia, and their relationship to embodiment. In an oft-quoted passage, Levi recounts the scene of a soccer match reported by a Hungarian Jewish pathologist, Miklós Nyiszli, who worked with Joseph Mengele. Nyiszli also worked alongside the last *Sonderkommando*, the 'Special Squad' of prisoners tasked with, amongst other things, leading Jews to the gas chambers, clearing and sorting bodies, and attending the crematoria. As a doctor who worked in a laboratory, Nyiszli would have enjoyed certain privileges denied to those responsible for more 'menial' tasks. Levi writes:

> in them [the *Sonderkommando*], they [the SS] recognized, to some extent, colleagues, by now as inhuman as themselves, hitched to the same cart, bound together by the foul link of imposed complicity. So, Nyiszli tells [*Nyiszli racconta dunque*] how during a "work" pause he attended a soccer match between the SS and the SK (*Sonderkommando*), that is to say [*vale a dire*], between a group representing the SS on guard at the crematorium and a group representing the Special Squad. Other men of the SS and the rest of the squad are present at the game; they take sides, bet, applaud, urge the players on as if, rather than at the gates of hell, the game were taking place on the village green. (*DS*, 38)

Levi employs a number of different linguistic markers to draw attention to his mediation of this scene. He notes that the German SS guards treated veteran *Sonderkommando* members with a kind of respect, as "colleagues," who are "now as inhuman as themselves, hitched to the same cart, bound together by the foul link of imposed complicity." This false equivalence between the SS and the *Sonderkommando* is a form of what Debarati Sanyal calls "coerced mimesis," in which the soccer match provides "the illusion of a mimetic relation between persecuted and persecutor."[54] This implied representational frame is then punctuated with a form of reported speech ("Nyiszli tells") that provides the entry point to the soccer match story. Levi also uses the conversational *dunque*, which appears frequently in spoken Italian, thus directing our attention to the act of telling (or *raccontare*). The markers of conversational language and reported speech highlight how this passage is a representation of testimony. They foreground the function of language as a system of representation. It thus resists naturalizing the relationship of representation the SS seeks to impose on the *Sonderkommando*, which simultaneously exculpates the SS and reviles the SK. The conventions

---

54 Sanyal, *Memory and Complicity*, 24. I am indebted to Sanyal's nuanced reading of the gray zone and her mobilization of aesthetic figures, such as allegory, for understanding how embodied trauma and the representation of trauma overlap and differ.

of conversational language interrupt this solemn reflection upon the way the gray zone scrambles the rules of a normal moral universe by drawing attention to the way Levi is himself reporting what Nyiszli has previously recounted.

Levi also places "work" in quotation marks, which defamiliarizes the camp's deformation of work and provides another frame for the representation of speech. This deformation is, in turn, embodied in the figure of Nyiszli, a specialist of autopsies turned into a producer of corpses. Placing "work" in quotation marks disrupts the linguistic chain of signification, in which the signifier "work" only derives meaning from its difference from related signifiers, namely "play," such that one could almost mistake a soccer match conducted in Auschwitz alongside other normal 'matchday' behaviors, like taking sides, betting, and cheering for a game that takes "place on the village green." The implicit critique of representation achieved by defamiliarizing "work" – and, by extension, 'play' – becomes slightly more pronounced in the clause that follows. Through the qualifier "that is to say" [*vale a dire*], Levi corrects the mimetic falsity of "a soccer match between the SS and the SK," qualifying that the match is "between a group *representing* the SS [. . .] and a group *representing* the Special Squad" (my italics). Just as work is separated from its normal function, so too do these groups become figures; as Sanyal argues, they are "representatives of each squad and yet seemingly detachable from their real tasks."[55] Levi thus accentuates how the SS and SK function as figures for the way representation no longer 'works' as a normative figural force in the camps, just as words like 'play,' or even 'victim' or 'perpetrator' become increasingly indistinct. If soccer (*calcio* in Italian) is a game governed by strict rules in which players must find their footing on the field of play, here Levi transforms the certainty of this game, normally governed by strict rules, into a terrain of aporia that leads one to lose one's footing.

The allegorical nature of this aporetic 'work,' which disrupts the representational work of figuration, becomes more concrete in the actual aporia that opens the paragraph that follows the soccer anecdote:

> Nothing of this kind ever took place, nor would it have been conceivable, with other categories of prisoners [*Niente di simile è mai avvenuto, né sarebbe stato concepibile, con altre categorie di prigionieri*]; but with them, with the "crematorium ravens," the SS could enter the field on an equal footing, or almost. Behind this armistice one hears a satanic laughter: [. . .] We have embraced you, corrupted you, dragged you to the bottom with us. (*DS*, 38)

---

55 Sanyal, *Memory and Complicity*, 25.

This self-conscious reporting of Nyiszli's depiction of the soccer match draws attention to its mediated form: it can only exist to readers and even potential spectators as a representation. This sense of mediation is further emphasized through the odd formulation that "nothing of this kind ever took place, nor would it have been conceivable." Levi quickly adds the qualifier "with other categories of prisoners," and we can surmise that these categories of prisoners are themselves categories of representation. But it is also notable that he leads with an aporetic expression of doubt, and one that echoes many of his earlier statements about his continued difficulty believing what happened, and his anxiety that others will not listen to him.

As Sanyal writes in her astute analysis of the role representation plays in constructing the gray zone, this passage "illustrates the gray zone's function as an aporetic space where extreme and norm converge, and where victims, perpetrators, and witnesses seem to exchange positions with the fluidity of a soccer ball's course on the village green."[56] This "aporetic space" of representation transforms the camp's physical space into a wild formal terrain that throws up obstacles to both writing and reading. Kertész insists the concentration camp is knowable only through literary representation, even as this literary representation makes one lose one's footing. Similarly, Levi constructs the Lager as a rhetorical space of aporia that suspends the normal rules and conventions governing representation by throwing into relief how it falsely places SS and SK "on an equal footing." It operates as a space where SS and SK *seem*, as Sanyal points out, to fluidly exchange roles and position.

The Lager's representational dimension is characterized as a savage physical terrain, which blocks or suspends the normal rules of narrative, representation, and comprehension. The intersection of representation and physical materiality becomes even more pronounced in another equally incongruous event that Levi reports Nyiszli describing:

> Nyiszli describes [*racconta*] another episode that deserves to be meditated upon. In the gas chamber have been jammed together and murdered the components of a recently arrived convoy and the squad is performing its horrendous everyday work, sorting out the tangle of corpses, washing them with hoses, and transporting them to the crematorium, but on the floor they find a young woman who is still alive. The event is exceptional, unique; perhaps the human bodies formed a barrier around her, sequestered a pocket of air that remained breathable. The men are perplexed; death is their trade at all hours, death is a habit because, precisely, "one either goes crazy the first day or gets accustomed to it," but this woman is alive. They hide her, warm her, bring her beef broth, question her: the girl is sixteen years old,

---

56 Sanyal, *Memory and Complicity*, 25.

> she cannot orient herself in space or time, does not know where she is, has gone through without understanding it the sequence of the sealed train, the brutal preliminary selection, the stripping, the entry into the chamber from which no one had ever come out alive. She has not understood, but she has seen; therefore she must die, and the men of the squad know it just as they know that they too must die for the same reason. But these slaves debased by alcohol and the daily slaughter are transformed; they no longer have before them the anonymous mass, the flood of frightened, stunned people coming off the boxcars: they have a person. (*DS*, 38–39).

As with the soccer match story, Levi begins his representation of Nyiszli's story with the framing device of reported speech ("Nyiszli describes"), which is also implied when the men's thoughts are presented as being "perplexed." This device again draws attention to representation's mediating function, as well as the way it is mediated for the reader, and it is the first in a series of nested representational frames. The reported speech slides into free indirect discourse, but also comes up against other modes of speech, including the direct but anonymous quotation that "one either goes crazy the first day or gets accustomed to it." Levi reports what Nyiszli has witnessed, which is also a telling of what the other men seem to think. As opposed to the false sense of normality associated with the soccer game that takes place as if "on the village green," Levi here notes that this "event is exceptional, unique." And its exceptional nature disrupts the naturalized equilibrium of both the narrative of work and the work of narrative, in which death is a "trade" and a "habit." The *mis-en-abyme* nature of various narrative frames and represented voices lead the reader through the aporia of the gas chamber. This culminates not in doubt, but in certainty: the narrative voice expresses conviction about what the men think. The *Sonderkommando* "know" that the girl must die, as surely as "they know that they too must die," even as our only access to these thoughts is through the different layers of narration. These representational frames give form to the aporia that exists at the level of the girl's understanding, and, also, to our reading of the passage.

Just as it is hard to locate the source of the witnessing and the voice of authority within the aporia of the gray zone – a rhetorical space that throws up physical impediments to narrative progression and understanding ("the sealed train, the brutal preliminary selection, the stripping, the entry into the chamber from which no one had ever come out alive") – so too the girl "cannot orient herself in space or time, does not know where she is." She cannot make sense of the brutal death rituals she has undergone only to come out on the other side, however briefly, alive. The paragraph ends with the striking image of "slaves debased by alcohol and the daily slaughter" who are momentarily able to recognize the existence of a living figure amongst "the anonymous mass" they are condemned to lead to their deaths. Here the passage reverts to reported narration that both presents the men's thoughts as a form of certainty and points to the mediation of this representation. These multiple layers of narration transform the aporia of the gas chamber into the living, breathing certainty in front of them: "they have a person." Amongst the innumerable faceless figures the *Sonderkommando* lead to the gas chambers, they are finally confronted with a "*Mitmensch*, the co-man: the human being of flesh and blood standing before us, within the reach of our providentially myopic senses" (*DS*, 40). This fellow creature, incarnated as a corporeal reality, provides a landmark or a *peirata* that lights a way through aporia's chaos, enabling our "providentially myopic sense" to discern the path. Rather than revealing an abyssal experience, the imbricated representational frames and reported voices takes shape in the thickening effects of embodied form.

Levi's representation of these multiple layers of testimony leads to an embodied figure rather than the trace of a presence. Despite the enormous pressures the camps exerted on physical bodies, including deprivation, overwork, torture, and exhaustion, Levi presents the body here not as fragmented and unrecoverable, but as indisputable in its living, breathing form. The carefully constructed levels of testimony – the different layers of mimesis, mediation, and translation – returns embodiment as the corporeal, material anchor that steadies us within the wild formal terrain of aporia. It is not fragmented by representation. In translating the experience of a range of others into language, *The Drowned and the Saved*, as well as Levi's other testimonial literature, enacts a politics of representation. But whereas Holocaust studies scholarship has often associated the act of rendering another's experience in language as an act of violence,[57] Levi's mediation of testimony is a small act of agency; it identifies a "human being of flesh and blood" at the heart of witnessing. It does not turn away from speaking, witnessing, or writing, but turns *into* it, exploring language like a physical terrain in order to encounter the embodied presence of testimony at its core.

I draw two conclusions from Levi's reflection on the relationship between the gray zone and representation. First, he constructs the aporia of the Holocaust as a question of the representation of aporia, rather than an aporia that structures representation. This helps identify boundaries as well as continuities between the space of the camp, the space of language, and the 'real world.' Through the representation of multiple narrative and vocal frames, Levi reminds us we are reading a *representation*

---

57 See Mandel, *Against the Unspeakable*, Chapter 1 for a discussion of this view.

of testimony and points to the *rhetorical* function of aporia. It should also be noted that even when it appears like we have direct access to Levi's thoughts, actions, and experience, such as when he uses first-person narration, free-indirect discourse, or metaleptically interjects into the diegetic frame with a reflection on his experience of writing in that moment, these are still *representations* of speech – representations that Levi is often at pains to underscore as such. If the terrain of aporia is like "a badly plowed field" this is because bystanders, readers, and critics have refused to acknowledge testimony's representational dimension. Aporia, in this sense, is not an *a priori* quality of the experience of the camps – something that can never be fully captured in language or that points to the limits of testimony or representation – but rather a rhetorical effect of representing the speech of victims and survivors.[58]

Second, he posits the body and embodied experience as central to aporia. Embodiment helps carve a path through this rhetorical field, and it emerges at its center as he moves through multiple layers of doubt. That the lived experience of the concentration camp may only be given to us through literary mediation does not necessarily mean that this experience is unrepresentable, but rather that it is given to us through aporia's *form*. Literary representation and form are, in fact, the major means for grasping this experience. In layering representation upon representation upon representation, Levi's work gives testimony a materiality – an embodied weight. This is not a withdrawal from representation but an amplification of representational relations. It reminds us that all speech, even thought, is a form of representation that emerges from and translates embodied experience.

Body Objects

In the previous section, I argued that aporia is a physical space of literary form. It is constructed from multiple layers of the representation of testimony. The embodied subject stands at the center. Levi is at pains throughout works like *If This Is a Man*, *The Truce*, and *The Drowned and the Saved*, to assert the veracity of his experience, but also to foreground the importance of representation. Embodiment can only be given to us through these forms of mediated speech. But this does not mean that the body escapes representation. On the contrary, these

---

58 See Mandel, *Against the Unspeakable*, 100–104, for a highly insightful discussion of the difference between survivor testimony and representations of survivor testimony, and the consequences of this crucial difference (that few scholars make) for our understanding of what is supposedly unspeakable in terms of the Holocaust or the witness.

multiple layers of representation accrete into an embodied presence that stands as a material rebuttal to the unspeakable, itself often embodied in the figure of the *Muselmann*, the 'true' witness who has lost the capacity for speech.

Yet the embodied witness needs help navigating aporia. One of the points of convergence between my characterization of aporia as a "badly plowed" physical terrain filled with physical obstacles and Levi's representation of his experience of the camps and his long return home is the importance of material objects like spoons, bowls, and shoes. They are threshold objects, maintaining the body's difference from its surroundings. They also metaphorically extend the body and help it navigate language. They thus play a central role in constructing testimony's embodied form. In this section, then, I will explore the relationship between the human body and the objects on which it depends for survival in the Lager, as well as the embodied rituals that revolve around the object world. These objects also throw into relief how representation seems to objectify bodies, a material symbol that stands in for an embodied absence. Yet for this reason the literal relationship between bodies and objects illuminates the *representational* relationship between them.

Objects are, of course, an important part of the Holocaust's iconography and material culture. Writing about the displays of objects confiscated from Jewish victims, Young notes the power of these displays that now form part of the visual and material vocabulary of the Holocaust, even as he is disturbed by them: "Armless sleeves, eyeless lenses, headless caps, footless shoes: victims are known only by their absence, by the moment of their destruction. In great loose piles, these remnants remind us not of the lives that once animated them, so much as the brokenness of lives."[59] Echoing the notion that objects act as prostheses for those who have been lost, Michael Bernard-Donals argues that "while we attach names to objects, and see objects as mnemonics for that which is irrevocably lost [...] what has been lost and what is absent exerts a terrible pressure upon both monument and name, and insinuates itself between the two."[60] Kristeva frames these objects in terms of the abject: "In the dark halls of the museum that is now what remains of Auschwitz, I see a heap of children's shoes [...] something I have already seen elsewhere under a tree, for dolls [...] The abjection of Nazi crime reaches its apex when death [...] interferes with" the

---

59 James E. Young, *The Texture of Memory: Holocaust Memorials and Meaning* (New Haven, CT: Yale University Press, 1994), 132.
60 Michael F. Bernard-Donals, *Forgetful Memory: Representation and Remembrance in the Wake of the Holocaust* (Albany, NY: SUNY Press, 2008), 6.

"living universe."⁶¹ Young, Bernard-Donals, and Kristeva express a common anxiety in Holocaust studies about the power of objects to replace human lives and the violence that results when humans are objectified. Such objects point to the absence of the bodies that once filled or used them; they gesture to the precarity of human agency and action.

However, I suggest reframing the relationship of bodies and objects from one of metonymic replacement to representational equivalence. To do so, I will return to Rancière's critique of the unrepresentable that I briefly touched on in the "Introduction." Across his writing, Rancière challenges the notion that some events, such as the Holocaust, are fundamentally unrepresentable and that, in turn, art and literature harbor within them an incapacity to make such events intelligible. He inverts appeals to the sublime or the abject, asking instead what perceptual conditions would render something unrepresentable.⁶² His demarcation of different regimes of art is key. The representative regime of art, which he associates roughly with early modernism, was governed by a hierarchy that positioned human action and knowledge at the pinnacle, and designated that only certain subject matters, classes of individuals, types of action, or kinds of stories could be told. But the aesthetic regime, or 'modern' art, demolishes these hierarchies and abrogates rules about what is an appropriate subject for representation: "everything is now on the same level, the great and the small, important events and insignificant episodes, human beings and things. Everything is equal, equally representable."⁶³ *Pace* Lyotard's notion of the unrepresentable, Rancière argues for the existence of "anti-representative" art, or an "art without unrepresentable things": "there are no longer any inherent limits to representation, to its possibilities."⁶⁴ This 'equality' of representation treats human consciousness, perception, and action with the same weight as the inconsequential, the insignificant, the non-human, and the passive, such

---

61 Kristeva, *Powers of Horror*, 4.
62 Rancière, "Are Some Things Unrepresentable?" 109.
63 Rancière, "Are Some Things Unrepresentable?" 120.
64 Rancière, "Are Some Things Unrepresentable?" 137. Rancière describes Levi's "paratactic writing" as exemplary of the realist mode that emerged during the nineteenth century and its rejection of representational hierarchies, in Rancière, "The Aesthetic Revolution and Its Outcomes," 150. By contrast, Hayden White argues that Levi represents a type of modernist writing that anticipates "a new form of historical reality, a reality that included, among its supposedly unimaginable, unthinkable, and unspeakable aspects, the phenomena of Hitlerism, the Final Solution, total war, nuclear contamination, mass starvation, and ecological suicide; a profound sense of the incapacity of our sciences to *explain*, let alone control or contain these; and a growing awareness of the incapacity of our traditional modes of representation even to *describe* them adequately," in White, "Historical Emplotment and the Problem of Truth," 52.

as the object world. In doing so, representation "expresses the structural features" of democracy, namely equality itself, refusing "the distinction between the poetic depiction of noble action and merely prosaic life."[65] The presence of these previously weightless, silent, or passive things emerges through an imposed materiality or gradual opacity – a kind of formal accretion – rather than through traditional representational media like visibility and speech.[66]

Rancière consistently illustrates his thinking on the unrepresentable with reference to the nineteenth-century realist novel, in particular *Madame Bovary*. In contrast to categories that would place Flaubert's naturalist text at the pinnacle of 'representational' art, Rancière argues it exemplifies the "paratactic style" particular to modern art, which privileges "description over action" and which does not prioritize human experience or consciousness over the object world. Parataxis (a term that Rancière uses somewhat loosely), or the listing of clauses without subordination, situates human and non-human experience on an equal footing, in which "minor perceptions" are added onto or equated with one another.[67] This type of literature focuses on "a concatenation of little perceptions and sensations," which subverts the "mediations and hierarchies" of the representative regime, in which human action stands at the zenith.[68] In the aesthetic regime, there is thus no hierarchy of language for describing uniquely human experience.

This seeming degradation of human action poses problems for Holocaust representation, in particular testimony. This is not because the event is implicitly unrepresentable or language is insufficient. It is because in a regime in which human action and speech is equated with "the absolute passivity of physical matter," the language used to convey the "extreme experience of the inhuman" is exactly the same as that used to describe the extreme experience of dehumanization.[69] Witnessing or testimony seems to require a hierarchy of subjects, and it relies upon human action and experience.[70] Thus, it is not that some experiences, such as the Holocaust, are unrepresentable, but that the language used to depict it is not specific to the event – an event that demands we recognize it as singular, unique, or even sacred.

---

65 Alison Ross, "Expressivity, Literary, Mute Speech," in *Jacques Rancière: Key Concepts*, ed. Jean-Philippe Deranty (Durham: Acumen, 2010), 138.
66 Rancière, "Are Some Things Unrepresentable?" 121.
67 Rancière, "Are Some Things Unrepresentable?" 125.
68 Rancière, "The Aesthetic Revolution and Its Outcomes," 150.
69 Rancière, "Are Some Things Unrepresentable?" 126.
70 Rancière is quite dismissive of the act of witnessing in "Are Some Things Representable?" He does revisit this question in "L'irreprésentable en question," offering a more nuanced approach.

And yet many representations of Holocaust testimony, including Levi's, rely upon paratactic modes of expression and paratactical relationships between the human and non-human world.[71] This paratactical mode is not without its problems. Often, the parataxis expresses ambivalence about its own mode of delivery by juxtaposing anxieties about representation with its production. Sometimes this emerges as an unease about the horizontal structure of 'equal' representation. At other times, it is revealed in the strange pleasures embodied experience offers at the most terrifying moments of human experience, such as the selection for the gas chambers, which brings embodiment into the realm of representation. Thus, even as Levi distributes objects and bodies on the same sensorial plane, he often draws attention to the pressures this puts on witnessing – an act that, by necessity, depends upon vertical relations of agency and authority. Rancière identifies a similar tension in realist fiction, in which characters "are still trapped in the old poetics with its combination of actions, its characters envisioning great ends, its feelings related to the qualities of person, its noble passions opposed to everyday experience," and the restructured perspective that brings such transcendental aims onto a plane of sensibility, "an eternal flood of atoms that keeps doing and undoing new configurations."[72] This anxiety is again not specific to representations of Holocaust testimony, but it is nevertheless amplified by the event's violence and its ethical demands for historical accuracy.

Throughout Levi's Holocaust testimony we are confronted with a topsy-turvy world in which the normal relations between humans and objects are continually being renegotiated. Levi details the interrelation between these embodied rituals and objects in the Lager's routine:

> The rites to be carried out were infinite and senseless: every morning one had to make the "bed" perfectly flat and smooth; smear one's muddy and repellent wooden shoes with the appropriate machine grease; scrape the mudstains off one's clothes (paint, grease and rust-stains were, however, permitted); in the evening one had to undergo the control for lice and the control of washing one's feet; on Saturday, have one's beard and hair shaved, mend or have mended one's rags; on Sunday, undergo the general control for skin diseases and the control of buttons on one's jacket, which had to be five. (*IM*, 40)

It is only in a world where the mimetic rules governing existence and appearance have been suspended ("there is no why here") that the object

---

71 Alongside Levi, Rancière offers the examples of Robert Antelme and Claude Lanzmann. I add to this list Jorge Semprún and Charlotte Delbo, amongst others.
72 Rancière, "Why Emma Bovary Had to Be Killed," 242–43.

world and human action and consciousness are leveled out. As with the soccer match, however, this process emerges through self-conscious forms of representation. Levi defamiliarizes commonplace objects like "bed," in the passage above, as well as more abstract concepts like "good" and "evil" (*IM*, 92), by placing them in quotation marks and inverted commas.[73] The paratactic syntax, like Levi's defamiliarization of self-evident objects brings embodiment and objects onto the same representational plane; it turns them into literary devices that hold equal weight.

For instance, Levi describes how only several weeks after his arrival in the Lager, he had already acquired "the prescribed hunger, that chronic hunger unknown to free men." He had "learnt not to let myself be robbed, and in fact if I find a spoon lying around, a piece of string, a button which I can acquire without danger of punishment, I pocket them and consider them mine by full right." These objects are equivalent in syntactical terms with his description of his body: "I push wagons, I work with a shovel, I turn rotten in the rain, I shiver in the wind; already my body is no longer mine: my belly is swollen, my limbs emaciated, my face is thick in the morning, hollow in the evening" (*IM*, 43). Embodied experiences like hunger and cold are paratactically placed on the same level as spoons, strings, buttons, while the body expresses the influence of the object world in its degradation. Objects distance Levi from his body, but return it to him as a representation, allowing him to perceive it, however unpleasantly, in a new light. The object world thus helps give the body a definite form through which it can be expressed. Objects render it readable and representable. The close relationship between objects and bodies in Levi's work, I argue, is not only about material survival and objectification, but rather about the ability to represent bodies concretely. On a thematic level, objects evoke a hierarchy upon which human experience is elided and replaced, pointing to the limits of both the body and the Holocaust. Yet on a formal and aesthetic level, the equivalence between object and human consciousness structures a different relation to the body.

There is no object more important – or that the Lager renders more unfamiliar – than shoes.[74] "Do not think that shoes form a factor of

---

[73] Jessica Lang argues that Levi's use of quotation marks around common terms, as well as his retention of foreign terms like *Häftling* and Lager, point to "how these normative meanings fall short" and thus to "the limitations attached to the best of their representation," in Lang, *Textual Silence: Unreadability and the Holocaust* (New Brunswick, NJ: Rutgers University Press, 2017), 39. I argue, by contrast, that this type of reading, far from distancing us from the normative effects of language, has the opposite effect: it returns us to the normative dimension of the unrepresentable, the unsayable, and the unreadable.

[74] See Lang, *Textual Silence*, 39–42, for an astute analysis of the relationship between the

secondary importance in the life of the Lager," Levi asserts early on in *If This Is a Man*, "death begins with the shoes; for most of us, they show themselves to be instruments of torture, which after a few hours of marching cause painful sores which become fatally infected" (*IM*, 40). The worst result is "a diagnosis of '*dicke Füsse*' (swollen feet) [...] because it is well known to all, and especially to the SS, that here there is no cure for that complaint" (*IM*, 41). The distribution of shoes – and thus the potential for survival – are also governed by the senseless ritual of "the ceremony of the changing of the shoes," which "tests the skill of the individual who, in the middle of the incredible crowd, has to be able to choose at an eye's glance one (not a pair, one) shoe, which fits. Because once the choice is made, there can be no second change" (*IM*, 40). The shoe represents a material barrier between the body and the Lager's harsh world, without which "a naked and barefoot man feels that all his nerves and tendons are severed; he is helpless prey" (*DS*, 90).

This is nowhere better illustrated than in a passage in *The Truce*, at once moving and humorous, when Levi finds himself stranded on the side of the road with a fellow survivor, Mordo Nahum, the venerable "Greek." Levi's "curious foot-coverings" made "of extremely delicate leather" (*T*, 214) have disintegrated, leaving him unable to continue their journey on foot. The Greek, by contrast, is in possession of "exceptional" shoes, "leather, almost new, of elegant design: a real portent, given the time and the place" (*T*, 209). The Greek dismisses Levi's feeble protestations as "words [...] Anyone can talk," for "a man who has no shoes is a fool" (*T*, 215). Both the representation of direct speech and the dismissal of normative language as mere "words" point to shoes' mimetic relationship with the body. Shoes are more concrete than words, but they are also given to us through speech, in a reciprocal relationship in which object and word mutually reinforce each other. The shoe is the foot's inverse (one might say 'logical') form and extends the body into space. This intertwined material and mimetic relationship is captured in the way even the crudest shoes form "a tenuous but indispensable defence," which constructs the body's boundaries. Without them one "no longer perceives himself as a human being, but rather as a worm: naked, slow, ignoble, prone on the ground. He knows he can be crushed at any moment" (*DS*, 90). Shoes thus demonstrate not merely

---

representation of shoes and the economy of unreadability in Levi's work. Whereas Lang focuses on how Levi's defamiliarization of the signifier "shoes" from its normal signification points to a the unreadability of experience, I explore how shoes reveal a different aesthetic regime in which the human and the object are brought together on the same plane of representation. This leads to more possibilities for representation – whether understood in terms of reading or writing – rather than less.

the embodied subject's dependence on the object world, but the body's mimetic *correspondence* to it, even as this equivalence provokes a great deal of unease, captured in the image of a human transformed into a grotesque worm that lies "prone" on the ground.

Paratactic form thus redraws the representational relations between human consciousness and embodiment and the non-human world. Anxieties about this re-formation are also evident in the way extreme experiences of terror are brought down to the level of minute sensorial experience. I earlier cited a passage from Levi in which he writes that "if the Lagers had lasted longer a new, harsh language would have been born; and only this language could express what it means to toil all day in the wind, with the temperature below freezing, wearing only a shirt, underpants, cloth jacket and trousers, and in one's body nothing but weakness, hunger and knowledge of the end drawing near" (*IM*, 129). It is arguable that a new language *did* emerge to describe the specific experience of the camps, not least in terms like the *Muselmann*, which has become a conceptual paradigm for Holocaust studies.[75] In addition to a new language, a new sensorium specific to the Lager appears. While existence in the Lager is an eternal struggle to overcome hunger, cold, fatigue, and illness, this sensorium is not necessarily marked by terror or extreme violence. It is remarkable because it provides the constant experiential background, an almost banal backdrop. Life in Lager is characterized by an embodied pattern: "go out and come in; work, sleep and eat; fall ill, get better or die" (*IM*, 42). This routine is both purely sensorial and obscures its sensorial regime; it is "the hypnosis of the interminable rhythm, which kills thought and deadens pain" (*IM*, 57). Only when one is afforded the rare opportunity to escape this interminable world of being riveted to the senses does one become aware of them. This occurs when Levi is sent to Ka-Be, the medical ward, after injuring his foot: "Ka-Be is the Lager without its physical discomforts. So that, whoever still has some seeds of conscience, feels his conscience re-awaken." Yet even this conscience cannot escape embodiment: "the memories of the world outside crowd our sleeping and our waking hours, we become aware, with amazement, that we have forgotten nothing, every memory evoked rises in front of us painfully clear" (*IM*, 61). The language that evokes the pain of memory closely resembles the language used to describe the body's pain – there is no difference, in other words, between human consciousness and the physical world of sensation. The realization of this equivalence is itself painful, coalescing

---

75 Oster notes terms like *Muselmann* do signal the emergence of a new language, in Oster, "Impossible Holocaust Metaphors," 304.

in the warning that "no one must leave here and so carry to the world, together with the sign impressed on his skin, the evil tidings of what man's presumption made of man in Auschwitz" (*IM*, 61). Testimony is marked on the surface of the skin, an embodied stigmata of parataxis. Language is not insufficient; it is unexceptional.

Similar feelings of unease emerge in a scene depicting the selection, when the Nazis choose who will be kept for forced labor and who will be sent to the gas chambers. Yet rather than describing this experience in terms of abject embodiment or sublime terror – the terms that have generally accompanied critical responses to the gas chambers – Levi brings these 'unspeakable' affects down to the minute, immersive flow of sensorial experience. The "crowd of frightened, naked people" is driven into a small holding room. The sense of fear recedes. It is replaced by "the feeling of warm flesh pressing all around," a "warm compact human mass" that fills "all the corners" of the room (*IM*, 133). Instead of inspiring horror, this sense of warmth "is unusual and not unpleasant," though "one has to take care to" preserve a sense of quotidian pragmatism, and "hold up one's nose so as to breath, and not to crumple or lose the card in one's hand" (*IM*, 133). After emerging from this not unpleasant sensorial experience, however, Levi observes with disgust an old prisoner loudly praying in gratitude for being saved in front of a young prisoner who has been selected for the gas chamber: "Does Kuhn not understand that what has happened today is an abomination, which no propitiatory prayer, no pardon, no expiation by the guilty, which nothing at all in the power of man can ever clean again?" (*IM*, 136). Once again the flow of embodied and perceptual sensation seems to break against the testimonial imperative to provide a record of the event as an "abomination" existing beyond human comprehension.

As one last example, I will explore the tension between horizontal relations of representational equivalence, expressed at the level of syntax and form, and vertical relations of human agency and action, in which the subject must rise above the passivity of the non-human world. After only several weeks in the camp, Levi notes that he lost "the instinct for cleanliness" (*IM*, 46). Wandering aimlessly, he comes across his friend Steinlauf, who is scrubbing his body with "great energy" despite the fact "he has no soap." Steinlauf reproaches Levi for not washing. But to Levi the ritual is senseless; it is "a mechanical habit, or worse, a dismal repetition of an extinct rite" (*IM*, 46), to which Steinlauf replies:

> precisely because the Lager was a great machine to reduce us to beasts, we must not become beasts; that even in this place one can survive, and therefore one must want to survive, to tell the story, to bear witness; and that to survive we must force ourselves to save at least the skeleton, the scaffolding, the form

of civilization [*lo scheletro, l'impalcatura, la forma della civiltà*]. We are slaves, deprived of every right, exposed to every insult, condemned to certain death, but we still possess one power, and we must defend it with all our strength for it is the last – the power to refuse our consent. So we must wash our faces without soap in dirty water and dry ourselves on our jackets. We must polish our shoes, not because regulation states it, but for dignity and propriety. We must walk erect, without dragging our feet, not in homage to Prussian discipline but to remain alive, not to begin to die. (*IM*, 47)

The language of testimony – the need "to tell the story, to bear witness" – is delivered in a paratactic syntax that draws a structural equivalence between this imperative and the "great machine to reduce us to beasts." This conflicting horizontal syntactical structure and vertical righteous pursuit is captured in the triplet of "the skeleton, the scaffolding, the form of civilization," in which the body's denuded structure is reincarnated in the fragile props and behaviors of human culture, signaled by the dual meaning of *civiltà* as both civilization and civility. (This could also be the stage on which both the body and civilization are hanged.) And precisely because the prisoners are "slaves, deprived of every right," who exist at the same level of the objects they depend upon for survival, they must grasp any small act of agency, itself expressed in the body's vertical posture: "we must walk erect, without dragging our feet." In other words, one must rise above the horizontal plane on which humans and objects merge together in the camp, and on which the figure of the *Muselmann* eventually succumbs in a posture of abasement. There thus exists a structural, formal tension between the horizontal plane of the physical, material world and the vertical plane of human action and agency. Embodiment bridges these two planes. It organizes the arrangement of words and phrases in a paratactic mode, and it acts as the site of agency and resistance.

In shifting the relationship between objects and bodies in the Holocaust away from absence, replacement, and loss, I have sought to redraw embodiment's connection to representation. My aim here is to not become embroiled in whether the Holocaust is a unique event or whether it is appropriate to depict it in language that is not specific to it. Rather, I have reoriented the debates about Holocaust representation away from moral injunctions about proper types, as well as from the evocation of limits that is, as Rancière reminds us, normative (or ethical) rather than descriptive.[76] Levi's work, by far the most 'realist' of the literature in *Formal Matters*, thus offers an opportunity to revisit the

---

[76] Rancière makes the repeated point that the unrepresentable inscribes "in the practice of art the necessity of the ethical detour," in Rancière, "The Aesthetic Revolution and Its Outcomes," 150.

terms upon which the body is seen as inherently escaping representation. Levi's distribution of embodiment – ranging from extreme deprivation to minor aggravations, as well as the constant background hum of hunger, cold, and fatigue – along the same horizontal axis as objects and non-human experience does not condemn the body to insufficient representation. It *amplifies* the opportunities for representing the body. More qualities, practices, and modes can be harnessed to bring the body into the field of representation. This, in turn, asserts the body's authority, agency, and presence, rather than its absence or silence. This is not a redemptive act, however. Or rather, it is redemptive to the degree that it brings the body into representation and language, rather than placing it beyond expression. But this re-presentation of the body continues to harbor anxieties about the relationship between humans and objects within the very ambivalence of its form. Indeed, my analysis of Levi in this chapter points to another way of understanding the body's relationship to representation. Rather than trying to provide a complete representation, literary form can draw our attention to the possibility (indeed, the ethical necessity) of historically and contextually determined forms of representation – particularly of the body.

The Matter of Representation

In his essay "Communicating" in *The Drowned and the Saved*, Levi writes:

> I never liked the term "incommunicability," so fashionable during the 1970s [...] In today's normal world, which by convention and contrast we call from time to time "civilized" or "free," one almost never encounters a total linguistic barrier: that is, finding oneself facing a human being with whom one must absolutely establish communication or die, and then is unable to do so. (*DS*, 68)

Despite Levi's defamiliarization of the "civilized" and "free" world, the deadly linguistic barrier he describes seems to belong more to the camp, a place where a failure to communicate truly could lead to death rather than mere misunderstanding. Barriers to communication certainly exist at every turn in the camps; yet these are not unsurmountable: "to say that it is impossible to communicate is false; one always can. To refuse to communicate is a failing; we are biologically and socially predisposed to communication, and in particular to its highly evolved and noble form, which is language. All human species speak, no non-human species knows how to speak" (*DS*, 69). If a prisoner failed to understand what a camp guard said, then violence filled its place: physical blows "were a variant of the same language." This signaled that the "use of words to communicate thought, this necessary and sufficient mechanism for man to be man, had fallen into disuse," even that "those people were no longer men" (*DS*, 70–71). In this context, language is embodied in a physical object oriented purely towards pain: "the rubber truncheon was called *der Dolmetcher*, the interpreter: the one who made himself understood by everybody" (*DS*, 71).

Like the other works I have explored in this chapter, "Communication" both demonstrates a rearrangement of the relationship between the body and representation and manifests deep anxieties about this change. Only humans, Levi insists, have the capacity for language, separating them from the non-human world. Yet at the same time, a rubber truncheon communicates when words fall into "disuse." What mediates between the two poles of human intentionality and the extreme passivity of the object world is embodiment. It is the common denominator – the discursive and material ground – that ties them together. This can take place through aesthetic phenomena like speech and noise, or through compulsive bodily drives like hunger. This recalls Levi's metaphor about memory as a magnetic tape equivalent to a body that digests food: "At a distance of forty years we still remember in a purely acoustic form, words and sentences pronounced around us in language we did not know and did not learn afterwards." This sonic experience "became engraved on our memories as on an empty, blank magnetic tape; in the same manner, a famished stomach rapidly assimilates even indigestible food." This odd shift from the metaphor of language recorded via technological means to the body's absorption of language as if it was food is part of the meaning-making, even chiastic process, in which embodiment incorporates, digests, and disgorges language at the same time that it translates, records, and testifies. These processes were part of an "effort to carve a meaning or sense out of the senseless" (*DS*, 73).

Communication, language, discourse, and representation are fragile and open to abuse. But they are not impossible, precisely because they emerge from the locus of speech: the body. Whereas Blanchot's notion of the disaster is something that exists beyond language, Levi explicitly seeks to 'write the disaster.' He wants to give it a name, to bring it into the field of representation so that it can be understood (even if that does not guarantee something similar will not happen again). Even those bodies who seem most at risk of silence, such as the *Muselmänner*, have a capacity for speech, precisely *because* it is rendered through the representation of speech as an embodied act. The failure in communication comes, then, not from the limits of language but from a refusal to listen, from the act of 'emptying' out of the *Muselmann*.

In this chapter, I have sought to reorient debates about the representation of the body away from absence, immateriality, and limits. By transforming aporia into the material space of the Lager, Levi provides a representational domain for exploring the mimetic relationship between embodiment and testimony beyond lack. In turn, I have demonstrated how embodiment is not only central to his representation of the Holocaust, but also to the rhetorical, aesthetic, and formal *structure* of his testimony. By exploring testimony as a formal structure and related figures, such as aporia, through the lens of embodiment, I expand my analysis of embodied form beyond experimental literature to take in types of discourse and writing that have a strongly representational dimension. Unlike prosopopoeia in Garréta's *Sphinx* or metalepsis in Beckett's *How It Is*, testimony has an expressly representational and political function. Testimonial literary texts frequently pronounce their mimetic relationship to reality. Verisimilitude, for instance, is a fundamental part of the act of witnessing. Testimony is also a form of evidence, in which an individual makes a declaration of fact in a court, literally representing themselves before the law. Accordingly, whereas the previous chapters followed embodiment's close relationship with form, this chapter has theorized the relationship between embodiment and representation. This was necessary because Levi himself frames the role that representation plays in testimony through strategies that draw attention to their own mimetic processes via the body. In anchoring testimony and its related figures in embodiment, I challenge the notion that the Holocaust designates a limit event or a crisis of representation.

By way of conclusion, I would like to turn to Levi's short story "Carbon," the final chapter of *The Periodic Table*, in which each of the twenty-one chapters takes on the characteristics and names of a chemical element. *The Periodic Table* is at once an autobiography, a scientific treatise, and a reflection upon the natural world. But it also composed of many of the fundamental elements that make up embodiment, including hydrogen, potassium, and iron. The most important of these is carbon: the primary building block of both human and non-human life, as essential to the body's blood and bones as it is to the crystalline existence of a diamond. It is "the key element of living substance."[77] Carbon is both completely "not specific" (*PT*, 188), in the sense that all life is based upon it, while also being a "singular element," the only one "that can

---

77 Primo Levi, *The Periodic Table*, trans. Raymond Rosenthal (London: Penguin, 2001), 190. Hereafter cited parenthetically using the abbreviation *PT*.

bind itself in long stable chains without a great expense of energy." This is precisely what "life on earth" (*PT*, 190) requires. The story follows the voyage of a single carbon atom, from the "limestone rock ledge" from which it is dislodged by a pickax (an object, Levi is at pains to point out, that is "the most important intermediar[y] in the millennial dialogue between the elements and man"), before being plunged into a "lime kiln" where the fire separates it from its fellow element calcium. "Still firmly clinging to two of its three former oxygen companions" (*PT*, 189), it floats out of the chimney, taking to the open air. From there it follows a "tumultuous" (*PT*, 190) fate, penetrating the bodies of animals, being swept on the wind, and dissolved in the sea. As Marco Caracciolo notes in his beautiful reading of this passage, its "kinetic patterns" make it read "like a roller-coaster ride."[78] This twisting, trope-like movement follows the carbon atom until it becomes part of the long binding chain of its elemental destiny, carbon dioxide, allowing it to become part of the structural "architecture" (*PT*, 191) of life, "from tiny algae to small crustaceans to fish" (*PT*, 194). Finally, this tiny carbon atom makes its way into "a very complex, long chain" whose links are nevertheless "all acceptable to the human body." This substance is milk. Someone drinks this milk, and Levi details the way

> it migrates, knocks at the door of a nerve cell, enters, and supplants the carbon which was part of it. This cell belongs to a brain, and it is my brain, the brain of the *me* who is writing; and the cell in question, and within it the atom in question, is in charge of my writing, in a gigantic minuscule game which nobody has yet described. It is that which at this instant, issuing out of a labyrinthine tangle of yeses and nos, makes my hand run along a certain path on the paper, mark it with these volutes that are signs [*la segni di queste volute che sono segni*]: a double snap, up and down, between two levels of energy, guides this hand of mine to impress on the paper this dot, here, this one. (*PT*, 195)

I began this book with an image of prehistoric man pressing his hand against a cave wall, blowing paint like the breath of language over it to leave behind an imprint of his body's absence. The book subsequently sought to fill in the gap between index and the body through an attention to form, the aesthetic flesh that unites signifier and signified, subject and object, the body and representation. I finish this book with an image of a hand from a remarkably different historical context – a context present to us through written history – but one that is nevertheless connected to the Chauvet caves, not least through their equal dependency on carbon. Far from the image of a hand withdrawing and leaving

---

78 Caracciolo, *Embodiment and the Cosmic Perspective*, 76.

behind an imprint of the body's absence, Levi builds the very structure of representation – its most elemental symbols and signs – from bodily material. The pressure of the hand renders itself material in the paratactic accumulation of chemical elements, physical objects, animal figures, and natural forms.[79] But also, perhaps most importantly, in the syntactical accumulation of "signs." The original Italian presents us with a near chiasmus, in which the verb 'to sign' (*segni*, translated in English as "mark" in the passage) turns itself over into the noun "signs." Like Keats' "living hand" we are presented here with an index of indexes – of signs that inscribe themselves as material signs. The carbon atom – an aesthetic figure or metaphor for the fundamental processes of organic, biological life – transpierces the boundaries of the body, while the body's expressive energies suffuse representation with a sense of limitless potential. By bringing embodiment into the very structure of representation, and endowing representation with an embodied architecture, Levi's work demonstrates how we can read not only for embodied form, but also for representations of the body.

---

79 Caracciolo argues that this passage depicts an "ontological metalepsis" in which the narrative frames between material, natural history and embodied, performative autobiography break down, merging together, in Caracciolo, *Embodiment and the Cosmic Perspective*, 77.

Afterword

Against the Unrepresentable: The Common Sense of Embodied Form

In tracing the relationship between embodiment and form, *Formal Matters* has established an alternative approach to the body that does not place it beyond representation or expression. I have explored how poetic, rhetorical, and formal figures are grounded in embodied experience, and I have demonstrated the way this embodied experience is an integral part of their figurative processes. My recourse to formalist figures has reinstated their embodied form, either implicit but ignored by formalism or explicit but dispatched by postmodernism. This reading of embodied form has charted a course between these two poles in order to demonstrate both literary form's inseparable relationship to embodiment and the way embodiment takes shape in form. By explicitly attending to the embodied foundation of literary form and, in turn, using poetic figures to read embodiment, I have provided a methodology for grasping embodiment beyond a text's representational, thematic, propositional, or discursive content. At the same time, I have argued that there is no essential, natural embodiment that pre-exists our reading for it. The organic, holistic, unified nature of embodied form emerges through interpretation, which brings together seemingly disconnected elements of representation.

Some may remain unconvinced that my focus on form offers an alternative to representation and that the problematics that plague the body's relationship to representation haunt its connection to form. Does literary form merely stand in for or extend embodiment in a similar manner to representation? Can the body's corporeality and materiality – its reality as living 'flesh' – be rendered in form more fully than in representation? It remains true that the body's material form and the senses cannot be directly 'injected' into literature without some translation, mediation, or transposition that entails a kind of dematerialization of the brute 'stuff' of matter. Rather than seeing this process as a failure, however, I have sought to demonstrate that what results in this transposition of embodied experience into literature is a new type of materiality: embodied form. Through formal constellations and poetic figures, embodied form projects the body's organization of perceptual experience into meaningful patterns. Literary form – as well as other aesthetic objects – both take their shape from and mediate bodily experience, even if this process will never be complete, like the constant vacillation of chiasmus. This would, after all, go against the body's processes, whether in the constant, minute, almost indiscernible adjustments the body makes to move through space or in longer term changes like ageing. The concept of form enables us to comprehend embodiment in ways that are not possible when we frame our engagement with the body in terms of representation.

In addition to demonstrating the embodied foundation of poetic and literary form, one of *Formal Matters* major interventions has consisted in questioning the paradigm of the unrepresentable, whether as a limit on thought and language or a barrier to expressing embodiment. This materiality may never (thankfully!) be fully present to us, but form affords us more opportunities for understanding the way language expresses embodiment and how embodiment structures language, than the paradigm of representation allows. This, in turn, has political implications. As philosophers like Arendt and Rancière, as well as new formalist and older critical theorists, have reminded us, aesthetic experience is inseparable from the political realm.[1] By reconceiving of perceptual relations, aesthetic mediums like literature are capable of conceiving of new political forms. Yet it is important to explicitly theorize the inherently bodily locus of this aesthetic experience in relationship to literature and other creative forms. *Aesthesis* does not emerge out of the ether into a pure consciousness. If we place the body outside of linguistic or semiotic representation, we risk repeating postmodernism's error of form, which has left bodily materiality fragmented and irrecoverable. I have explicitly engaged with the embodied foundations of this aesthetics in order to understand how certain bodies are left out of forms of political representation, and how, in turn, attending to language's embodied origins enables some bodies to signify more fully.

Up until now, however, I have largely focused on individual embodied and sensory experience. Yet I have also touched upon the way individual bodies form the basis of collective forms, exemplified by the figure of the body politic. In order to think through the way the embodied

---

1 The relationship between aesthetics and politics is not, of course, the preserve of thinkers who largely conceive of their connection in productive terms, such as Arendt and Rancière. Those who viewed the aesthetic dimension of the political in more agonistic terms include Walter Benjamin, Theodor Adorno, and Slavoj Žižek.

experience of certain subjects remains unrepresentable in political forms – even those forms ostensibly organized around the principle of equal representation and transparency – I now want to turn towards more collective modes of sensory perception. To do so, I will explore the work of Hannah Arendt and her notion of "common sense." This is a shared realm of aesthetic and perceptual experience, which forms the collective faculty of the body politic. I pair this concept with her insistence that language is able to bridge the divide between the 'invisible' world of individual sensory experience and the public realm of speech, action, and belonging – of politics, in other words. Against models of destituency, she argues that the breakdown of "common sense" and the medium of language that communicates it results in the worst political forms, namely totalitarianism. In this sense, aestheticization does not lead to fascism or totalitarianism. Aesthetics is what these political movements must destroy in order to constitute themselves. For this reason, aesthetic forms, in particular literature for Arendt, are necessary for reconstructing spaces where a plurality of perspectives can be imagined and encountered, without subsuming these different viewpoints to one indistinguishable mass.

The 'Reality' of Common Sense

Arendt begins *The Life of the Mind* with a reflection on the world's phenomenal nature: "the world men are born into contains many things, natural and artificial, living and dead, transient and sempiternal, all of which have in common that they *appear* and hence are meant to be seen, heard, touched, tasted, and smelled, to be perceived by sentient creatures endowed with the appropriate sense organs."[2] Individuals are thus both sensing spectators and 'appearances,' or objects of perception. Echoing Merleau-Ponty, she says this duality of "subject and objects – perceiving and being perceived" guarantees their existence in the world. At the same time, this plurality of spectators and their perspectives is what assures the existence of a common world.[3] The common world, what she often calls the "space of appearance," is the basis of political activities like speech and action. The *polis* "is not the city-state in its physical location; it is the organization of the people as it arises out of acting and speaking together." This collective aesthetic action constitutes "the space of appearance in the widest sense of the world." It is "where I

---

2 Arendt, *The Life of the Mind*, 19.
3 Arendt, *The Life of the Mind*, 20.

appear to others as others appear to me, where men exist not merely like other living or inanimate things but make their appearance explicitly."[4] Aesthetic appearance is concrete; it is *embodied*.

However, individual sensory experience is not enough to secure the existence of plurality and a shared world. Although all beings ostensibly share the same ability to see, hear, taste, touch, and smell, the experience of these sensations is private. A "sixth sense," what Arendt calls "common sense," is thus needed to coordinate and integrate this perceptual experience into a shared framework. Common sense is not connected to a particular body; it unites the five senses and assimilates them into a cohesive reality. It bridges the divide between the internal, private realm of sense experience and the external realm of shared reality. This "sixth sense" is what ensures, for instance, that when I bite into an apple, its taste, smell, odor, and visual appearance all unite in one sensory experience and that, in turn, I can be relatively sure the experience of another person biting into a similar apple will be comparable to my own. If each of the five senses corresponds to a particular property of the apple (it is "visible because we have vision"), then the property that corresponds to the way this sensory experience fits into the world is the "*sensation* of reality." Common sense is the world's sensorial dimension of "*realness*."[5] It is thus the political sense *par excellence*; it integrates private experience into a common framework broadly understood and shared by the whole community, even when the world is perceived through radically different political and ideological perspectives. Common sense, in other words, is the sense of the body politic.

But common sense does not have to be homogenizing. Indeed, Arendt was suspicious of political discourses of assimilation, believing it can destroy difference.[6] Nevertheless, she recognized the need to find the "viewpoint from which to look upon, to watch, to form judgments [. . .] to reflect upon human affairs."[7] Since the political realm is composed of the multiple perspectives of those who act and speak within it, it is

---

4 Arendt, *The Human Condition*, 198–99.
5 Arendt, *The Life of the Mind*, 50–51. Italics in the original.
6 In "We Refugees," for instance, Arendt is highly critical of cosmopolitanism, which she identifies as a kind of assimilationist identity, although she does not explicitly use those terms. See Hannah Arendt, "We Refugees," in *The Jewish Writings*, ed. Jerome Kohn and Ron H. Feldman (New York: Schocken books, 2007). For a discussion of Arendt's treatment of assimilation see Andreea Ritivoi, "Reading (with) Hannah Arendt: Aesthetic Representation for an Ethics of Alterity," *Humanities* 8, no. 155 (September 24, 2019), 8–10.
7 Hannah Arendt, *Lectures on Kant's Political Philosophy* (Chicago: University of Chicago Press, 1990), 44.

necessary to try and understand as many of these viewpoints as possible. Common sense enables members of a community to agree on a common identity for things – the taste of an apple, for instance – even if they do not share the same opinion on it. By constellating the plurality of different viewpoints, this shared 'multi-dimensionality' constitutes the experience and sense of realness.

The problem, as Arendt argues, is that reality is not perceived like vision, taste, or smell. Reality surrounds us but cannot be reduced to a specific act or moment of recognition. There are certain things, however, that provide a sense of realness or throw reality into relief. One of the things that does this is the medium of language, which translates the invisible world of sensory experience and thinking into the concrete space of appearance. Language does not constitute a limit or an aporia in Arendt's thinking. It is a *bridge*, a connecting structure between thought and speech, perception and action, the senses and appearing.

Language and Metaphor

In *Formal Matters*, I have argued that the unrepresentable is the overriding paradigm of postmodernism, the imperfect umbrella term that groups together both critical schools of thought and cultural changes. As Arendt reminds us, however, the notion that truth is ineffable extends as far back as ancient philosophy, and perhaps even farther through its association with the invisibility of God in Judaism.[8] Arendt's analysis of poetic language provides another way of approaching the unrepresentable, or what she terms the "ineffable." Indeed, like Rancière, Arendt associates the ineffable with the Western metaphysical tradition, which she argues is no longer a credible model for understanding the world.[9] She critiques this tradition through the metaphysical separation of the realm of ideas – *eidos* in Platonic thinking – and the concrete world of things and sensory experience. What bridges these two things is language. Like the formalists, she distinguishes between 'everyday' and poetic language. Unlike the formalists, however, she does not treat poetic language as autonomous. Rather, metaphorical language – from the Greek *metapherein*, or 'carrying over' – connects the realm of sensory experience and perception to the space of appearance. Arendt quotes Shelley

---

8 For instance, she notes that Heidegger's characterization of speech as inauthentic, to the extent that it separates thought from language, parallels Plato's notion of mimesis, in Arendt, *The Life of the Mind*, 118–19.
9 John Tambornino, *The Corporeal Turn: Passion, Necessity, Politics* (Lanham: Rowman & Littlefield Publishers, 2002), 16.

to illustrate this process: the poet's language "marks the before unapprehended *relations* of things and perpetuates their apprehension."[10] This metaphorical, or even chiastic, carrying over of sensory perception into the space of appearance and back again produces the phenomenal character of existence: "*Being and Appearing coincide.*"[11]

Metaphor is important for Arendt in two ways: first, it is essential for "common-sense thinking."[12] Language is what guarantees and communicates the common sense of the body politic. It 'carries over' individual sensory data into a shared framework of understanding, meaning, and belonging, connecting the "realm of the invisible," which relates to sensory perception and thinking, to the space of appearance, in which individuals act, speak, and are recognized by others. Second, metaphor demonstrates the falsity of the metaphysical separation of "being and appearance," into a transcendental realm of eternal forms and an immanent realm of physical sensation and experience: "language, by lending itself to metaphorical usage, enables us to think, that is, to have a traffic with non-sensory matters, because it permits a carrying-over, *metapherein*, of our sense experience. There are not two worlds because metaphor unites them."[13]

Arendt's thinking, then, provides an alternative to both postmodernism's suspicion of language and its ability to convey material, bodily experience and the metaphysical tradition that postmodernism rightly critiques, which denigrates sensory life and situates 'true' thinking in a transcendental realm of eternal forms. However, it would be incorrect to argue that Arendt sees language as able to fully express the body's sheer physicality and intensity. Language more easily communicates thinking, willing, and judging – activities of the mind.[14] Even though she recognizes that sensory, phenomenological experience emerges from a bodily locus, she remains quite wary of the body itself. Its material need for food, water, and shelter can tether the individual to the cyclical process of labor,[15] preventing them from engaging in activities like aesthetic work and political action. Without a common world, individuals are returned to the "cruel privacy [of] the experience of bodily processes."[16] Arendt is almost always oriented towards the public realm as a way of

---

10 Arendt, *The Life of the Mind*, 102. Emphasis in original.
11 Arendt, *The Life of the Mind*, 19. Emphasis in original.
12 Arendt, *The Life of the Mind*, 103.
13 Arendt, *The Life of the Mind*, 110.
14 See Tambornino, *The Corporeal Turn*, 26.
15 Arendt, *The Human Condition*, 117. Arendt discusses labor and work or fabrication extensively in Chapters III and IV, respectively.
16 Arendt, *The Human Condition*, 117.

constellating these 'private' sensory existences into a shared framework of understanding.

The Aestheticization of Politics

Arendt is thus suspicious of the kind of subjective forms of embodied experience I have explored throughout *Formal Matters*, which, in the absence of a shared perceptual world, can result in isolation, alienation, and atomization. These, in turn, are affects exploited and perpetuated by the worst political movements of the twentieth century: the totalitarianism of Nazism and Stalinism. She closely explores the relationship between sensory and perceptual experience and language in *The Origins of Totalitarianism*, in which she demonstrates how Nazism's flattening of language went hand in hand with its destruction of shared aesthetic experience, such that it isolated each individual in their own world. Totalitarian propaganda sought to sever the link between what people perceive through the senses and what they hear, read, or say. Reflecting back on the Eichmann trial, she writes that "clichés, stock phrases, adherence to conventional, standardized codes of expression and conduct" absolve people from thinking and thus judging.[17] Viktor Klemperer dubs this propagandistic language of Nazism *Lingua Tertii Imperii*, in which conventional usages were turned upside down, anodyne euphemisms were used to describe radically violent acts, causality and action were inverted, and neologisms produced new political categories and acts naturalized through an appeal to scientific language.[18]

This language was often in direct opposition to the world individuals perceived through their sensory experience, making them distrustful of reality. When Nazism's official language insisted on the existence of *Der jüdische Krieg* (The Jewish War),[19] even as Jewish neighbors and friends simply undertook everyday activities, then people began to stop believing "in anything visible, in the reality of their own experience."[20] Totalitarianism thus gradually fragments common sense, "the experience of the materially and sensually given world [. . .] which regulates and controls the other senses," into a vast undifferentiated daze of

---

17 Arendt, *The Life of the Mind*, 4.
18 Victor Klemperer, *The Language of the Third Reich: LTI Lingua Tertii Imperii: A Philologist's Notebook*, trans. Martin Brady (London; New York: Bloomsbury Academic, 2013). Klemperer describes how Nazi reshaped the very structure of language, for example through the use of prefixes or punctuation.
19 Klemperer, *The Language of the Third Reich*, 178.
20 Arendt, *The Origins of Totalitarianism*, 351.

"unreliable and treacherous" data. This leaves people not only unable to trust their own "immediate sensual experience" but also the plural experiences of others.[21] Totalitarian ideology thus becomes "emancipated from the reality that we perceive with our five senses"; it "insists on a 'truer' reality concealed behind all perceptible thing, dominating them from this place of concealment and requiring a sixth sense that enable us to become aware of it."[22] This ideological "supersense" replaces "common sense," offering the hollowed-out form of plurality – an ossified shell of senseless cohesion.

In destroying common sense and language, totalitarianism begins to produce atomization and isolation. Total terror – the "essence of totalitarian government" – "substitutes for the boundaries and channels of communication between individual men a band of iron which holds them so tightly together that it is as though their plurality had disappeared into One Man of gigantic dimensions."[23] In language that is strikingly resonant of Beckett's description of a body politic oriented only towards the reduction of language to violence, or in Levi's description of the way violence emerges when communication breaks down, Arendt writes that violence – pure force – transforms language's sense-making system into the "murderous alphabet" of totalitarian logic,[24] an arbitrary arrangement of letters and signs that results in a genocidal "fiction."[25] This both squeezes individuals into one undifferentiated mass and prevents them from communicating with each other. The result is a loneliness that becomes the defining existential condition under totalitarianism, in which everyone is at once identical and sealed off from others. Arendt often describes this experience in terms of 'homelessness,' a condition that comes about when common sense is destroyed. It is the experience of having "no place in the world, recognized and guaranteed by others."[26]

This is a world that resembles Kofman's description of aporia, a limitless space buffeted by violent winds. According to Arendt, totalitarianism seeks to abolish the "boundaries," "channels of communication," and "fences of laws between men," thus destroying "the living space of freedom." Without language's physical structure, or what Steinlauf calls "the skeleton, the scaffolding, the form of civilization" in *If This Is a Man*, we are left with "the lawless, fenceless wilderness of fear and

---

21 Arendt, *The Origins of Totalitarianism*, 475–76.
22 Arendt, *The Origins of Totalitarianism*, 470–71.
23 Arendt, *The Origins of Totalitarianism*, 465–66.
24 Arendt, *The Origins of Totalitarianism*, 472.
25 Arendt, *The Origins of Totalitarianism*, 392.
26 Arendt, *The Origins of Totalitarianism*, 475.

suspicion." Totalitarianism even sets this "desert itself in motion, to let loose a sand storm that could cover all parts of the inhabited earth," obliterating all difference.[27] The sandstorm is a metaphor for totalitarianism's destruction of the material infrastructure of communication and language, which immerses each individual in the swirling sands of their own unlocatable sensory perception; they are unable to see or touch those around them who remain just out of reach. Similarly, the loss of defined spaces, walls, and boundaries parallels the ruination of cultural forms. Both denote a destruction of the human subjects that inhabit, create, and move between them.[28] A world without boundaries and fences is one where humanity is cast perpetually to the peripheries – it is a world of profound loneliness. Its corresponding aesthetic space would be a kind of formlessness – like shifting sands – unanchored by tangible markers of worldliness and shelter, where "no-sense" rather than "common sense" reigns.[29] In this world given over to formlessness, the only concrete entity that emerges is the 'total' form of the concentration camp – a monolith in both senses of the word.

This account of the relationship between aesthetic experience and totalitarianism is quite different from the one offered by Arendt's friend Walter Benjamin, who decried the "aestheticization of politics," which offers the visual and phenomenal appearance of political recognition without any of the rights that politics should guarantee.[30] Benjamin's critique of aesthetics found remarkable purchase across a range of twentieth- and twenty-first century thinkers. This critique of aesthetics as *"l'art pour l'art"* associated it with totalizing or "bounded" forms and, indeed, forms of totalitarianism.[31] As I have noted throughout this book, against the perceived dangers of assimilation, absorption, order, and containment, scholars have wielded modes of counterviolence that seek to dissemble and dismantle forms. Yet what Arendt describes here

---

27 Arendt, *The Origins of Totalitarianism*, 478. See also Hannah Arendt, *The Promise of Politics* (New York: Schocken Books, 2005), 202.
28 See Susannah Young-ah Gottlieb, *Regions of Sorrow: Anxiety and Messianism in Hannah Arendt and W. H. Auden* (Stanford, CA: Stanford University Press, 2003), 30.
29 Arendt, *The Origins of Totalitarianism*, 458.
30 Walter Benjamin writes: "Fascism attempts to organize the newly created proletarian masses without affecting the property structure which the masses strive to eliminate. Fascism sees its salvation in giving these masses not their right, but instead a chance to express themselves. The masses have a right to change property relations; Fascism seeks to give them an expression while preserving property. The logical result of Fascism is the introduction of aesthetics into political life. [. . .] All efforts to render politics aesthetic culminate in one thing: war," in Benjamin, "The Work of Art in the Age of Mechanical Reproduction," in *Illuminations*, ed. Hannah Arendt, trans. Harry Zohn (New York: Schocken Books, 1986), 241.
31 See Kornbluh, *The Order of Forms*, 3.

is how totalitarianism *destroys* aesthetic experience, common sense, and language, the 'scaffolding' of human existence and civilization. Far from an aestheticization of politics, totalitarianism and fascism destroy aesthetic experience. Indeed, aesthetic representation is necessary for the (re)construction of political communities, precisely because it helps reinstate the "boundaries" and "lines of communication" between individuals. It rebuilds plurality by allowing people to imagine the viewpoints and perspectives of others without the false comforts of compassion and empathy.[32] Against the destituency of fascism and totalitarianism, aesthetic fabrication offers a sense of stability and realness. Aesthetics is thus necessary for the construction of political communities – of forms, in other words – that provide a 'home' in which one's place in the world can be guaranteed by shared forms of sensory perception and language.

Constructing Forms

Hannah Arendt was a builder. Over and over again she returns to images and figures for construction: walls, lines, boundaries, and blueprints. These are not exclusionary spaces designed to keep people out, however. Instead, they are oriented towards providing a 'home.' Though she may not have put it in these terms, she advocated building stable, lasting forms against the violent destituency of fascism and totalitarianism. But where is the body's place in this world? Although she decries the violence totalitarianism wrought on the body, reducing people to pure sensing animals, "bundles of reactions,"[33] she was suspicious of the body's demands, of its physical fragility and existence, what in postmodernist terms would be called its 'immanence.' The cyclical nature of labor and reproduction tethers the body to its biological needs. Against this, Arendt advocates for work, which produces aesthetic objects, or for action, the basis of political activity.

Yet, precisely because the body, in all its vulnerability and immanence, is both the locus of sensory experience and the object of political domination, we must find a way to fit it into more lasting forms of representation. Embodied form helps integrate this fragile, bodily experience into a more endurable form, and in doing so it also provides a more stable foundation for progressive political configurations, which are dependent on shared forms of sensory perception. Embodied form helps individual

---

32 Arendt considers these affects the enemy of judgment, because they destroy the critical distance needed to allow the imagination to work. See, for instance, Hannah Arendt, "On Humanity in Dark Times," in *Men in Dark Times* (San Diego, CA: Harvest Books, 1970).
33 Arendt, *The Origins of Totalitarianism*, 438, 456.

bodily experience fit into the body politic of representation. This does entail a kind of aestheticization. Indeed, as I have argued throughout this book, the 'aestheticization' of embodiment – that is, the way in which poetic language renders bodily experience apprehensible – is not only necessary, it is *inescapable*. Political movements from totalitarianism to Trumpism have sought to empty everyday life of its aesthetic dimension. They have operated by cutting off individuals' perceptual experience from the world around them, creating atomized spheres of existence ('echo chambers') that language cannot 'carry over' into a shared realm. In the face of this hollowing-out of aesthetic experience, the aestheticization of the body is more vital than ever. Aestheticization is what enables the body to appear and be counted in the world – to be represented politically. The body cannot escape representation. Rather, representation should not be thought of without the body.

Common sense can provide this more integrative model of representation, whether aesthetic or political. The trick comes in being able to recognize the embodied experiences of those most excluded from the political realm. Like Bertolt Brecht, one of her favorite writers, Arendt advocated for "a passionate longing for a world in which all can be seen and heard, the passionate wrath against a history that remembered a few and forgot so many, a history that under the pretense of remembering caused us to forget."[34] Put in terms that may be more familiar to readers today, Arendt sought to "recover marginalized or repressed perspectives."[35] Literature, art, and other aesthetic forms help to do so, not by providing *representations* of such bodies but by integrating their sensorial experiences and experiential worlds into the common sense – the sensorial form – of the body politic. Incorporating this embodied experience into common sense may help change the body politic's *reality*.

Literary form embodies common sense. It infuses individual embodied experience into literary language and endows the specificity of literature with bodily expression. But it not only brings these two things together, it also fits them into a shared framework that provides the sense of

---

34 Hannah Arendt, "Beyond Personal Frustration: The Poetry of Bertolt Brecht," in *Reflections on Literature and Culture*, ed. Susannah Young-ah Gottlieb (Stanford, CA: Stanford University Press, 2007), 141.

35 Ritivoi, "Reading (with) Hannah Arendt," 2. It is nevertheless important to recognize Arendt's own ethical failings when it came to recognizing the rights of some of these excluded voices, such as African Americans in the United States. Her essay "Reflections on Little Rock," which address school integration, is stunning in its insensitivity and verges on overt racism. For a critique of this see Kathryn T. Gines, *Hannah Arendt and the Negro Question* (Bloomington, IN: Indiana University Press, 2014). Arendt was also highly critical of what we would today call 'identity politics,' which she associated with a myopic turning into an experience, instead of gazing outwards.

reality that permeates literature, from the most experimental literature of Garréta or Beckett to the most sincerely 'representational,' like Levi's. By this I do not mean that it provides a sense of verisimilitude, or a reality effect. Rather, literary language seems immediately available and meaningful to us, even before we may have understood its propositional or discursive content, precisely because it is able to communicate common forms of sensory perception. Embodied form provides this shared realm of sense perception and language. It constructs a 'home' for the body, to reprise Arendt's interest in building forms, or a space in which the experiences of many can be integrated and made to speak without assimilation or absorption, just as multiple aesthetic modes and devices can exist at the same time within the same text without logical contradiction. By making manifest the embodied foundation of politics – the way it emerges from individual bodies and coalesces into shared forms of common sense – literary form can help model the translation, mediation, and *carrying over* of embodied experience into forms that are not entirely coincident with it but that are, nevertheless, inseparable. This work will always be speculative to an extent; indeed, as the work of both Beckett and Levi demonstrates, an exact equivalence between form and politics can be highly destructive. But poetic language not only connects embodied experience and political forms, it also renders embodiment apprehensible in the political sphere. In doing so, it demonstrates how politics is composed through bodily relations. Literature, in a sense, *embodies* this connection between bodies and politics through its (metaphorical) form. Conversely, by embodying the senses, movement, and presence into a shared form, literature and other aesthetic modes provide the property of *realness* associated with common sense. This leads me to turn my statement above into a chiasmus: it is not only that literary form embodies common sense, embodied form is the *sensus communis* of literature.

Bibliography

Abrams, Meyer Howard. *The Mirror and the Lamp: Romantic Theory and the Critical Tradition*. Oxford: Oxford University Press, 1953.
Adorno, Theodor W. "Cultural Criticism and Society." In *Prisms*. Cambridge, MA: MIT Press, 1983.
Agamben, Giorgio. *Homo Sacer: Sovereign Power and Bare Life*. Translated by Daniel Heller-Roazen. Stanford, CA: Stanford University Press, 1998.
Agamben, Giorgio. *Remnants of Auschwitz: The Witness and the Archive*. Translated by Daniel Heller-Roazen. New York: Zone Books, 2002.
Ahmed, Sara. *Strange Encounters: Embodied Others in Post-Coloniality*. London; New York: Routledge, 2000.
Ahmed, Sara. *The Cultural Politics of Emotion*. London: Routledge, 2013.
Alaimo, Stacy. *Bodily Natures: Science, Environment, and the Material Self*. Bloomington, IN: Indiana University Press, 2010.
Alaimo, Stacy, and Susan J. Hekman, eds. *Material Feminisms*. Bloomington, IN: Indiana University Press, 2008.
Alaimo, Stacy, and Susan J. Hekman "Trans-Corporeal Feminisms and the Ethical Space of Nature." In *Material Feminisms*, edited by Stacy Alaimo and Susan J. Hekman. Bloomington, IN: Indiana University Press, 2008.
Althusser, Louis. *Reading Capital*. Translated by Etienne Balibar. New York: Pantheon Books, 1971.
Altieri, Charles. "The New Criticism." In *The Edinburgh Encyclopedia of Modern Criticism and Theory*, edited by Julian Wolfreys. Edinburgh: Edinburgh University Press, 2002.
Altieri, Charles. *The Particulars of Rapture: An Aesthetics of the Affects*. Ithaca, NY: Cornell University Press, 2003.
Améry, Jean. *At the Mind's Limits: Contemplations by a Survivor on Auschwitz and Its Realities*. Translated by Sidney Rosenfeld and Stella P. Rosenfeld. Bloomington, IN: Indiana University Press, 1980.
Antonello, Pierpaolo. *Il ménage a quattro: Scienza, filosofia, tecnica nella letteratura italiano del novecento*. Florence: Le Monnier, 2005.
Appelfeld, Aharon. *Beyond Despair: Three Lectures and a Conversation with Philip Roth*. New York: Fromm International, 1994.
Arendt, Hannah. "Beyond Personal Frustration: The Poetry of Bertolt Brecht." In *Reflections on Literature and Culture*, edited by Susannah Young-ah Gottlieb. Stanford, CA: Stanford University Press, 2007.

Arendt, Hannah. *Lectures on Kant's Political Philosophy*. Chicago: University of Chicago Press, 1990.
Arendt, Hannah. "On Humanity in Dark Times." In *Men in Dark Times*. San Diego, CA: Harvest Books, 1970.
Arendt, Hannah. "Preface." In *Men in Dark Times*. San Diego, CA: Harvest Books, 1970.
Arendt, Hannah. *The Human Condition*. Chicago: University of Chicago Press, 1958.
Arendt, Hannah. *The Life of the Mind*. New York: Harvest Books, 1971.
Arendt, Hannah. *The Origins of Totalitarianism*. New York: Harcourt Brace Jovanovich, 1973.
Arendt, Hannah. *The Promise of Politics*. New York: Schocken Books, 2005.
Arendt, Hannah. "We Refugees." In *The Jewish Writings*, edited by Jerome Kohn and Ron H. Feldman. New York: Schocken Books, 2007.
Aristotle. *Aristotle's "Politics."* Translated by Carnes Lord. Chicago: University of Chicago Press, 1984.
Attridge, Derek. *The Singularity of Literature*. London: Routledge, 2004.
Auerbach, Erich. *Mimesis: The Representation of Reality in Western Literature*. Princeton, NJ: Princeton University Press, 2003.
Bari, Shahidha Kazi. "Feeling Friendship: Reading Keats's 'This Living Hand' and the Sonnets on the Elgin Marbles." In *The Hand of the Interpreter: Essays on Meaning After Theory*, edited by G. F. Mitrano and Eric Jarosinski. Berlin: Peter Lang, 2009.
Baroghel, Elsa. "Samuel Beckett, lecteur de Sade: *Comment c'est* et *Les cent vingt journées de Sodome*." Samuel Beckett, no. 4 in *La Revue des lettres modernes*. Paris: Classiques Garnier, 2017.
Bauer Wise, Susan. *The History of the Ancient World: From the Earliest Accounts to the Fall of Rome*. New York: W. W. Norton & Company, 2007.
Beckett, Samuel. *Comment c'est*. Paris: Les Editions de Minuit, 1961.
Beckett, Samuel. *Compagnie*. Paris: Les Editions de Minuit, 1980.
Beckett, Samuel. "Company." In *Nohow On: Company, Ill Seen Ill Said, Worstword Ho*. New York: Grove Press, 1996.
Beckett, Samuel. *Disjecta: Miscellaneous Writings and a Dramatic Fragment*. Edited by Ruby Cohn. New York: Grove Press, 1984.
Beckett, Samuel. *Dream of Fair to Middling Women*. Edited by Eoin O'Brien and Edith Fournier. London: Calder Publications, 1993.
Beckett, Samuel. *How It Is*. Edited by Edouard Magessa O'Reilly. London: Faber and Faber, 2009.
Beckett, Samuel. "Ill Seen Ill Said." In *Nohow On: Company, Ill Seen Ill Said, Worstword Ho*. New York: Grove Press, 1996.
Beckett, Samuel. *Malone Dies*. Harmondsworth: Penguin Books, 1975.
Beckett, Samuel. *Molloy*. London: Faber and Faber, 2009.
Beckett, Samuel. *Murphy*. London: Calder Publications, 2003.
Beckett, Samuel. *Proust*. New York: Grove Press, 1978.
Beckett, Samuel. *The Complete Dramatic Works*. London: Faber and Faber, 1990.
Beckett, Samuel. *The Complete Short Prose, 1929–1989*. Edited by S. E. Gontarski. New York: Grove Press, 2000.

Beckett, Samuel. *The Letters of Samuel Beckett*. Edited by Martha Fehsenfeld, Lois More Overbeck, George Craig, and Daniel Gunn. Vol. I: 1929–1940. Cambridge: Cambridge University Press, 2009.

Beckett, Samuel. *The Unnamable*. London: Faber and Faber, 1958.

Benardete, Seth. *The Argument of the Action: Essays on Greek Poetry and Philosophy*. Chicago: University of Chicago Press, 2000.

Benjamin, Walter. "The Work of Art in the Age of Mechanical Reproduction." In *Illuminations*, edited by Hannah Arendt, translated by Harry Zohn. New York: Schocken Books, 1986.

Bennett, Andrew. "Language and the Body." In *The Cambridge Companion to the Body in Literature*, edited by David Hillman and Ulrika Maude. Cambridge: Cambridge University Press, 2015.

Bernard-Donals, Michael F. *Forgetful Memory: Representation and Remembrance in the Wake of the Holocaust*. Albany, NY: SUNY Press, 2008.

Bernard-Donals, Michael F., and Richard R. Glejzer. *Between Witness and Testimony: The Holocaust and the Limits of Representation*. Albany, NY: SUNY Press, 2001.

Bernini, Marco. *Beckett and the Cognitive Method: Mind, Models, and Exploratory Narratives*. New York; Oxford: Oxford University Press, 2021.

Bersani, Leo. *Balzac to Beckett: Center and Circumference in French Fiction*. Oxford: Oxford University Press, 1970.

Best, Stephen, and Sharon Marcus. "Surface Reading: An Introduction." *Representations* 108, no. 1 (2009): 1–21.

Bishop, Cécile. "Photography, Race and Invisibility." *Photographies* 11, no. 2–3 (September 2, 2018): 193–213.

Blackman, Lisa. *Hearing Voices: Embodiment and Experience*. London; New York: Free Association Books, 2001.

Blackman, Lisa. *Immaterial Bodies: Affect, Embodiment, Mediation*. Los Angeles: Sage, 2012.

Blackman, Lisa. *The Body: The Key Concepts*. Oxford; New York: Berg, 2008.

Blanchot, Maurice. *Faux pas*. Translated by Charlotte Mandell. Stanford, CA: Stanford University Press, 2001.

Blanchot, Maurice. *L'Instant de ma mort*. Montpellier: Fata Morgana, 1994.

Blanchot, Maurice. *The Infinite Conversation*. Translated by Susan Hanson. Minneapolis, MN: University of Minnesota Press, 1993.

Blanchot, Maurice. *The Space of Literature*. Translated by Ann Smock. Lincoln, NE: University of Nebraska Press, 1989.

Blanchot, Maurice. *The Writing of the Disaster*. Translated by Ann Smock. Lincoln, NE: University of Nebraska Press, 1995.

Blanchot, Maurice, and Jacques Derrida. *The Instant of My Death /Demeure: Fiction and Testimony*. Translated by Elizabeth Rottenberg. Stanford, CA: Stanford University Press, 2000.

Bloom, Harold. *A Map of Misreading*. Oxford: Oxford University Press, 2003.

Bois, Yve-Alain and Rosalind E. Krauss. *Formless: A User's Guide*. New York; Cambridge, MA: Zone Books, 1997.

Bolens, Guillemette. *The Style of Gestures: Embodiment and Cognition in Literary Narrative*. Translated by Alain Berthoz. Baltimore, MD: Johns Hopkins University Press, 2012.

Boxall, Peter. "Samuel Beckett: Towards a Political Reading." *Irish Studies Review* 10, no. 2 (August 2002): 159–70.
Brackney, Kathryn L. "Remembering 'Planet Auschwitz' During the Cold War." *Representations* 144, no. 1 (November 1, 2018): 124–53.
Braidotti, Rosi. *Nomadic Subjects: Embodiment and Sexual Difference in Contemporary Feminist Theory.* New York: Columbia University Press, 1994.
Braiterman, Zachary. "Against Holocaust-Sublime: Naive Reference and the Generation of Memory." *History and Memory* 12, no. 2 (2000): 7–28.
Breu, Christopher. *Insistence of the Material: Literature in the Age of Biopolitics.* Minneapolis, MN: University of Minnesota Press, 2014.
Brienza, Susan D. *Samuel Beckett's New Worlds: Style in Metafiction.* Norman, OK: University of Oklahoma Press, 1987.
Brinkema, Eugenie. *The Forms of the Affects.* Durham, NC: Duke University Press, 2014.
Brooks, Cleanth. "The Formalist Critics." *The Kenyon Review* 13, no. 1 (1951): 72–81.
Brooks, Cleanth. *The Well Wrought Urn: Studies in the Structure of Poetry.* New York: Houghton Mifflin Harcourt, 1947.
Brooks, Peter. *Body Work: Objects of Desire in Modern Narrative.* Cambridge: Harvard University Press, 1993.
Brown, Llewellyn, ed. *La violence dans l'œuvre de Samuel Beckett: Entre langage et corps.* Paris: Lettres Modernes Minard, 2017.
Bruns, Gerald L. *Maurice Blanchot: The Refusal of Philosophy.* Baltimore, MD: Johns Hopkins University Press, 1997.
Butler, Judith. *Bodies That Matter: On the Discursive Limits of "Sex."* New York: Routledge, 1993.
Butler, Judith. *Excitable Speech: A Politics of the Performative.* New York: Routledge, 1997.
Butler, Judith. "Foucault and the Paradox of Bodily Inscriptions." *The Journal of Philosophy* 86, no. 11 (November 1, 1989): 601–7.
Butler, Judith. *Gender Trouble: Feminism and the Subversion of Identity.* New York: Routledge, 1990.
Butler, Judith. "Sexual Ideology and Phenomenological Description: A Feminist Critique of Merleau-Ponty's Phenomenology of Perception." In *The Thinking Muse: Feminism and Modern French Philosophy*, edited by Jeffner Allen and Iris Marion Young. Bloomington, IN: Indiana University Press, 1989.
Butler, Judith. *The Psychic Life of Power: Theories in Subjection.* Stanford, CA: Stanford University Press, 1997.
Cairns, Lucille. "Queer Paradox/Paradoxical Queer: Anne Garréta's *Pas un jour* (2002)." *Journal of Lesbian Studies* 11, no. 1–2 (August 2007): 70–87.
Caracciolo, Marco. *Embodiment and the Cosmic Perspective in Twentieth-Century Fiction.* New York; Abingdon: Routledge, 2020.
Carroll, David. "The Limits of Representation and the Right to Fiction: Shame, Literature, and the Memory of the Shoah." *L'Esprit Créateur* 39, no. 4 (1999): 68–79.
Caruth, Cathy. *Unclaimed Experience: Trauma, Narrative, and History.* Baltimore, MD: Johns Hopkins University Press, 1996.

Chabert, Pierre. "The Body in Beckett's Theatre." *Journal of Beckett Studies* 8 (1982): 23–28.
Chernavin, Georgy, and Anna Yampolskaya. "'Estrangement' in Aesthetics and Beyond: Russian Formalism and Phenomenological Method." *Continental Philosophy Review* 52, no. 1 (March 2019): 91–113.
Clark, Michael, ed. *Revenge of the Aesthetic: The Place of Literature in Theory Today*. Berkeley, CA: University of California Press, 2000.
Cohen, S. M. "Hylomorphism and Functionalism." In *Essays on Aristotle's De Anima*, edited by Martha Craven Nussbaum and Amélie Rorty. Oxford: Clarendon Press, 1992.
Cohen, William A. *Embodied: Victorian Literature and the Senses*. Minneapolis, MN: University of Minnesota Press, 2009.
Cohn, Ruby. *Back to Beckett*. Princeton, NJ: Princeton University Press, 1974.
Cohn, Ruby, "Foreword." In *Disjecta: Miscellaneous Writings and a Dramatic Fragment*, by Samuel Beckett, edited by Ruby Cohn. New York: Grove Press, 1984.
Coleridge, Samuel Taylor. *The Poetical Works of Samuel Taylor Coleridge*. New York: Appleton, 1857.
Conboy, Katie, and Nadia Medina, eds. *Writing on the Body: Female Embodiment and Feminist Theory*. New York: Columbia University Press, 1997.
Connor, Steven. *Beckett, Modernism and the Material Imagination*. New York; Cambridge: Cambridge University Press, 2014.
Connor, Steven. *Samuel Beckett: Repetition, Theory, and Text*. Oxford: Basil Blackwell, 1988.
Connor, Steven. "Shifting Ground," accessed 7 September 2021, http://stevenconnor.com/beckettnauman.html.
Connor, Steven. "The Matter of Beckett's Facts." *Journal of Beckett Studies* 28, no. 1 (April 2019): 5–18.
Coole, Diana, and Samantha Frost. "Introducing the New Materialisms." In *New Materialisms: Ontology, Agency, and Politics*, edited by Diana Coole and Samantha Frost. Durham, NC: Duke University Press, 2010.
Coole, Diana, and Samantha Frost, eds. *New Materialisms: Ontology, Agency, and Politics*. Durham, NC: Duke University Press, 2010.
Cools, Arthur. "Intentionnalité et singularité: Maurice Blanchot et la phénoménologie." In *Blanchot et la philosophie*, edited by Eric Hoppenot and Alain Milon. Paris: Presses Universitaires de Paris 10, 2010.
Crowther, Paul. *Art and Embodiment: From Aesthetics to Self-Consciousness*. Oxford: Oxford University Press, 1993.
Csordas, Thomas J. *Body/Meaning/Healing*. New York: Palgrave Macmillan, 2007.
Csordas, Thomas J. "Embodiment as a Paradigm for Anthropology." *Ethos* 18, no. 1 (March 1, 1990): 5–47.
Csordas, Thomas J. "Introduction: The Body as Representation and Being-in-the-World." In *Embodiment and Experience: The Existential Ground of Culture and Self*, edited by Thomas J. Csordas. Cambridge: Cambridge University Press, 1994.
Culler, Jonathan. "Commentary." *New Literary History* 6, no. 1 (1974): 219–29.

Culler, Jonathan. *Saussure*. London: Fontana, 1976.
Culler, Jonathan. *The Pursuit of Signs: Semiotics, Literature, Deconstruction*. London: Routledge, 2002.
Cummings, Brian. "Metalepsis: The Boundaries of Metaphor." In *Renaissance Figures of Speech*, edited by Sylvia Adamson, Gavin Alexander, and Katrin Ettenhuber. Cambridge: Cambridge University Press, 2011.
Cusset, François. *French Theory: How Foucault, Derrida, Deleuze, & Co. Transformed the Intellectual Life of the United States*. Translated by Jeff Fort. Minneapolis, MN: University of Minnesota Press, 2008.
Daniel, E. Valentine, and Jeffrey M. Peck, eds. *Culture/Contexture: Explorations in Anthropology and Literary Studies*. Berkeley, CA: University of California Press, 1996.
Davis, Thomas S. "Neutral War: *L'Instant de ma mort*." In *Clandestine Encounters: Philosophy in the Narratives of Maurice Blanchot*, edited by Kevin Hart. Baltimore, MD: Johns Hopkins University Press, 2004.
Dennis, Amanda. "Radical Indecision: Aporia as Metamorphosis in *The Unnamable*." *Journal of Beckett Studies* 24, no. 2 (2015): 180–97.
Derrida, Jacques. "Living On." In *Deconstruction and Criticism*, by Harold Bloom, Paul de Man, Jacques Derrida, Geoffrey H. Hartman, and J. Hillis Miller. London: Seabury Press, 1979.
Derrida, Jacques. *Positions*. Translated by Alan Bass. Chicago: University of Chicago Press, 1998.
Derrida, Jacques. *Writing and Difference*. Translated by Alan Bass. London: Routledge, 2009.
Descombes, Vincent. *Modern French Philosophy*. Cambridge: Cambridge University Press, 1980.
Dewey, John. *Art as Experience*. New York: Perigee Books, 1934.
Diner, Hasia R. *We Remember with Reverence and Love: American Jews and the Myth of Silence after the Holocaust, 1945–1962*. New York: New York University Press, 2009.
Doane, Mary Ann. "Indexicality: Trace and Sign: Introduction." *Differences* 18, no. 1 (January 1, 2007): 1–6.
Driver, Tom. "Interview with Samuel Beckett." In *Samuel Beckett: The Critical Heritage*, edited by Lawrence Graver and Raymond Federman. London; Boston: Routledge & Kegan Paul, 1979.
Druker, Jonathan. *Primo Levi and Humanism After Auschwitz: Posthumanist Reflections*. New York: Palgrave Macmillan, 2009.
Dufrenne, Mikel. *The Phenomenology of Aesthetic Experience*. Translated by Edward S. Casey. Evanston, IL: Northwestern University Press, 1973.
Dukes, Hunter. "Beckett's Vessels and the Animation of Containers." *Journal of Modern Literature* 40, no. 4 (2017): 75–89.
Duncan, Dennis. *The Oulipo and Modern Thought*. Oxford: Oxford University Press, 2019.
Dupriez, Bernard. *A Dictionary of Literary Devices*. Translated by Albert W. Halsall. New York: Harvester Wheatsheaf, 1991.
Eagleton, Terry. *Criticism and Ideology: A Study in Marxist Literary Theory*. London: Verso, 1978.
Eagleton, Terry. *Literary Theory: An Introduction*. Minneapolis, MN: University of Minnesota Press, 2008.

Erlich, Avi. *Russian Formalism: History – Doctrine*. The Hague: Mouton Publications, 1955.
Ernout, Alfred, Antoine Meillet, and Jacques André. *Dictionnaire étymologique de la langue latine: histoire des mots*. Fourth edition. Paris: Klincksieck, 2001.
Featherstone, Mike, Mike Hepworth, and Bryan Turner, eds. *The Body: Social Process and Cultural Theory*. London: Sage, 1991.
Felman, Shoshana. *The Juridical Unconscious: Trials and Traumas in the Twentieth Century*. Cambridge, MA: Harvard University Press, 2002.
Felski, Rita. *The Limits of Critique*. Chicago: University of Chicago Press, 2015.
Forth, Christopher E. "The Body." In *Writing the Holocaust*, edited by Jean-Marc Dreyfus and Daniel Langton. London: Bloomsbury Academic, 2011.
Foucault, Michel. "A Preface to Transgression." In *Language, Counter-Memory, Practice: Selected Essays and Interviews*, translated by Donald. F. Bouchard and Sherry Simon. Ithaca, NY: Cornell University Press, 1977.
Foucault, Michel. *Discipline and Punish: The Birth of the Prison*. London: Vintage, 1995.
Foucault, Michel. *The History of Sexuality, Vol. 1: An Introduction*. Translated by Robert Hurley. New York: Vintage, 1990.
Foucault, Michel. *The History of Sexuality, Vol. 2: The Use of Pleasure*. Translated by Robert Hurley. New York: Vintage Books, 1990.
Foucault, Michel. *The History of Sexuality, Vol. 3: The Care of the Self*. Translated by Robert Hurley. New York: Vintage, 1990.
Foucault, Michel. "The Order of Discourse." In *Untying the Text: A Post-Structuralist Reader*, edited by Robert Young. Boston; London: Routledge & Kegan Paul, 1981.
Foucault, Michel. *The Order of Things*. London; New York: Routledge, 2002.
Frank, Arthur W. *The Wounded Storyteller: Body, Illness, and Ethics*. Chicago: University of Chicago Press, 1997.
Friedlander, Saul. "Introduction." In *Probing the Limits of Representation: Nazism and the "Final Solution,"* edited by Saul Friedlander. Cambridge, MA: Harvard University Press, 1992.
Froula, Christine. *Modernism's Body: Sex, Culture, and Joyce*. New York: Columbia University Press, 1996.
Fuss, Diana. *Essentially Speaking: Feminism, Nature, and Difference*. New York: Routledge, 1989.
Gallagher, Catherine, and Stephen Greenblatt. *Practicing New Historicism*. Chicago: University of Chicago Press, 2000.
Garréta, Anne. *Sphinx*. Paris: Grasset, 1986.
Garréta, Anne. *Sphinx*. Translated by Emma Ramadan. Dallas, TX: Deep Vellum Publishing, 2015.
Garréta, Anne, and Eva Domeneghini. "Entretien avec Anne F. Garréta" [Interview with Anne F. Garréta], October 13, 2000. http://cosmogonie.free.fr/index2.html
Gasché, Rodolphe. "Reading Chiasms: An Introduction." In *Readings in Interpretation: Hölderlin, Hegel, Heidegger*, by Andrzej Warminski. Minneapolis, MN: University of Minnesota Press, 1987.
Gaskill, Nicholas. "The Close and the Concrete: Aesthetic Formalism in Context." *New Literary History* 47, no. 4 (2016): 505–24.

Geertz, Clifford. *Works and Lives: The Anthropologist as Author*. Stanford, CA: Stanford University Press, 1988.
Genette, Gérard. *Narrative Discourse: An Essay in Method*. Translated by Jane Lewin. Ithaca, NY: Cornell Univ. Press, 1980.
Geroulanos, Stefanos. *Transparency in Postwar France: A Critical History of the Present*. Stanford, CA: Stanford University Press, 2017.
Gibson, Andrew. *Samuel Beckett*. London: Reaktion Books, 2010.
Gibson, Andrew. *Towards a Postmodern Theory of Narrative*. Edinburgh: Edinburgh University Press, 1996.
Gines, Kathryn T. *Hannah Arendt and the Negro Question*. Bloomington, IN: Indiana University Press, 2014.
Gontarski, S. E, and Anthony Uhlmann. *Beckett after Beckett*. Gainesville, FL: University Press of Florida, 2006.
Graver, Lawrence, and Raymond Federman, eds. *Samuel Beckett: The Critical Heritage*. London; Boston: Routledge & Kegan Paul, 1979.
Grosz, Elizabeth. *Volatile Bodies: Toward a Corporeal Feminism*. Bloomington, IN: Indiana University Press, 1994.
Gunzberg, Lynn M. "Down among the Dead Men: Levi and Dante in Hell." *Modern Language Studies* 16, no. 1 (1986): 10–28.
Hanssen, Beatrice. *Critique of Violence: Between Poststructuralism and Critical Theory*. London; New York: Routledge, 2000.
Haraway, Donna. *Simians, Cyborgs and Women: The Reinvention of Nature*. London: Free Association Books, 1991.
Hariman, Robert. "What Is a Chiasmus? Or, Why the Abyss Stares Back." In *Chiasmus and Culture*, edited by Boris Wiseman and Anthony Paul. New York: Berghahn Books, 2014.
Harrison, Nicholas. *Postcolonial Criticism: History, Theory, and the Work of Fiction*. Malden, MA; Cambridge: Polity, 2003.
Heathcote, Owen. "Beyond Antoinette Fouque (*Il y a deux sexes*) and Beyond Virginie Despentes (*King Kong Théories*)? Anne Garréta's Sphinxes." In *Women's Writing in the Twenty-First Century: Life as Literature*, edited by Amaleena Damlé and Gill Rye. Cardiff: University of Wales Press, 2013.
Henry, Michel. *Philosophy and Phenomenology of the Body*. Translated by Girard Etzkorn. The Hague: Martinus Nijhoff, 1975.
Hill, Leslie. *Bataille, Klossowski, Blanchot: Writing at the Limit*. New York: Oxford University Press, 2001.
Hill, Leslie. *Beckett's Fiction: In Different Words*. Cambridge: Cambridge University Press, 1990.
Hill, Leslie. *Maurice Blanchot and Fragmentary Writing: A Change of Epoch*. London; New York: Continuum, 2012.
Hill, Leslie. *Maurice Blanchot: Extreme Contemporary*. London: Routledge, 1997.
Hillman, David, and Ulrika Maude. "Introduction." In *The Cambridge Companion to the Body in Literature*, edited by David Hillman and Ulrika Maude. Cambridge: Cambridge University Press, 2015.
Hillman, David, and Ulrika Maude, eds. *The Cambridge Companion to the Body in Literature*. Cambridge: Cambridge University Press, 2015.
Hollander, John. *The Figure of Echo: A Mode of Allusion in Milton and After*. Berkeley; Los Angeles, CA: University of California Press, 1981.

Isar, Nicoletta. "Undoing Forgetfulness: Chiasmus of Poetical Mind – a Cultural Paradigm of Archetypal Imagination." *Europe's Journal of Psychology* 1, no. 3 (August 28, 2005), https://doi.org/10.5964/ejop.v1i3.370.
Iser, Wolfgang. *The Act of Reading: A Theory of Aesthetic Response*. Baltimore, MD: Johns Hopkins University Press, 1994.
Jameson, Fredric. *The Cultural Turn: Selected Writings on the Postmodern, 1983–1998*. London; New York: Verso, 1998.
Jameson, Fredric. *The Political Unconscious: Narrative as a Socially Symbolic Act*. Ithaca, NY: Cornell University Press, 1982.
Jancovich, Mark. *The Cultural Politics of the New Criticism*. Cambridge; New York: Cambridge University Press, 1993.
Karamanolis, George, and Vasilis Politis. "Introduction." In *The Aporetic Tradition in Ancient Philosophy*, edited by George Karamanolis and Vasilis Politis. New York: Cambridge University Press, 2018.
Keats, John. "This Living Hand." In *The Complete Poems*, edited by John Barnard. London: Penguin, 2003.
Kenner, Hugh. *Samuel Beckett: A Critical Study*. New York: Grove Press, 1961.
Kertész, Imre. *Dossier K*. Translated by Tim Wilkinson. Brooklyn, NY: Melville House, 2013.
Kertész, Imre. *Gályanapló*. Budapest: Holnap Kiadó, 1992.
Kertész, Imre. "Who Owns Auschwitz?" Translated by John MacKay. *The Yale Journal of Criticism* 14, no. 1 (2001): 267–72.
Kim, Annabel L. *Unbecoming Language: Anti-Identitarian French Feminist Fictions*. Columbus, OH: Ohio State University Press, 2018.
Klemperer, Victor. *The Language of the Third Reich: LTI Lingua Tertii Imperii: A Philologist's Notebook*. Translated by Martin Brady. London; New York: Bloomsbury Academic, 2013.
Knowlson, James. *Damned to Fame: The Life of Samuel Beckett*. London: Bloomsbury, 1997.
Kofman, Sarah. "Beyond Aporia?" In *Post-Structuralist Classics*, edited by Andrew E. Benjamin. London; New York: Routledge, 1988.
Kornbluh, Anna. *The Order of Forms: Realism, Formalism, and Social Space*. Chicago: University of Chicago Press, 2019.
Kott, Jan. "Introduction." In *This Way for the Gas, Ladies and Gentlemen*, by Tadeusz Borowski. New York: Penguin Books, 1976.
Kristeva, Julia. *Powers of Horror: An Essay on Abjection*. Translated by Leon S. Roudiez. New York: Columbia University Press, 1982.
Lacan, Jacques. *Seminar III: The Psychoses, 1955–1956*. Edited by Jacques-Alain Miller. Translated by Russell Grigg. New York; London: W.W. Norton & Company, 1997.
LaCapra, Dominick. *Representing the Holocaust: History, Theory, Trauma*. Ithaca, NY: Cornell University Press, 1996.
Lacoue-Labarthe, Philippe. "Fidelities." *The Oxford Literary Review* 22 (2000): 132–51.
Lang, Jessica. *Textual Silence: Unreadability and the Holocaust*. New Brunswick, NJ: Rutgers University Press, 2017.
Langer, Susanne K. *Problems of Art*. New York: The Scribner Library, 1957.
Lanzmann, Claude, Cathy Caruth, and David Rodowick. "The Obscenity of

Understanding: An Evening with Claude Lanzmann." *American Imago* 48, no. 4 (1991): 473–95.

Lauretis, Teresa de. "The Violence of Rhetoric: Considerations on Representation and Gender." *Semiotica* 54, no. 1–2 (1985): 11–31.

Lee, Crispin T. *Haptic Experience in the Writings of Georges Bataille, Maurice Blanchot and Michel Serres*. Oxford; New York: Peter Lang, 2014.

Lefkovitz, Lori Hope, ed. *Textual Bodies: Changing Boundaries of Literary Representation*. Albany, NY: SUNY Press, 1997.

Leighton, Angela. *On Form: Poetry, Aestheticism, and the Legacy of a Word*. Oxford; New York: Oxford University Press, 2007.

Lentricchia, Frank. *After the New Criticism*. Chicago: University of Chicago Press, 1994.

Levi, Primo. *I sommersi e i salvati*. Torino: Einaudi, 1986.

Levi, Primo. *If This Is a Man/The Truce*. Translated by Stuart Woolf. London: Abacus, 1991.

Levi, Primo. *La tregua*. Torino: Einaudi, 1971.

Levi, Primo. "Note to the Theatre Version of *If This Is a Man*." In *The Black Hole of Auschwitz*. Cambridge: Polity Press, 2005.

Levi, Primo. *Se questo è un uomo*. Edited by Alberto Cavaglion. Torino: Einaudi, 2012.

Levi, Primo. *The Drowned and the Saved*. Translated by Raymond Rosenthal. London: Abacus, 2002.

Levi, Primo. *The Periodic Table*. Translated by Raymond Rosenthal. London: Penguin, 2001.

Lévinas, Emmanuel. *Totality and Infinity: An Essay on Exteriority*. Translated by Alphonso Lingis. The Hague: Martinus Nijhoff, 1979.

Levine, Caroline. *Forms: Whole, Rhythm, Hierarchy, Network*. Princeton, NJ: Princeton University Press, 2015.

Levine, Michael G. *The Belated Witness: Literature, Testimony, and the Question of Holocaust Survival*. Stanford, CA: Stanford University Press, 2006.

Leys, Ruth. *Trauma: A Genealogy*. Chicago: University of Chicago Press, 2000.

Lindsay, Cecile. "Lyotard and the Postmodern Body." *L'Esprit Créateur* 31, no. 1 (1991): 33–47.

Littell, Jonathan. *Les Bienveillantes*. Paris: Gallimard, 2006.

Loshitzky, Yosefa. *Spielberg's Holocaust: Critical Perspectives on Schindler's List*. Bloomington, IN: Indiana University Press, 1997.

Lucy, Niall. *A Derrida Dictionary*. Malden, MA; Oxford: Blackwell Publishers, 2004.

Lyotard, Jean-François. *Dérive à partir de Marx et Freud*. Paris: Galilée, 1994.

Lyotard, Jean-François. *Heidegger and "the Jews."* Translated by Andreas Michel and Mark S. Roberts. Minneapolis, MN: University of Minnesota Press, 1990.

Lyotard, Jean-François. *Libidinal Economy*. Translated by Iain Hamilton Grant. Bloomington, IN: Indiana University Press, 1993.

Lyotard, Jean-François. *The Postmodern Explained: Correspondence 1982–1985*. Translated by Don Barry, Bernadette Maher, Julian Pefanis, Virginia Spate, and Morgan Thomas. Minneapolis, MN: University of Minnesota Press, 1992.

Lyotard, Jean-François. *The Differend: Phrases in Dispute*. Translated by Georges Van Den Abbeele. Manchester: Manchester University Press, 1988.

Lyotard, Jean-François. *The Inhuman: Reflections on Time*. Translated by Geoffrey Bennington and Rachel Bowlby. Stanford, CA: Stanford University Press, 1991.

Lyotard, Jean-François. *The Postmodern Condition: A Report on Knowledge*. Manchester: Manchester University Press, 2005.

Macksey, Richard, and Eugenio Donato. "The Space Between – 1971." In *The Structuralist Controversy: The Languages of Criticism and the Sciences of Man*, edited by Richard Macksey and Eugenio Donato. Baltimore, MD: Johns Hopkins University Press, 1970.

Macksey, Richard, and Eugenio Donato, eds. *The Structuralist Controversy: The Languages of Criticism and the Sciences of Man*. Baltimore, MD: Johns Hopkins University Press, 1970.

Magessa O'Reilly, Edouard. "Preface." In *How It Is*, by Samuel Beckett, edited by Edouard Magessa O'Reilly. London: Faber and Faber, 2009.

Malina, Debra. *Breaking the Frame: Metalepsis and the Construction of the Subject*. Columbus, OH: Ohio State University Press, 2002.

Man, Paul de. *Allegories of Reading: Figural Language in Rousseau, Nietzsche, Rilke, and Proust*. New Haven, CT: Yale University Press, 1979.

Man, Paul de. "Autobiography as De-Facement." *MLN* 94, no. 5 (1979): 919–30.

Man, Paul de. "The Epistemology of Metaphor." *Critical Inquiry* 5, no. 1 (1978): 13–30.

Man, Paul de. *The Resistance to Theory*. Minneapolis, MN: University of Minnesota Press, 1986.

Man, Paul de. *The Rhetoric of Romanticism*. New York: Columbia University Press, 1984.

Mandel, Naomi. *Against the Unspeakable: Complicity, the Holocaust, and Slavery in America*. Charlottesville, VA; London: University of Virginia Press, 2006.

Maude, Ulrika. *Beckett, Technology and the Body*. Cambridge: Cambridge University Press, 2009.

McMullan, Anna. *Performing Embodiment in Samuel Beckett*. Abingdon: Routledge, 2010.

McMullan, Anna. "Versions of Embodiment/Visions of the Body in Beckett's '... but the Clouds ...'" *Samuel Beckett Today / Aujourd'hui* 6 (1997): 353–64.

McNaughton, James. *Samuel Beckett and the Politics of Aftermath*. Oxford: Oxford University Press, 2018.

Merleau-Ponty, Maurice. *Phenomenology of Perception*. Translated by Colin Smith. London: Routledge, 2002.

Merleau-Ponty, Maurice. *The Primacy of Perception*. Translated by William Cobb. Evanston, IL: Northwestern University Press, 1964.

Merleau-Ponty, Maurice. *The Structure of Behavior*. Translated by Alden L. Fisher. Boston, MA: Beacon Press, 1967.

Merleau-Ponty, Maurice. *The Visible and the Invisible: Followed by Working Notes*. Edited by Claude Lefort. Translated by Alphonso Lingis. Evanston, IL: Northwestern University Press, 1975.

Miller, J. Hillis. "Line." In *The J. Hillis Miller Reader*, edited by Julian Wolfreys. Stanford, CA: Stanford University Press, 2005.

Mitchell, W. J. T. "Representation." In *Critical Terms for Literary Study*, edited by Frank Lentricchia and Thomas McLaughlin, Second Edition. Chicago: University of Chicago Press, 1995.

Mitchell, W. J. T. "The Commitment to Form; Or, Still Crazy after All These Years." *PMLA* 118, no. 2 (2003): 321–25.

Morier, Henri. *Dictionnaire de poétique et de rhétorique*. Paris: Presses Universitaires de France, 1961.

Morot-Sir, Edouard. "Samuel Beckett and Cartesian Emblems." In *Samuel Beckett: The Art of Rhetoric*, edited by Edouard Morot-Sir, Howard Harper, and Douglas McMillan III. Chapel Hill, NC: University of North Carolina Press, 1976.

Motte, Warren. "Shapes of Things." *L'Esprit Créateur* 48, no. 2 (2008): 5–17.

Murphy, Peter John, Werner Huber, Rolf Breuer, and Konrad Schoell. *Critique of Beckett Criticism: A Guide to Research in English, French, and German*. Columbia, SC: Camden House, 1994.

Norris, Christopher. *Contest of Faculties: Philosophy and Theory after Deconstruction*. New York; London: Routledge, 2009.

Oster, Sharon B. "Impossible Holocaust Metaphors: The Muselmann." *Prooftexts* 34, no. 3 (2014): 302–48.

Oster, Sharon B. "The Female Muselmann in Nazi Concentration Camp Discourse." *The Journal of Holocaust Research* 34, no. 3 (July 2, 2020): 198–219.

Pelkey, Jamin R. *The Semiotics of X: Chiasmus, Cognition and Extreme Body Memory*. London; New York: Bloomsbury, 2017.

Plato. *Plato's Timaeus*. Translated by Peter Kalkavage. Newburyport, MA: Focus Publishing, 2001.

Poovey, Mary. *Making a Social Body: British Cultural Formation, 1830–1864*. Chicago: University of Chicago Press, 1995.

Rabaté, Jean-Michel. *The Future of Theory*. Oxford: Blackwell Publishers, 2002.

Rabaté, Jean-Michel. *Think, Pig! Beckett at the Limit of the Human*. New York: Fordham University Press, 2016.

Rae, Gavin. "Forming the Individual: Castoriadis and Lacan on the Socio-Symbolic Function of Violence." In *Violence and Meaning*, edited by Lode Lauwaert, Laura Katherine Smith, and Christian Sternad. Cham: Palgrave Macmillan, 2019.

Raengo, Alessandra. *On the Sleeve of the Visual*. Hanover, NH: Dartmouth College Press, 2013.

Rancière, Jacques. "Are Some Things Unrepresentable?" In *The Future of the Image*, translated by Gregory Elliott. London: Verso, 2009.

Rancière, Jacques. *Disagreement: Politics and Philosophy*. Minneapolis, MN: University of Minnesota Press, 1999.

Rancière, Jacques. "L'irreprésentable en question. Entretien avec Jacques Rancière." *Europe*, no. 926–927 (2006): 425–54.

Rancière, Jacques. "The Aesthetic Revolution and Its Outcomes: Emplotments of Autonomy and Heteronomy." *New Left Review*, no. 14 (April 2002): 133–51.

Rancière, Jacques. *The Politics of Aesthetics*. Translated by Gabriel Rockhill. New York: Continuum, 2006.
Rancière, Jacques. "Why Emma Bovary Had to Be Killed." *Critical Inquiry* 34, no. 2 (January 1, 2008): 233–48.
Ransom, John Crowe. *The World's Body*. Baton Rouge, LA: Louisiana State University Press, 1938.
Rapport, Nigel. *The Prose and the Passion: Anthropology, Literature, and the Writing of E.M. Forster*. Manchester: Manchester University Press, 1994.
Renfrew, Alastair. *Towards a New Material Aesthetics: Bakhtin, Genre and the Fates of Literary Theory*. Oxford: Legenda, 2006.
Ricks, Christopher. *Beckett's Dying Words: The Clarendon Lectures 1990*. Oxford: Oxford University Press, 1995.
Ricoeur, Paul. *Freud and Philosophy: An Essay on Interpretation*. Translated by Denis Savage. New Haven, CT: Yale University Press, 1970.
Ricoeur, Paul. *Oneself as Another*. Translated by Katherine Blamey. Chicago: University of Chicago Press, 1995.
Ricoeur, Paul. *The Course of Recognition*. Translated by David Pellauer. Cambridge, MA: Harvard University Press, 2005.
Ricœur, Paul. *The Rule of Metaphor: The Creation of Meaning in Language*. London: Routledge, 2006.
Riffaterre, Michael. "Prosopopeia." *Yale French Studies*, no. 69 (1985): 107–23.
Ritivoi, Andreea. "Reading (with) Hannah Arendt: Aesthetic Representation for an Ethics of Alterity." *Humanities* 8, no. 155 (September 24, 2019).
Robinson, Douglas. *Estrangement and the Somatics of Literature: Tolstoy, Shklovsky, Brecht*. Baltimore, MD: Johns Hopkins University Press, 2008.
Rooney, Ellen. "Form and Contentment." *MLQ: Modern Language Quarterly* 61, no. 1 (March 1, 2000): 17–40.
Rose, Nikolas. "The Human Sciences in a Biological Age." *Theory, Culture & Society* 30, no. 1 (January 2013): 3–34.
Ross, Alison. "Expressivity, Literarity, Mute Speech." In *Jacques Rancière: Key Concepts*, edited by Jean-Philippe Deranty. Durham: Acumen, 2010.
Ross, Charlotte. *Primo Levi's Narratives of Embodiment: Containing the Human*. Abingdon: Routledge, 2010.
Ross, Stephen. "Introduction: The Missing Link." In *Modernism and Theory: A Critical Debate*, edited by Stephen Ross. New York: Routledge, 2009.
Rothberg, Michael. *The Implicated Subject: Beyond Victims and Perpetrators*. Stanford, CA: Stanford University Press, 2019.
Rye, Gill. "Uncertain Readings and Meaningful Dialogue: Language and Sexual Identity in Anne Garréta's *Sphinx* and Tahar Ben Jelloun's *L'Enfant de sable* and *La Nuit sacrée*." *Neophilologus* 84, no. 4 (2000): 531–40.
Santagostino, Giuseppina. *Primo Levi: metamorfosi letterarie del corpo*. Moncalieri: Centro interuniversitario di ricerche sul viaggio in Italia, 2004.
Sanyal, Debarati. *Memory and Complicity: Migrations of Holocaust Remembrance*. New York: Fordham University Press, 2015.
Sanyal, Debarati. *The Violence of Modernity: Baudelaire, Irony, and the Politics of Form*. Baltimore, MD: Johns Hopkins University Press, 2006.
Sartre, Jean-Paul. *Existentialism Is a Humanism*. Edited by John Kulka. Translated by Carol Macomber. New Haven, CT: Yale University Press, 2007.

Scarry, Elaine. *Resisting Representation*. New York: Oxford University Press, 1994.
Scarry, Elaine. *The Body in Pain: The Making and Unmaking of the World*. New York; Oxford: Oxford University Press, 1987.
Sedgwick, Eve Kosofsky. *Touching Feeling*. Durham, NC: Duke University Press, 2003.
Serjeantson, R. W. "Testimony: The Artless Proof." In *Renaissance Figures of Speech*, edited by Sylvia Adamson, Gavin Alexander, and Katrin Ettenhuber. Cambridge: Cambridge University Press, 2011.
Shenker, Israel. "An Interview with Samuel Beckett." In *Samuel Beckett: The Critical Heritage*, edited by Lawrence Graver and Raymond Federman. London; Boston, MA: Routledge & Kegan Paul, 1979.
Shklovsky, Viktor. "Art, as Device." Translated by Alexandra Berlina. *Poetics Today* 36, no. 3 (September 2015): 151–74.
Sodi, Risa B. *A Dante of Our Time: Primo Levi and Auschwitz*. New York: Peter Lang, 1990.
Steiner, Peter. *Russian Formalism: A Metapoetics*. Ithaca, NY: Cornell University Press, 1984.
Stewart, Susan. *On Longing: Narratives of the Miniature, the Gigantic, the Souvenir, the Collection*. Durham, NC: Duke University Press, 1993.
Tajiri, Yoshiki. *Samuel Beckett and the Prosthetic Body: The Organs and Senses in Modernism*. Basingstoke: Palgrave Macmillan, 2007.
Tambornino, John. *The Corporeal Turn: Passion, Necessity, Politics*. Lanham, MD: Rowman & Littlefield Publishers, 2002.
Tanaka, Mariko Hori, Yoshiki Tajiri, and Michiko Tsushima, eds. *Samuel Beckett and Trauma*. Manchester: Manchester University Press, 2018.
Terdiman, Richard. *Body and Story: The Ethics and Practice of Theoretical Conflict*. Baltimore, MD: Johns Hopkins University Press, 2007.
Thomas, Edmund. "Chiasmus in Art and Text." *Greece & Rome* 60, no. 1 (2013): 50–88.
Trezise, Thomas. *Into the Breach: Samuel Beckett and the Ends of Literature*. Princeton, NJ: Princeton University Press, 1990.
Turner, Aaron. "Embodied Ethnography. Doing Culture." *Social Anthropology* 8, no. 1 (January 19, 2007): 51–60.
Turner, Bryan. *The Body and Society*. Los Angeles: Sage, 2008.
Turner, Mark. *Reading Minds: The Study of English in the Age of Cognitive Science*. Princeton, NJ: Princeton University Press, 2021.
Tyler, Stephen A. *The Unspeakable: Discourse, Dialogue and Rhetoric in the Postmodern World*. Madison, WI: University of Wisconsin Press, 1987.
Vivero García, María Dolores. "Humour, engagement et création littéraire chez Anne Garréta." *Women in French Studies* 19, no. 1 (2011): 85–93.
Vries, Hent de. "'Lapsus Absolu': Notes on Maurice Blanchot's *The Instant of My Death*." *Yale French Studies*, no. 93 (January 1, 1998): 30–59.
Wall, Thomas Carl. *Radical Passivity: Lévinas, Blanchot, and Agamben*. Albany, NY: State University of New York Press, 1999.
Warminski, Andrzej. *Readings in Interpretation: Hölderlin, Hegel, Heidegger*. Minneapolis, MN: University of Minnesota Press, 1987.
Warren, Calvin L. *Ontological Terror: Blackness, Nihilism, and Emancipation*. Durham, NC: Duke University Press Books, 2018.

Wasser, Audrey. *The Work of Difference: Modernism, Romanticism, and the Production of Literary Form*. New York: Fordham University Press, 2016.
Watson, David. *Paradox and Desire in Samuel Beckett's Fiction*. Basingstoke: Palgrave Macmillan, 1991.
Waugh, Patricia. "Writing the Body: Modernism and Postmodernism." In *The Body and the Arts*, edited by Corinne J. Saunders, Ulrika Maude, and Jane Macnaughton. Basingstoke; New York: Palgrave Macmillan, 2009.
Waxman, Zoë. *Writing the Holocaust: Identity, Testimony, Representation*. Oxford: Oxford University Press, 2006.
Weiss, Gail. *Refiguring the Ordinary*. Bloomington, IN: Indiana University Press, 2008.
Welch, John W. *Chiasmus in Antiquity: Structures, Analyses, Exegesis*. Provo, UT: Neal A. Maxwell Institute for Religious Scholarship, 1998.
Wellek, René. *Concepts of Criticism*. New Haven, CT: Yale University Press, 1975.
Wellek, René. "The New Criticism: Pro and Contra." *Critical Inquiry* 4, no. 4 (1978): 611–24.
Wellek, René. *Theory of Literature*. San Diego, CA: Harcourt Brace Jovanovich, 1984.
White, Hayden. "Historical Emplotment and the Problem of Truth." In *Probing the Limits of Representation: Nazism and the "Final Solution,"* edited by Saul Friedländer. Cambridge, MA: Harvard University Press, 1992.
Wiesel, Elie. *From the Kingdom of Memory: Reminiscences*. New York: Summit Books, 1990.
Williams, Raymond. *Keywords: A Vocabulary of Culture and Society*. New York; Oxford: Oxford University Press, 1985.
Witz, Anne. "Whose Body Matters? Feminist Sociology and the Corporeal Turn in Sociology and Feminism." *Body & Society* 6, no. 2 (June 2000): 1–24.
Wolff, Francis. "Polis." In *Dictionary of Untranslatables: A Philosophical Lexicon*, edited by Barbara Cassin, Steven Rendall, and Emily S. Apter. Princeton, NJ: Princeton University Press, 2014.
Wolfson, Susan J. *Formal Charges: The Shaping of Poetry in British Romanticism*. Stanford, CA: Stanford University Press, 1997.
Wolfson, Susan J., and Marshall Brown, eds. *Reading for Form*. Seattle, WA: University of Washington Press, 2006.
Young, James E. "Interpreting Literary Testimony: A Preface to Rereading Holocaust Diaries and Memoirs." *New Literary History* 18, no. 2 (1987): 403–23.
Young, James E. *The Texture of Memory: Holocaust Memorials and Meaning*. New Haven, CT: Yale University Press, 1994.
Young-ah Gottlieb, Susannah. *Regions of Sorrow: Anxiety and Messianism in Hannah Arendt and W. H. Auden*. Stanford, CA: Stanford University Press, 2003.
Zarader, Marlène. *L'Etre et le neutre: A partir de Maurice Blanchot*. Paris: Verdier, 2001.

Index

Note: 'n' indicates footnote number

abjection, 20, 39–42, 106, 107, 111, 114, 155, 164, 179–80, 186
absence, 1, 6–11, 19, 23, 26, 34, 47, 53, 57, 60–2, 64
   and Garréta's *Sphinx*, 83–6, 84n30, 89, 135
   and Levi's testimonial works, 152, 154, 157, 159, 159n30, 160, 162, 165, 171, 179, 180, 187, 188, 190–2
   and the work of Beckett, 98, 107, 119
   and the work of Blanchot, 139, 141–6, 148, 149
Adorno, Theodor, 151
aesthetics, 43, 55–6, 65, 67
   and embodied form, 5–6, 19, 45, 51, 52, 55–6, 59, 61, 64–7, 204
   and form, 3n8, 5–7, 12, 14, 16–18, 16n42, 30–3, 35, 45, 71, 74, 94, 116, 194–5, 203
   and Garréta's *Sphinx*, 71, 74, 81, 86, 87, 94–6
   and Levi's testimonial works, 151, 151n2, 155, 157, 161, 164–5, 171
   and the work of Arendt, 194–6, 194n1, 198, 199–203
   and the work of Beckett, 98–9, 102, 109, 109n32, 110, 114, 116, 117, 119, 121n63
   and the work of Blanchot, 147
   and the work of Rancière, 12, 12n34, 155, 180–1, 194, 194n1
aesthetics of failure (failure of language), 64, 73, 98–9, 102, 109, 109n32, 110, 116–17, 119, 121n63, 123
Agamben, Giorgio, 42n134, 62, 153, 153n12, 159n28, 164
Ahmed, Sara, 5n17
Alaimo, Stacy, 28
Améry, Jean, 152
anamnesis, 77, 77n20
anthropology, 5, 5n17, 66–7, 67n49
aporia, 7, 14, 18, 64–5, 73–4, 77, 78, 117–18, 117n50, 165–71, 179, 200
   in Levi's testimonial works, 153–5, 158–60, 159n28, 164–79
Appelfeld, Aharon, 152
Arendt, Hannah, 12, 87, 155–6, 194, 194n1, 202–3, 202n32, 203n35
   The Life of the Mind, 195–9
   The Origins of Totalitarianism, 199
   "We Refugees," 196n6
Aristotle, 2, 2n4
assimilation, 3, 44, 120, 135, 196, 196n6, 201, 204; *see also* difference
Auerbach, Erich, 2n6

Baker, Josephine, 79n23
Bari, Shahidha Kazi, 10n31

Bataille, Georges, 25n65
Beckett, Samuel, 19, 45, 98–137, 99n5, 100n11, 138, 150
   The Calmative, 105
   Company, 105, 107–8, 111, 112, 113
   Dream of Fair to Middling Women, 111
   Endgame, 113
   First Love, 105
   Footfalls, 111
   Happy Days, 112–13
   How It Is, 111, 112, 113, 122–32, 123nn65–7, 135, 150
   "Lessness," 113
   Malone Dies, 105, 110, 112, 113
   Molloy, 105, 110, 112, 113
   Murphy, 107, 110–11, 114
   Not I, 105, 106–7, 112
   Proust, 110, 111, 112
   Three Dialogues, 98, 98n1
   The Unnamable, 105, 106, 107, 108, 109, 111, 112, 113, 114, 115–18, 136, 144
belonging, 102, 104, 120, 124, 136, 195, 198
Benjamin, Walter, 3n8, 201
Bennett, Andrew, 10n30
Bernard-Donals, Michael F., 152, 179–80
Bersani, Leo, 98n1
Blackman, Lisa, 5n17
blackness, 70, 79–82, 84, 88–93, 88n38
Blanchot, Maurice, 45, 138–50
   The Infinite Conversation, 146
   The Instant of My Death, 139, 141–6, 141n15, 142n16, 142n19, 146n24
   The Writing of the Disaster, 142n17, 148–50, 148n29
body parts, 61, 92, 94, 104–19; *see also* hands
body politic, 2, 4, 12, 13, 123, 130–2, 136, 155, 194–8, 203
Boxall, Peter, 120–1
Brackney, Kathryn L., 151n2
Braidotti, Rosi, 4, 26–7
Brecht, Bertolt, 203

Breu, Christopher, 15n38
Brinkema, Eugenie, 16n42, 17n44
Brooks, Cleanth, 29n83, 31, 35n104, 52–3, 54, 59, 66, 111
Brooks, Peter, 34
Butler, Judith, 4, 26–8, 27n76, 41, 42, 43, 44n140, 70

Caracciolo, Marco, 191, 192n79
Caruth, Cathy, 102n16
catachresis, 7, 14, 61–2, 63, 65, 117–18, 135
   in Garréta's *Sphinx*, 71, 83, 84, 87–97, 88n38, 89n42
Chabert, Pierre, 100n11
chiasmus, 8–11, 8n22, 10n31, 13–14, 23, 59–62, 68, 117–18, 204
   in the work of Blanchot, 138–41, 143–50
   in the work of Merleau-Ponty, 9, 22–3, 59, 117, 138, 141, 147
close reading, 30–3, 35n104, 38, 68
Cohn, Ruby, 98n1, 123n66
common sense, 193–204
Connor, Steven, 100, 100n9, 114
containment, 51, 110–12, 111n38, 114, 116, 120, 159n29
   the body as bounded container, 31, 53–5, 65
counterviolence, 42–4, 101, 103, 120–2, 128, 131, 132, 134, 135, 201
Csordas, Thomas J., 23
Cusset, François, 38

De Man, Paul, 38, 60, 60n25, 60n27, 83, 88, 95–6, 109, 109n21, 140–1
deconstruction, 15, 33, 35–6, 35n105, 64–5, 70, 83, 96, 109n32, 121, 135–6, 139, 140, 142n19
Derrida, Jacques, 35–9, 35n105, 41, 65, 141, 141n15, 142n19, 142nn16–17
Dewey, John, 17–18, 56, 56n10, 59
difference, 1–3, 13, 14, 19, 27, 37, 54, 55, 140, 196, 201

difference (*cont.*)
  and Garréta's *Sphinx*, 79–80,
    79n22, 82n25, 88n38, 89, 91,
    94, 95
  and the work of Beckett, 120, 131,
    133n78
  see also assimilation
Diner, Hasia, 163n36
discourse, 3–6, 12–15, 20, 22, 24–8,
    24n64, 27n76, 29n82, 30, 32–4,
    37, 40–5, 50, 51, 52, 54, 58,
    193, 196, 204
  discursive violence, 4, 120, 124,
    130, 132–4
  and Garréta's *Sphinx*, 70, 76n19,
    78–80, 82, 82n25, 94
  and Levi's testimonial works, 154,
    156, 169, 170, 189, 190
  and the work of Beckett, 99,
    100n11, 101, 116, 120–2, 124,
    127, 130, 132–6
  and the work of Blanchot, 139,
    148
Doane, Mary Ann, 7–8
Donato, Eugenio, 37n114
Druker, Jonathan, 168
Dukes, Hunter, 111n38

embodied form, 4–8, 4n16, 11,
    14, 18–20, 35, 45, 49, 51, 52,
    55–68, 193–4, 202–4
  and Garréta's *Sphinx*, 69, 69n2,
    72, 73–4, 86, 87, 91
  and Levi's testimonial works, 165,
    177, 179, 190, 192
  and the work of Beckett, 103–4,
    115, 119, 122, 129–32, 135–6
  and the work of Blanchot, 138,
    139, 141–50
embodiment, 1, 3–7, 5n17, 9, 10n31,
    11–21, 12n34, 23, 27–9, 31–2,
    34, 41, 44, 45, 49–50, 51,
    55–62, 64, 65, 193–4, 203, 204
  and aestheticization, 12, 154, 161,
    164–5, 171, 195, 199–202,
    203
  and Garréta's *Sphinx*, 69, 71–5,
    76n19, 78, 83–4, 87, 89–90,
    93–7
  as interpretation, 52, 54, 55,
    60n27, 64, 65–8, 138, 139, 143,
    146–8, 193
  and Levi's testimonial works,
    153–4, 156n25, 157–9, 159n30,
    160, 162–6, 168, 170–3, 177–8,
    182–3, 185–90, 192
  and representation, 15, 19, 20,
    27–8, 153, 157–65, 170–94,
    203
  and the work of Merleau-Ponty,
    27
  and the works of Beckett, 101–2,
    101n11, 104, 107, 109–10,
    109n32, 114–19, 122, 124,
    127–8, 130–3, 136
  and the works of Blanchot, 138–9,
    142–3, 142n19, 145–50

failure of language (aesthetics of
    failure), 64, 73, 98–9, 102, 109,
    109n32, 110, 116–17, 119,
    121n63, 123
fascism, 3n8, 155, 195, 202
Felman, Shoshana, 154
feminism, 5, 5n17, 15, 21, 26–8
figuration/figurality, 7, 55, 61–5,
    67, 84–8, 90–2, 94–7, 94n46,
    104–10, 114–18, 151, 164, 166,
    170, 174
  and ground, 110–14
Flaubert, Gustave, *Madame Bovary*,
    181
formalism, 6–7, 12, 14–16, 18–20,
    29–32, 36, 38, 51–3, 66, 69,
    71, 75, 75n17, 79, 193, 194,
    197
  New Criticism, 14, 14n36, 30,
    30n88, 35n104, 36, 36n106, 38,
    52–5, 65, 66, 68, 96, 103n20,
    109n32
  new formalism, 15–16, 16n42
  Russian Formalism, 29n85, 30,
    30n86
  and the work of Beckett, 103n20,
    110, 111, 123, 131, 134, 135
formlessness, 16, 18, 20, 31, 35–44,
    42n134, 89, 91, 149, 201
  and the work of Beckett, 100, 101,

110, 112, 112n41, 122, 124, 128, 131, 136, 137
Foucault, Michel, 3, 20, 24–6, 24n64, 25n65, 27, 41
fragmentation of the body, 4, 20, 39–40, 42–3, 49, 64, 156, 177
   and Garréta's *Sphinx*, 71, 76–8, 95
   and the work of Beckett, 101, 105, 108–10, 113, 116, 117, 121–2, 128–9, 132, 133, 134, 136
Friedlander, Saul, 151
Fuss, Diana, 26

Gallagher, Catherine, 34
Garréta, Anne F., *Sphinx*, 45, 69–97, 69nn1–2, 73n11, 135–6, 138
Gasché, Rodolphe, 140
Geertz, Clifford, 66
gender, 13, 14, 19, 26–8, 42, 51–2, 135
   and Garréta's *Sphinx*, 69–78, 70n3, 76n19, 80–1
Genette, Gérard, 62
Gibson, Andrew, 99
Glejzer, Richard, 152
Gray, Thomas, "Elegy Written in a Country Churchyard," 53
Greenblatt, Stephen, 34
Grosz, Elisabeth, 26–7

hands, 7, 9–11, 19–20, 22–3, 59, 191–2
   Chauvet cave paintings, 1, 6–9
Hanssen, Beatrice, 42–4, 101, 102, 133
Heidegger, Martin, 197n8
Helen of Troy, 62–3
Hill, Leslie, 99
historicism *see* New Historicism
Holocaust, 40, 43, 44, 49, 64, 148–58, 148n29, 151n2, 153n12
   testimony, 152–8, 152n11, 163n36, 165, 182
   see also Levi, Primo
Holocaust studies, 152n5, 156n23, 156n25, 164n41, 165, 177, 180, 185
Homer, 2, 2n6, 8, 140

interpretation, 17, 52, 54, 55, 60n27, 64, 65–8, 138, 139, 141, 143, 146–8, 193

Jameson, Fredric, 29n82

Keats, John, "This Living Hand," 9–11, 10nn29–31, 111, 192
Kertész, Imre, 171, 175
Kim, Annabel L., 69n2, 79nn22–3
Klemperer, Viktor, 199, 199n18
Kofman, Sarah, 166–8, 200
Kornbluh, Anna, 3n8, 15–16, 16n41
Kristeva, Julia, 39–40, 41, 179–80

Lacan, Jacques, 102n15
LaCapra, Dominick, 154–5
Lang, Jessica, 183nn73–4
Langer, Susanne K., 55, 56, 56n10, 57, 59
Lanzmann, Claude, 151, 161
Lauretis, Teresa de, 41
Lee, Crispin T., 139n3
Lentricchia, Frank, 14n36, 32n94
Levi, Primo, 45, 138, 150, 151–92, 159nn29–30, 180n64
   The Drowned and the Saved, 152–3, 152n11, 154, 158, 172–8, 184, 188–9
   If This Is a Man, 153n13, 154, 158, 162–70, 163n36, 164n41, 169nn48–9, 178, 182–7, 183nn73–4, 200
   The Periodic Table, "Carbon," 190–2, 192n79
   The Truce, 153, 153n13, 158, 162, 163, 178, 184
Lévinas, Emmanuel, 24n62
Levine, Caroline, 15, 52n1, 53
Levine, Michael G., 156n25, 163
lightness, 47, 141, 143–6, 145n21, 148, 149
Lindsay, Cecile, 40
listening, 161–5, 190
logical forms, 55–9, 70–1, 74, 83, 114, 118, 120, 184
Lyotard, Jean-François, 17, 38–41, 151–2, 152n5, 152n11, 180

Macksey, Richard, 37n114
McMullan, Anna, 100n11, 107
Malina, Debra, 121
Mandel, Naomi, 156–7
maps, 57–8, 57n15
Marlow, Christopher, 62
Maude, Ulrika, 99n6, 108n31
Merleau-Ponty, Maurice, 5, 9, 20, 21–4, 28, 59, 117, 138, 141, 147, 195
metafigures, 109, 109n32, 118
metalepsis, 14, 62–5, 150, 160, 178, 192n79
  in the work of Beckett, 101–4, 114, 116–22, 120n54, 124–9, 131–7
metaphor, 9, 61, 118, 197–9
metaphysics, 36, 42, 43, 197
Miller, J. Hillis, 65
mimesis, 71, 93, 171–8
Mitchell, W. J. T., 4n16
Motte, Warren, 71

narrative voice, 146–8
narratology, 101–2, 120, 122
New Criticism, 14, 14n36, 30, 30n88, 35n104, 36, 36n106, 38, 52–5, 65, 66, 68, 96, 103n20, 109n32
new formalism, 15–16, 16n42
New Historicism, 33, 38, 52–4
Norris, Christopher, 36n106

objects, 160, 178–88, 183n74, 189
Oster, Sharon B., 164n41, 185n75
Oulipo (*Ouvroir de littérature potentielle*; Workshop for a Potential Literature), 31, 31n89, 71–2, 72n8

pathos, 84–5, 84n28
phenomenology, 5, 23–4, 29–30, 29n85, 52, 54, 56n10, 58, 63, 66, 67, 95, 138, 142n19, 148, 153, 158
Plato, 38, 64, 77n20
  Timaeus, 139–40
polis, 2, 2n7, 54, 123, 195
political violence, 43, 103, 133, 135

politics, 40–1, 43, 45, 194–5, 194n1, 199–204
  body politic, 2, 4, 12, 13, 123, 130–2, 136, 155, 194–8, 203
  and embodied form, 4n16, 6, 7, 14, 18–20, 58, 66, 68, 69, 87, 104, 130–1, 136, 202–3
  and form, 1–4, 3n8, 6–7, 12–17, 19, 26, 44–5, 49, 102–4, 122, 124, 132–6, 194–5, 204
  and Garréta's *Sphinx*, 69–72, 80, 87, 95–7
  and Levi's testimonial works, 154–5, 161, 172, 177, 190
  and the work of Beckett, 102–4, 120, 122, 129–36
Poovey, Mary, 52, 53–4
postmodernism, 14–20, 15n38, 32–5, 32n93, 36, 51–2, 54, 60n27, 64, 193
  and Garréta's *Sphinx*, 70–3, 77–8, 95
  and Levi's testimonial works, 151, 153, 155–7, 159n30, 163
  and the unrepresentable, 17–20, 35, 38–44, 73, 77–8, 95, 133, 155–7, 156n23, 163, 194, 197
  and the work of Beckett, 101–2, 103n20, 113, 120, 120n54, 121–2, 131–2, 135–6
  and the work of Blanchot, 138–40
poststructuralism, 15, 16, 24, 26, 27, 35, 35n105, 37n114, 43, 64–5, 99–100, 103n20, 124
power, 15, 24–6, 24n64, 40, 42–4, 42n134, 52, 149, 171
  and the works of Beckett, 101, 102, 121, 122, 124, 129–30, 133, 134, 136
prosopopoeia, 7, 14, 60–2, 60n25, 60n27, 65, 164, 165, 170
  in Garréta's *Sphinx*, 71, 83–7, 84n30, 90–1, 95–7
Proust, Marcel, 99, 100, 109n32, 112
Puttenham, George, 62

Rabaté, Jean-Michel, 114
race, 14, 19, 42, 51–2, 135

blackness, 70, 79–82, 84, 88–93, 88n38
and Garréta's *Sphinx*, 69–72, 78–83, 82n25, 83n26, 87–95, 88n38, 89n42
whiteness, 79, 81, 88n38, 135–6
racism, 133, 133n77, 155
Raengo, Alessandra, 61, 89, 91n43
Rancière, Jacques, 12, 12n34, 13n35, 155, 157, 160, 180–2, 180n64, 181n70, 182n71, 187, 187n76, 194, 194n1
rhetoric, 7, 8, 13, 14, 23, 40, 42, 57, 59, 62–5, 67
in Garréta's *Sphinx*, 83–8, 95–7
and Levi's testimonial works, 157, 158, 178
rhetorical violence, 41, 43, 44, 87, 104, 126, 128, 133, 150
and the work of Beckett, 101, 103, 104, 122, 124–8, 131, 132, 133–4, 136
and the work of Blanchot, 138, 150
Ricks, Christopher, 99
Riffaterre, Michael, 60n27, 61, 84n30
Rose, Nikolas, 17
Ross, Charlotte, 159n29
Ross, Stephen, 45
Russian Formalism, 29n85, 30, 30n86

Sanyal, Debarati, 129n75, 134, 173, 173n54, 174, 175
Saussure, Ferdinand de, 2n3
semiotics, 18, 32, 37, 41, 92, 194; *see also* signs and signification
Shelley, Percy Bysshe, 197–8
Shklovsky, Viktor, 30, 31
signs and signification, 2, 2n3, 3, 8, 192
in Garréta's *Sphinx*, 71–3, 78, 79, 83, 87, 88n38, 89, 91, 93, 94–6
Sophocles, *Oedipus Tyrannus*, 73n12
speech, 64, 86, 87, 195, 197, 197n8
and Levi's testimonial works, 153, 154, 156–8, 156n23, 169–71, 178, 179, 189–90

the unspeakable, 156–8, 156n23, 179
and the work of Beckett, 103–7, 112, 117–20, 122, 123, 126–9, 133, 134
Stewart, Susan, 53
syntax, 72, 94, 144–5, 186–7, 192

Tajiri, Yoshiki, 100
testimony *see* Holocaust: testimony; Levi, Primo
totalitarianism, 3n8, 131, 136–7, 155–6, 195, 199–202
totality, 43, 131, 132–7, 141
Trezise, Thomas, 98n1, 103n20
Turner, Aaron, 67
Tyler, Stephen, 67

unrepresentability of the body, 4, 35–44
and Garréta's *Sphinx*, 73, 74–8, 76n19, 92, 95
and Levi's testimonial works, 155–7, 156n23, 160, 161, 163, 178, 180
and postmodernism, 17–20, 35, 38–44, 73, 77–8, 95, 133, 155–7, 156n23, 163, 194, 197
and the work of Beckett, 99, 110, 116, 122, 133, 134
urn, the, 52–5, 52n1, 111, 113–14

violence, 3, 4, 15, 19, 20, 35–44, 200
counterviolence, 42–4, 101, 103, 120–2, 128, 131, 132, 134, 135, 201
discursive violence, 4, 120, 124, 130, 132–4
and Garréta's *Sphinx*, 73, 77–8, 96
and Levi's testimonial works, 150, 151, 160, 171, 177, 180, 182, 185, 189
political violence, 43, 103, 133, 135
rhetorical violence, 41, 43, 44, 87, 104, 126, 128, 133, 150
and the work of Beckett, 101–4, 102nn15–16, 113, 120–37, 121n63, 129n75

Warminski, Andrezj, 141
Wasser, Audrey, 98n1
Waugh, Patricia, 34, 34n103
Wellek, René, 29n83
White, Hayden, 180n64

whiteness, 79, 81, 88n38, 135–6
Wiesel, Elie, 152

Young, James E., 154, 179–80

EU representative:
Easy Access System Europe
Mustamäe tee 50, 10621 Tallinn, Estonia
Gpsr.requests@easproject.com